T0285375

ALSO BY DAVID STEINBERG

The Book of David

INSIDE COMEDY

INSIDE COMEDY

THE SOUL, WIT, AND BITE OF COMEDY AND COMEDIANS OF THE LAST FIVE DECADES

DAVID STEINBERG

UNIVERSITY PRESS OF KENTUCKY

2023 edition published by The University Press of Kentucky,
scholarly publisher for the Commonwealth,
serving Bellarmine University, Berea College, Centre
College of Kentucky, Eastern Kentucky University,
The Filson Historical Society, Georgetown College,
Kentucky Historical Society, Kentucky State University,
Morehead State University, Murray State University,
Northern Kentucky University, Spalding University,
Transylvania University, University of Kentucky,
University of Louisville, University of Pikeville, and
Western Kentucky University.

Editorial and Sales Offices: The University Press of Kentucky
663 South Limestone Street, Lexington, Kentucky 40508-4008
www.kentuckypress.com

Reprinted by arrangement with Alfred A. Knopf, an imprint of
The Knopf Doubleday Publishing Group, a division of Penguin
Random House LLC

Cataloging-in-Publication data for the 2021 Knopf edition is
available from the Library of Congress.

ISBN 978-0-8131-9756-2 (pbk: alk. paper)
ISBN 978-0-8131-9758-6 (pdf)
ISBN 978-0-8131-9757-9 (epub)

This book is printed on acid-free paper meeting
the requirements of the American National Standard
for Permanence in Paper for Printed Library Materials.

Manufactured in the United States of America

Member of the Association
of University Presses

For my wife, Robyn,
to whom I leave the empire when I'm gone

CONTENTS

INSIDE COMEDY

CHAPTER 1

DISGUISED AS A NORMAL PERSON

Insecurity combined with arrogance is good DNA for a comedian. So is anger, aggression, and sadness. If you've had a great life and a wonderful bar mitzvah and you've been given a lot of money, you'd make a lousy comedian. You're better off being the comedian's lawyer.

I've had, and continue to have, a great career in comedy, first in stand-up, and over the last few decades, as a director of television comedy series, from *Designing Women* to *The Bob Newhart Show, Golden Girls, Mad About You, Seinfeld, Friends,* and *Curb Your Enthusiasm,* TV movies, my series of interviews with comedians called *Inside Comedy,* with several stops in between. But there were also doldrums along the way—personal and professional. What got me through them was my love of comedy—life itself—and my friendship with, admiration for, and work with other comedians. I knew most of them. I interviewed, worked with, directed, kvetched with, broke bread with, opened for, headlined for, and directed the best of them.

This book is not just my story, it's their stories.

Why me? Besides *being there,* there are things I'm too modest to tell you—that I may be the only comedian to have made Elie Wiesel laugh; that I was admired by the great *New Yorker* writer and humorist S. J. (Sid) Perelman, and by Philip Roth, Kenneth Tynan, and Harold Pinter. And that I was virtually adopted by Groucho Marx and many

A rare moment sitting by myself on the
set of *Inside Comedy* and waiting for Larry
David, 2014.

of the legendary old-timers (such as Jack Benny and George Burns) at
Hillcrest Country Club. I also directed Burt Reynolds at the height of
his considerable fame, before he self-destructed. Johnny Carson was
my mentor and invited me to be a guest on or host *The Tonight Show*
140 times. I believe I am now at the cutting edge of comedy as one
of the directors of *Curb Your Enthusiasm,* with my old friend and fellow kvetcher Larry David. And my series over the last few years, *Inside
Comedy,* is a documentary interview show, a conversation with, if you
will, more than seventy-five comedians and comic actors.

It's a funny thing about comedy: when you give your life to it,
it can become a serious business. I spent my life in and outside the
comedy world, and it *is* a world, a universe unto itself. I was a popular stand-up comic for three decades. I was twenty-five when I first
appeared at the Bitter End on Bleecker Street in Greenwich Village. I
usually prowled the tiny stage in a worn brown corduroy jacket—this

was 1968—and I did things like improvising sermons based on the Old Testament. (That wasn't too much of a reach, because I had been a pre-rabbinical student at Hebrew Theological College near Chicago before comedy found me.)

But this book is not just about my life in comedy—it's about my life and comedy in the last half of the last century. I lived through a time when stand-up comedy was a poor relation to other forms of entertainment, when being on a successful sitcom was nothing to write home about. But I think I was one of a group of people—along with Steve Martin, Richard Pryor, George Carlin, and a few others—who pushed stand-up forward as an art form and made comedy an important part of the culture. A comic hosting a television show used to be rare, but I hosted three—*Music Scene,* which featured artists like Crosby, Stills, Nash & Young and Joe Cocker; *Noonday,* a half-hour midday talk show; and *The David Steinberg Show,* about making a TV talk show and thus a precursor to Garry Shandling's *The Larry Sanders Show.*

But being successful at something I loved didn't always make me happy. Like many comics, I struggled with bouts of depression. And despite the affections of beautiful, accomplished women like Tuesday Weld, Mary Ellen Mark, Susan Sarandon, and Carly Simon, I, too often, thought of the book of Job, when I should have had my mind on other things. It must've been my Talmudic training (I had the only little black book in Hollywood that was written in Aramaic). Unlike many comics of my generation, however, I did manage to avoid heavy drug and alcohol use. With some luck I was able to dodge the heroin that floated through Second City and *Saturday Night Live,* killing John Belushi; the cocaine that undid Richard Pryor; and the alcoholic demons that brought down Chris Farley and George Carlin. But I was there, and I saw it all. To paraphrase the Beat poet Allen Ginsberg, I saw the best comedy minds of my generation destroyed by an angry fix.

Then I started to talk about my life. I had a little bit of the Lenny Bruce storytelling in me. On some level, that was hard and painful—you're giving a lot of yourself, and you're showing that your ego is bigger than anybody else's. Still, the actual performing was enjoyable to me. I opened for jazz greats like Miles Davis, pop stars like Dionne Warwick and Frankie Valli, and folkies like John Denver. The musicians were fans of mine because they identified with what I was doing. I started out with audiences of five hundred people, and before I knew it, there were crowds of two thousand.

The kind of stand-up that emerged from Second City, from Lenny Bruce, and that had moved away from vaudeville was uniquely American. The early comics, who were mostly Eastern European Jews, gave way to the Irish, like George Carlin. Their comedy carried a whiff of optimism, and some of a madman's tenderness. Robin Williams had it. Richard Pryor and George Carlin had it. Just consider, while Dostoevsky was writing *Crime and Punishment,* halfway around the world, Mark Twain was writing *The Celebrated Jumping Frog of Calaveras County.*

Stand-up comedy in the '70s was different from what it is now. Now, everyone wants to be a stand-up comedian. There were clubs, most of the comedians were close friends of mine like Richard Pryor, and all the other guys were just good friends. At all the clubs that we worked at in the '60s in New York, we were opening for jazz or folk musicians, not comedians. I performed at the Bitter End, opening for Jerry Jeff Walker. I also opened for Miles Davis (we spoke for hours after each show we'd done, and I never understood a word he said, as he talked so quietly). Once, Miles did a benefit at Lincoln Center and asked me to emcee it. It was sold out because he was so popular. All he cared about was music, so he went onstage, with thousands of people there to see him, and he turned his back on them to experience the music with his band of six musicians. The music was incredible—it was so atonal, as he was so ahead of everything with abstract, obscure music. When, after the performance, I said, "Thank you, Miles, I'll be humming that for weeks," he took me offstage in a headlock. That was the atmosphere that I loved to be in, with artists. I also happened to love the storytelling atmosphere of the country western singers. You were always in a creative community, and what could be better than that?

What is hard and painful about doing comedy, for me? Well, the actual performing, the "doing"—no, that was enjoyable to me. I would sometimes get a little nervous, but I never had much stage fright. There is a tradition of a kind of Jewish angst explored kinetically by these mentors of mine. They didn't mentor me by discovering me, but I was aware of them and read their stuff, and I realized that I was already in that kind of rhythm of talking about Jewish princesses and political stuff. And I held court every morning at the coffee shop, and after a while you just couldn't get into the place.

I dealt with the only material I had, which was my life. I didn't think it was an exceptional life, but it was the only way that I knew how to be funny and witty. I didn't think of it as being funny. I never thought of it as being a clown, and I never thought of it as a career. I used to go to the Gate of Horn in Chicago to hear the folk music I loved (I played the guitar). If there were more than two or three people, I would play, and they would all sing along.

I never had a comedian's range. I couldn't do impressions like comedians do. I wasn't a particularly good singer, although I was musical. But when you put me onstage, I would leave the script, just use it as a sort of springboard to whatever I wanted to say. The cast would stop, and I would literally do a monologue about what was going on in the play. It would be amateurish and embarrassing, but it was totally original. I performed at the Bitter End after Second City, with very small audiences, but I started to build a following. And when they moved on, this new guy came in, and that was Richard Pryor.

Once you're doing stand-up comedy on the level that we were doing it then, you're letting everyone know everything about you. So when you meet afterward, you sort of up the ante, and, well, yeah, "I fucked up this, I wanted to do that." It became like musicians talking about what they were doing. And Richard Pryor (I called him Richie until the day he died) wasn't quite Richie to the extent that he was going to be, but certainly heading there. He was at the Cafe Au Go Go, and I walked in to see what he was doing, which was brilliant Black-white stuff that no one would go near. It was outrageous then, but it wouldn't be outrageous now. Richie was a whole other level of writing genius because he was drawing from some authentic part of himself. Basically, it's writing. Then you improvise, you exaggerate; you only have one job, which is to connect with the audience and have them feel that they got their money's worth. Your job isn't to make them feel, oh, "we Blacks are marching down the street," or "I can't believe David Steinberg said that about Jews."

Comedians "steal" from each other all the time—not material, but ideas. There's no good comedian that hasn't stolen ideas from someone. And you don't really "steal" material. You do your own version of it. And so that's a bar code. So Shelley Berman on the phone—I guarantee you Nichols and May had their comedic "on the phone" piece before him. Bob Newhart was on the phone in a way no one else was. And Shelley Berman was on the phone—he just held his fingers to his mouth to give the audience the impression he had a prop there. And those comedians were so good at it, you believed that was a phone.

But it doesn't matter. It comes down to your thumbprint—how your version of that works. It's impossible for comedians not to "borrow" from each other. There is no way there would be Dave Chappelle if there hadn't been Richard Pryor. And there probably would be no Key & Peele (Keegan-Michael Key and Jordan Peele) if there weren't a Dave Chappelle. Keegan-Michael Key and Jordan Peele created the number one show on Comedy Central between 2012 and 2015, fifty-three socially conscious episodes in which they wrote, acted in, and directed sketches. In one, Keegan played Luther, President Obama's anger management translator, against Jordan playing Obama. In another, "East/West Collegiate Bowl," they created a parody of college football players and the way they present themselves. The show won a Peabody Award. It was irreverent, it was edgy, it totally pushed the envelope. Jordan Peele is now a producer/director/writer with great success. His first movie, *Get Out,* a horror movie rooted in social ills, won an Oscar for Best Screenplay, and was nominated for Best Picture and Best Director that same year. Keegan-Michael Key has since debuted on Broadway in Steve Martin's *Meteor Shower* with Amy Schumer. Both Keegan and Jordan were on my show *Inside Comedy* and were very insightful, funny; it's one of my favorite episodes. Years ago, in 2007, I directed Keegan in a wonderful pilot called *Frangela* (it was obvious then that Keegan had a gift), written by and starring the brilliant comedic duo Frances Callier and Angela V. Shelton, all Second City alumni, naturally. A comedy that dealt with race, it was clearly before its time, and it scared the network, but we were so proud of it. Time to remake it.

After comedy, my greatest passion was always language, which led me, many years later, to conversations with most of the greatest living comedians in America. I produced and hosted a show called *Inside*

Comedy, where I interviewed comedians like Jerry Seinfeld, Don Rickles, Chris Rock, Steve Carell, Billy Crystal, Martin Short, Brad Garrett, Larry David, Sarah Silverman, Garry Shandling, Mel Brooks, Carl Reiner, Ellen DeGeneres, Kathy Griffin, Steven Wright, Robin Williams, Louis C.K., Judd Apatow, Tiny Fey, Drew Carey, Martin Mull, Stephen Colbert, Jon Stewart, Steve Martin, Lily Tomlin, Jim Carrey, Will Ferrell, Betty White, Keenen Ivory Wayans, Richard Lewis, Keegan-Michael Key, Jordan Peele, Gilbert Gottfried, Bill Maher, Jimmy Fallon, Robert Klein, Zach Galifianakis, and, one of my all-time favorites, the great Jonathan Winters.

That is the history of comedy right there. Winters, by the way, was also a muse for the lately departed genius Robin Williams. Robin and I traveled the country together from 2012 through 2014 in a show that began as a onetime benefit for the Cleveland Clinic—the fabled heart hospital that had once saved Robin's life—and eventually turned into

On set with Jordan Peele (*left*) and Keegan-Michael Key (*center*). Many years ago, I directed Keegan in the pilot *Frangela* and subsequently became a big fan of Key & Peele. I was lucky to have Keegan and Jordan on *Inside Comedy* and to get to know these two amazingly talented people.

a two-year tour of America. For me it was a tour inside the heart and mind of one of America's greatest improvisational comedians and actors, who so sadly took his life. That was, and is, an unbearable loss for this uniquely American art form, and for the many who loved him. Like me.

So what have I learned from five decades inside comedy? I'm still finding out. All I know for sure is that I've gotten the greatest pleasure from it all—doing stand-up, hosting shows, directing sitcoms and movies, and doing *Inside Comedy*. One thing I found out about myself is that I like listening to other people and giving them the chance to talk about themselves. I'm an appreciative listener, and nothing pleases me more than to listen to great comics talk about their work, their life, their unpaid bills. Oh, yeah—and their anecdotes, insider stories, private ruminations (big word for "secrets"), and thoughtful reflections. That is what you will find on these pages. I found that people seem to want to climb into the minds of comedians. And now that the era of Trumpism had suddenly fallen on our heads, and as the independent press is suppressed and discredited, we needed our comedians to remind us that the emperor had no clothes. I should know—a big part of my early success came from satirizing Nixon and his gang, a necessary service to the nation, even though it put me on the Enemies List.

Groucho Marx liked to tell the story of how, when the Marx Brothers played a small town in Ohio, a man came up to the box office and asked, "Before I buy a ticket, I'd like to know one thing: Is it sad or high kickin'?" I remember Groucho saying, "That's the best line I ever heard about show business." For Groucho, "sad or high kickin'" said all there was to say, not just about show business, but about life itself. My hopes for this book is that it will be mostly high kickin'.

Where did it all begin? In Canada, of course. That's where some of our most inventive, most beloved comedians have come from over the last several decades—Martin Short, Eugene Levy, John Candy, Andrea Martin, Mike Myers, Dan Aykroyd, Jim Carrey, Norm Macdonald, Seth Rogen, Ryan Reynolds (who is not a comedian but a great comic actor), Lorne Michaels, Michael J. Fox, Tom Green, Catherine O'Hara,

Howie Mandel, Leslie Nielsen, Will Arnett, Samantha Bee, Tommy Chong, Caroline Rhea. How can such a buttoned-down place produce so many unbuttoned comedians? The return of the repressed? Taking moderation to an extreme?

Obviously, Jews seem to do well in Canada. They do even better than the Frenchmen. I come from Winnipeg, and I was around Jews a lot because we lived in the North End. But because I was a good athlete as a kid, I was always playing with the goyim, often late into Shabbat, the Jewish Sabbath. My family was not very orthodox, but we were traditional and spoke at the shul all the time, so I was used to people getting up and talking. After all, the Jews have always been great talkers. (It's probably not a coincidence that psychiatry—the "talking cure"— was invented by a Jew.)

My Russian parents had escaped pogroms in their country, and they were grateful to be in Canada. My father and his brothers and sisters were all grocers, and though no one was making much money, they were very supportive of one another. They weren't observers of Shabbat because they couldn't take the day off, but during the holidays, they'd all be at the shul. My favorite uncle, Israel (they would later name a country after him), was a Communist. I would walk around with him, talk with him, amuse him. He laughed at so much of what I said. I have no idea what that was about, because back then I wasn't trying to be funny at all.

I went to a private Hebrew school in Winnipeg, which was unusual in the late '40s and early '50s. I was taught Hebrew in the morning and English in the afternoon—no humor there. We had a small class of eight people, just two boys and six girls. Everyone from my class turned out to be much more accomplished than me (they're all millionaires now). Not a millionaire, me—but a few years ago I was asked to receive the Order of Canada. Shocking, since in my mind all I've done is make people laugh. The Order of Canada is a Canadian national order and the second-highest honor for merit in the system of orders, decorations, and medals.

Here's the story:

To coincide with the centennial of Canadian Confederation, the three-tiered order was established in 1967 as a fellowship recogniz-

David with Her Excellency the Right Honourable Julie Payette,
Governor General of Canada.

ing the outstanding merit or distinguished service of Canadians who
make a major difference to Canada through lifelong contributions in
every field of endeavor. Membership is accorded to those who exemplify the order's Latin motto, *desiderantes meliorem patriam,* meaning
"they desire a better country," a phrase, strangely enough, taken from
Hebrews 11:16. The three tiers of the order are Companion, Officer,
and Member. Appointees to the order are recommended by an advisory
board—people like scientists, musicians, politicians, artists, athletes,
businesspeople, film stars, benefactors—and, apparently, a comedian.
The ceremony, which also honored Mike Myers some years before me,
and Alex Trebek at the same time as me, was unforgettable—the military in uniform, music, a dignified ceremony, all at Rideau Hall, the
home of the Governor General of Canada.

Getting the Order of Canada was one of the most important
moments of my life. Remember, my father (a rabbi/grocer) and mother
were Russian immigrants, with very little. My only regret is that they
were not there to see me get one of the highest honors of my beloved

country. I do hope that my parents and teachers, especially Ms. McCrumb, who tried so desperately to make me amount to something, are all shocked—and kvelling—with pride and disbelief.

I know I am.

After I got out of Hebrew school, I went to the West Kildonan Collegiate Institute, a high school in a Winnipeg suburb. It wasn't very big, but it was my first time in a public school, my first time seeing these gorgeous girls and boys who were all taller than I was. Despite these handicaps, I could still control the class. I wouldn't say I was a "shit disturber," but I had a way of talking to the whole group, and I was funny. I wasn't aggressive. I was even voted class president. Well, president of my homeroom. Why? Because I could talk. And they could laugh.

I can remember when it first dawned on me that it was important to make people laugh. I had an older brother named Hymie who was killed in the Second World War when he was nineteen. I was around three or four when it happened. Of course, my mother never got back to a normal life after my brother's death.

When I was in my thirties, I went to a psychiatrist because I'd had sporadic depressions throughout my life. This guy was eighty years old, and during our sessions, he kept saying, "Tell me about your family."

And I would reply, "Well, my brother Fishy was a shoe salesman. Couldn't have had a more lovable brother. My brother and my sister, Tammy, were it. And then there were my parents . . ."

"Well, is that it for your family?"

So I told him, "When I was around three or four years old, I had an older brother whose plane crashed during the Second World War when he was coming back to Winnipeg from Iceland."

He asked, "What do you remember about your brother?"

And I said, "I don't remember a lot. There was a picture of him in our house wearing his air force uniform, my brother on one side, my sister on the other, and I'm a baby holding both of his hands. Whenever I looked at that picture, I thought I could feel his hands, even though I really didn't know him."

"Isn't there anything else you remember?"

"I remember the doorbell ringing in our house in Winnipeg. It was Passover, and we were all sitting around the table having a Seder.

My brother Hymie (in uniform; he was killed in
World War II), with (*left to right*) Tammy, me, and
Fishy, 1940s. Whenever I think of my brother Hymie
in uniform, I always imagine holding his hands. I
realize now it's because this picture, taken when I was
so young, was there all those years after World War II.
My brother Fishy loved comedy and would sneak me
into places I was too young to get into, and my sister,
Tammy, became a mother to me, as my mother had
an understandable breakdown after my brother was
killed.

I remember my dad saying, 'Duddy, go get it,' and I went, and there
was a telegram. I remember a lot of laughing had been going on in the
house, and I gave my dad the telegram, and then everyone suddenly
stopped laughing. We found out that my brother had been killed in the
war. Everyone started to cry."

The psychiatrist let me sit there for the longest time. After another long silence, he asked, "If you were a little kid bringing a message to your family that made them cry, don't you think that might have initiated your wanting to make people laugh?"

I remember thinking, "God, what an incredible insight. There's no way I would ever have thought of that on my own."

Fast-forward to one night when I was doing my one-man show in New York, and I closed with that story about the psychiatrist. It was different from the kind of topical material I usually did, and at the end there was silence. Then the audience just went crazy. The whole show made sense to them. That kind of visceral reaction from an audience might be why I'm so comfortable with comedy. That kind of reaction is all I care about. It's life-affirming.

By the way, Winnipeg was a great place to grow up.

Once, years ago, I flew from Los Angeles to Vancouver to direct a movie there. Actually, I'm the Martin Scorsese of Canada, on the A-list, always in demand, not because of my flawless camerawork or my impeccable ear for dialogue, but simply because I'm a Canuck. Canadian tax laws give a big tax credit to any film company for each Canadian point—meaning each Canadian they hire for an important position. (When I look into the bathroom mirror of my home in California, I'm shaving a face worth three Canadian points; by hiring me as a director, producer, and screenwriter, not to mention my walk-on as the Panicky Rabbi in scene 5, you get a ton of Canadian money and Canadian tax breaks.)

Anyway, here I am at the airport, shuffling along in a slow long line of fidgety travelers headed toward the US Immigration booth.

Someone says, "Are you who I think you are?"

"Probably not," I say, and keep moving.

"Booga Booga!" he shouts.

He is, of course, repeating my famous tagline, which was at its peak of popularity approximately halfway through the Gerald Ford administration.

"The psychiatrist bit! I have all your records!" he says.

The guy five briefcases ahead of me says he loves watching me on *The Tonight Show*. I thank him, even though I haven't been on *The

Tonight Show in ten years. He asks me if Jay Leno is as nice off-screen as he is on.

"Nicer," I say, and keep on moving.

Two distinct vibes permeate the room: one of recognition, the other of confusion. The members of the confused group are thinking: "Who is this guy, anyway?"

I don't mind that. The only reason I need to be on television these days is when I see that faraway look in a maître d's eyes. But even so, the phantom limb of my celebrity makes me act a certain way in public. A certain carriage. A way of walking without making eye contact. An expectation that you're going to be looked after. That's all fine for the people who know me, but to the people who don't know me, I'm just another nitwit with an attitude.

So as I approach the immigration officer, buoyed by the admiration of my two fans, he's thinking: "Why is this guy acting so strangely? And why does he look so vaguely familiar?"

These things happen to me a lot now. When I was really famous, which was from the very late '60s to the very early '90s, my life was a lot easier. And shallower—sure, you've got me there. On the road, for instance, airline employees would inevitably recognize me and whisk me immediately ahead of everybody else. You think I was embarrassed? Never. These days, when I go to the airport, I have to look for older and older airline employees each time. It's difficult being a semi-, quasi-, or—this hurts—formerly famous person.

One guy in a bookstore a few months ago stared at me for a few minutes, scratched his head, walked over, and said, "I know you from someplace."

I pulled out the always embarrassing "You probably know me from television."

"No, that's not it," he said, and walked away.

CHAPTER 2

THE APPRENTICESHIP OF DUDDY STEINBERG

*The most irresponsible student at the
University of Chicago sees the best comedian of all time—
Lenny Bruce—and finds his life's work.*

I had my own thumbprint when I was fifteen years old—and my own sense of humor. The strange thing is that in those times, the yeshiva (Chicago Jewish Academy) let me actually teach younger kids when I myself was a kid—fifteen years old!

One bleak day, my best friend, Moishe Postone, who was a brilliant scholar, looked up from his books and said, "You know, Duddy, there's a program at the University of Chicago that's just made for someone like you. It is called the Lab Program."

I'd never heard of it. Turns out the Lab Program was designed for bright students who hadn't gotten good grades, or even graduated from high school. The idea was that we'd be "stimulated" to learn by the ambiance and atmosphere at the university. We'd take an eclectic smorgasbord of advanced courses and graduate with an MA without even bothering with a BA. The program was designed for no more than six or seven students at a time. And, by the way, most Lab Program alumni have since gone on to do things like help unravel the DNA molecule or explore the meaning of the word "meaning."

Me? I got into a class taught by Philip Roth. Sort of. I had never seen a stand-up comedian, but this was the most witty, compelling, interesting human being. He was incredible! He was the Leonard

Cohen of his time. Then I got into a class led by Saul Bellow. Still in the Lab Program. Surprised? Me, too. He was amazing.

But first there was kind of an interview to get through. Afterward, they told me to wait outside the room for a few minutes. When I came back, they said, "We're giving you a Furstenberg."

It turned out I had won a Furstenberg Scholarship, which entitled me to free tuition at the university. Furstenberg Scholars like me had great latitude in choosing their course load. I chose to play a lot of basketball and occasionally to audit a class or two that interested me, provided that it had nothing to do with mathematics, physics, or biology. I found out a few years later that, soon after, very suddenly, they stopped giving out Furstenberg Scholarships.

My days at the University of Chicago followed a strict pattern. Every morning I went directly to Swift Hall. This was because I was broke all the time, and the library served breakfast on the honor system. I'd take some coffee and sweet rolls and donuts, engage some earnest theological students in a discussion about Saint Francis or Saint Thomas Aquinas, wait until they left, walk up to the change box, pick it up, shake the coins already in it, jingle the change in my pocket, and leave. (A few years later, when I performed at Mandel Hall on campus, I went back to Swift Hall, saw they still had breakfast on the honor system, and very cavalierly took out a $50 bill from my wallet and put it in the box.)

The rest of the day I spent in the student union coffee shop. The C Shop, it was cutely called. One morning, six great-looking female students walked past my table. And everything changed. Everything stopped because in the entire history of the University of Chicago, no one had ever seen six great-looking female students walking together. No one had even suspected that there were three beautiful women at the entire University of Chicago.

Anyway, six beautiful women, dressed beatnik-style with long dark hair, dark sweaters, black skirts, and black stockings, walked past my table. They went through a little door at the end of the cafeteria. I'd never noticed this door before. I stood up immediately, leaving the check for others, and followed them through it.

There was a sign on this door that said "U. of Chi. Theater." I climbed up a spiral staircase to a tiny attic-like space. Jammed into this attic was a very large man named Robert Benedetti, surrounded, unbelievably, by three more beautiful women. Bob ran the theater, had seen me do my "thing" in the coffee shop, and couldn't get over what I was doing.

"You've got to do more with this," he said.

I didn't really know what he meant. I wasn't doing anything except having fun, and I didn't think about turning it into an act or a theater piece. Stand-up comedy was not anywhere in my brain—you couldn't have a career in stand-up comedy; it would be ridiculous. No one planned it, no one would do it, you couldn't make enough money, and it wasn't a respectable thing to do . . .

So that's when Benedetti said, "You've got to go see Lenny Bruce." At the time, I'd never been to see a stand-up comedian. I was into folk music. I played the guitar and was a fan of the Weavers. I only knew comedians from the radio.

So I went to see Lenny Bruce when he was performing at the Gate of Horn, a folk/jazz music club on the North Side of Chicago, and he took my breath away. First of all, I liked the way he was dressed, in a Nehru jacket with a mandarin collar, and I liked the way he very gracefully walked the stage. He took the audience into his confidence. Later, I learned that this was the opposite of the Al Jolson/Eddie Cantor school of comedy, where the performer gives the audience anything to win them over, the "you ain't seen nothing yet" onslaught.

Lenny Bruce was cool, a precursor to Miles Davis, who'd play trumpet with his back to the audience. With a mic in hand, Lenny talked the language of a hipster. He was the first stream-of-consciousness comedian I ever saw. He was a revelation because he wasn't trying to be funny all the time. He was into the story, the way the character talked. Doing comedy is being smart, which I saw with Lenny. I suddenly knew that I wanted to be smart as much as I wanted to be funny. And then I realized that being funny is a version of being smart. That has stayed with me to this day. And as you will see, many comedians feel this way.

Lenny Bruce didn't talk loudly, so you'd have to really *listen*. At that point he'd only opened for jazz musicians, and he was really into the rhythms of jazz. He'd say, "Okay, dig this, da-da-da, dig that, dig this." I always thought that he secretly wanted to be a jazz musician, because they were the coolest people on earth (or maybe we didn't know if they were really cool or just on heroin all the time, which would make them seem cool). He was into the music of the rhythm of what he was saying.

The Lenny Bruce I saw that night was a very thin, very handsome man of about thirty. There were about three hundred people in the audience, and out of all of them, maybe six of us actually laughed at his material. The rest of the people, those who might have come to see Lenny Bruce and be titillated because they'd read about him in *Time* magazine, absolutely hated him, and they sat in sullen silence because he was saying things that offended and angered them. But we didn't care. And he didn't care. Because he was brilliant. I thought he was the coolest guy I'd ever seen as a performer.

At the time (although I didn't learn this until later), Lenny was at the height of his career. He was called the "Blue Boy" of comedy, notorious for saying "shocking" things. He didn't curse, didn't use words like "shit" or "fuck." And he used a lot of Yiddish on top of it. Yiddish was really dying out at that point, so when he was using Yiddish, no one knew what he was talking about. And since most of the audience couldn't understand him, he could say just about anything. He would tell the police to "kiss my tuchus"—and the police didn't know what he was saying, either (but they arrested him anyway and took him to jail).

That first time I saw him, I was sixteen and still at the yeshiva, and I still had my kippah on. No one had a kippah in those days because you could get beat up. The next time I saw him, several years later, I was one of the stars of Second City. That didn't mean anything to him, and I never told him about the kippah. Suddenly, as I was sitting there watching him, he singled me out and said, "David, where is the kippah? Where is the skullcap?" And I said, "I made it into a Frisbee since I was coming to see you."

So when Lenny was hauled into the police station, the other cops wanted to know what he'd said that had gotten him arrested, but he just repeated the words in Yiddish. When they asked him to explain, he said, "I don't have to explain. It's Yiddish." They called in a Yiddish cop who worked at night but had a delicatessen during the day, so at Lenny's trial, the Yiddish cop translated for the jury. That's how absurd the times were, but that rebelliousness got into my anti-establishment DNA bones big-time. (Little did I know that one day my own stand-up comedy routines on *The Smothers Brothers Comedy Hour* would be subject to the same kind of controversy and censorship.) Later, even after I saw other comedians—and there were some great ones then, like Mort Sahl and Shelley Berman, who were bringing in a newer, edgier, more sophisticated comedy style—I still couldn't get over Lenny Bruce, especially since, during that time, in '57 and '58, America was a very Calvinistic country, and public performances were censored. There were certain things you just couldn't say in those days—and not just profanity. Questioning Protestant values was pretty much off-limits, yet Lenny challenged the prevailing morality and was an equal opportunity offender. He would go at the police *and* he would go at the condescending liberals.

Thinking back on this brilliant presence, I realize that because he'd started as a Borscht Belt comedian, he had all the skills. He could sing, he could do impressions. Dead-on impressions. Just by curling a lip or finding the perfect change in his voice and posture, it was as if he was drawing a big cartoon of that person in the air right in front of him. But he used those skills in a new way. That's what was really shocking. At some point he'd decided, "I'm not playing the game. I won't kiss the audience's ass." He made the assumption, even though it wasn't true, that he and the audience all hated the same things. He hated any discrimination, any prejudice, any phoniness. He hated all public figures. What did he love? Talking about the hypocrisy that lay below the surface of '50s and early '60s society.

I remember a bit he did one night about a prison riot. He played the warden, the prisoners, a black Uncle Tom about to die, the Irish priest spouting phony platitudes, and a gay convict named Kiki who demanded a gay bar in the east wing for "the boys." The warden was Hume Cronyn. The priest was Barry Fitzgerald. And Uncle Tom—this might have been showing off a bit—was Paul Robeson. I didn't know then how difficult it was, how many years of failure and rejection and humiliation it took to reach the level on which he was operating. All I knew was that every routine, every line, every image, every word was absolutely the right one to convey his ideas. He flew seamlessly from one hilarious, absolutely correct, and mind-blowing insight to another. He was a jazz musician—only with words and thoughts instead of notes and chords.

In retrospect, he must have also been on some form of speed that night, but that isn't important. Neither is it important that he was "bombing," leaving most of his audience far behind. He stood alone onstage in his own impenetrable bubble of genius. There were moments I was so in awe that I was unable to laugh. And, after the arrest, he went from small audiences of about forty people to where you couldn't even get into the Gate of Horn. I saw him at least twice after—never the same show, but always supporting Blacks and calling the liberals on their phoniness.

And then I thought, "Is it possible that someday I can do something like this?"

In the end, it was both Lenny Bruce's brilliance and coolness that most impressed and inspired me. Plus, I'd heard that his girlfriend Honey was a stripper. I thought, "I *could* do this."

CHAPTER 3

GOD—WHOM I'M SURE YOU'LL REMEMBER FROM LAST WEEK'S SERMON

*My first years at Second City and
the other icons who joined*

One day, Bill Alton said to me, "You've got to see the guys in the touring company of Second City that is performing at the university." Second City, he explained patiently, was a Chicago-based "improvisational group" whose members took suggestions from the audience, improvised scenes out of them, and honed the ones that worked into comedy skits. They didn't use props or scenery. All they used was their minds. Of course I was going to go—but I didn't have money for a ticket, so I sneaked into the theater to see them.

The troupe I saw that first night consisted of Howard Alk (co-founder of Second City), Severn Darden, Andrew Duncan, Barbara Harris, Anthony Holland, Joan Rivers, Alan Arkin, and the great Elaine May and Mike Nichols. Nichols and May were young, intelligent, and funny. They tossed around intellectual, political, and literary references without a second thought. Elaine could play what today would be called a "bitchy woman," but do it with humor in a way that the audience was always on her side with whatever a male, usually Mike Nichols, had said to her. They were revolutionary in that they were able to make fun of hospitals, politics, funeral homes, and even motherhood, but the audience was not offended. They were not concerned with addressing the entire audience—what the two of them thought was funny and irreverent was what mattered, not what the audience responded to. Elaine and Mike revolutionized actual improvisational comedy as much as Second City did.

As I have said before, comedians still "steal" from each other all the time—not material, but ideas. It's like what T. S. Eliot once said, "Immature poets borrow; mature poets steal." That's a bar code. Even Lily Tomlin picked up from Elaine May her hilarious telephone operator routine, as Ernestine. (And Elaine May's hilarious telephone bits were inspired by an actress from the 1930s named Helen Troy.) But it doesn't matter. As I have said before, it comes down to your thumbprint—how your version of that works. It's stylistic.

Paul Sills, one of the founders of Second City, was good-looking and strong in a quiet way. He'd had a romance with the adorable comedic actress Barbara Harris, whom everyone at Second City yearned for. The Sillses were a whole family of improvisers, especially Paul's mother, Viola Spolin, who'd virtually created improvisation comedy with Paul. But Paul was my mentor, and his main advice to me was, "Don't work from the front of your mind. It's the subconscious stuff that matters."

Del Close was another mentor who also shaped a lot of great comedic actors—John Candy, Dan Aykroyd, John Belushi, Stephen Colbert, Bill Murray and Bill's brother Brian Doyle-Murray, Jon Favreau, Tina Fey, Amy Poehler, and Bob Odenkirk. There was something professorial about Del, who was thin and wore glasses. He seemed uncomfortable in his skin, maybe because he was so tall, and his comedy was similar to Woody Allen's, though I always felt Del's style might have been there before Woody's. He came up with something called "resistentialism"— like existentialism but about how objects resist people. He'd say, for example, "I want to sit in this chair, but the chair keeps moving away." He was an early and total beatnik. Once when I was interviewing Del during an improvisation, he fell asleep in the middle of the sketch. Unfortunately, I don't think it was verisimilitude; I think it was heroin, which he'd introduced to Second City. (Heroin had no appeal for me. The last thing I wanted to do was fall asleep onstage.) Del did so many hallucinatory drugs that he became a guru to all the people hitting hallucinogens back then. He was a brilliant guy and a great mentor.

When I was onstage with Del, my game improved, and the ideas came easier to me. He was incredibly smart, but he liked to show the audience how smart he was, a sort of show-offy smart, and that's not the kind of smart that mattered to me at all. I was after something else. Second City offered that, for here were people being funny about things I'd been trying to be funny about—anger, loneliness, repression, and pretentious people forcing their opinions down your throat.

The most amazing thing of all was that they worked together as a team. They were like a little family. I was twenty years old, and for the first time in my life, I'd found something that I really truly wanted to do. Something that I could do easily, that would be hard for just about everybody else. Because I'd snuck in under the circus tent and found magic. And I was on fire.

I thought to myself, "I can do that." And strangely enough, this time I could.

When I was at the University of Chicago, I was funny, but not aware that I was being funny. I would scroll through a newspaper, and I could feel something happening. The stories of the day were inspiration to me, and the jokes would just fly. It didn't hurt to be an outsider. If you're great at school, a nice kid, it's not good for comedy. It's not good for writers, either. A wound is what writers lean on to come to themselves. You need that. At Second City, you were forced into it because someone was improvising and you had to respond to it. Second City changed my mind—and my life.

I can say that it was made for me, since I loved improvisation. The first time I got onstage, I owned the place. It was like getting into a suit that fit exactly right.

Being at Second City was better than doing stand-up on the road, and back then it was the only game in town (*Saturday Night Live* hadn't started yet).

First, I was faster than anyone.

Second, I had more information that mattered to the culture at the time. I tried to read everything.

Third, I was at the right age, in my twenties. I was curious about things that I read, and I was interested in putting them onstage.

Fourth, I had grown up with radio. I had learned from listening to radio growing up in Winnipeg that when you're talking to the audience in any way, you create a picture for them. Basically, it's like writing. You create images. Then you improvise, and then you exaggerate.

Most of all, I had figured out that as a stand-up comedian, you only have one job, which is to connect with the audience and have them feel that they've gotten their money's worth. And then, truly, it's all the silences; it's not always what you say. It's in the looks. And moments in between. When I was younger watching movies in Canada, I didn't know that there was a director. I believed the movie. So the audience is getting a moral code from the movies. Which as a kid stays with you.

Here are the core principles of performing at Second City, principles I still follow today:

1. You work from the top of your intelligence.
2. You don't just play to the audience.
3. The more unique you are, the more interesting it's going to be.

In other words:

Don't dumb down for an audience.
Talk the way you would talk, and keep it as simple as it can be.
The ideal way for a comedian to talk is to verbally create visual images. So you're not just watching your guy stand alone onstage, you're hearing the world he's creating from it.

Just those three little rules.

And then I started something no one else was doing: at the insistence of Paul Sills, I would take a suggestion from the Old Testament and do a mock sermon on it. No one had touched the Bible in stand-up. What made me funny was that I was doing the sermons as a Reform rabbi who doesn't really know what he's talking about. But even when you don't know what you're talking about, you have to know something well to make fun of it. Thank God for those years I studied to be a rabbi. And because Second City was five hundred seats, and it was always filled, you had to do a different sermon every time.

The sermons went something like this:

"Solomon was a king and he lived in a big palace, and Solomon had a wonderful rapport with God . . . whom I'm sure you will remember from last week's sermon [that's how they all started].

"And God said to Solomon, 'You could have anything that your heart desires because you're the king of Israel.'

"And Solomon said, 'Oh, God, grant me wisdom that I might be the wisest man of all.' So God gave Solomon His anthropomorphic zap [a term I used a lot then], and Solomon became all wise and knowing, and *that's* when he knew he should have asked for money."

Then I did one on Moses:

"God is talking to Moses.

"And Moses says,

"'Who should I say sent me?'

"And God said,

"'Whom.'"

Now, believe this (or not), the McCormick Theological Seminary was a block away from Second City, and when I started to do these sermons, the theology students started to come to see me in droves. They wore those little white collars, but they weren't *Catholic* Catholic—more like the equivalent of Reform Jews—and they would challenge me on my sermons. They would try to catch me out with some biblical figure they thought I wouldn't know. They were stunned that they couldn't stump me on any of it. One night, when I was being recorded for my first comedy album, *The Incredible Shrinking God,* my dad was in the audience. One of the theology students suggested that I do a sermon on Onan, and I said, "I can't do Onan for you tonight, but I suggest you go home and try it yourself." Everyone laughed. My dad couldn't get over it. When he went back to Winnipeg, he told everyone, "Even the priests like him!"

I knew I had arrived when *Newsweek* did a piece on me doing those sermons at Second City, and that gave me some national recognition. But mostly, Second City helped define me as a person and established rules for comedy that are still a part of me today.

My first album was *The Incredible Shrinking God*. Sermons included "Moses," "Cain and Abel," "Onan and Jonah" (Jonah was swallowed by a whale; however, whales have tiny gullets and cannot swallow whole prophets, and the Christians, as is their wont from time to time, threw the Jew overboard), and "Esther and Joshua," all of which originated from suggestions from the audience at Second City. And almost every sermon ended with: "Let's get the Christ back into Christmas and the 'Huh' back into Chanukah." People loved it.

Suddenly I was hot. I was doing my stand-up and loving every minute of it. I never had stage fright, even though on some level, talking about your own life is hard, and can be painful—you're giving a lot of yourself, and you're showing that your ego is bigger than anybody else's. Still, the actual performing was totally enjoyable to me. Moreover, musicians were fans of mine.

A couple of years ago, I was looking at Bob Woodward's book on John Belushi because I saw my name there, and it was an incredible story that Judy Belushi had mentioned to me years earlier that I had forgotten. Judy remembers that when she and John went to see Second City, he couldn't get over how I went into the audience and didn't care what I said to them and that I wasn't hostile.

"John couldn't get over you, David. It wasn't Second City. It was you."

And I said, with real curiosity, "What was it?"

She explained, "The combative way in which you dealt with the audience."

So I asked, "Was I putting them down?"

"No, you let them talk, and then you'd improvise off of what they said. John couldn't get over the boldness of it all." And John went nuts for it, and he couldn't wait to get into Second City. I remember that Kurosawa *Rashomon* sketch I did, called "Roshashanamon." And I threw in all these Yiddish words that sounded Japanese, like *"tahka tahka."* Years later, John Belushi asked me if he could "borrow" it from me, and that became his samurai character on *Saturday Night Live*.

I stayed at Second City for six years. Some of the happiest of my life.

CHAPTER 4

FROM SECOND CITY TO BROADWAY

Little Murders, *Elliott Gould, Lily Tomlin,*
and other memories, from delight to disaster

After Second City, I worked in a club in New York called the Bitter End. Across the street was a place called Cafe Au Go Go.

One night, I put on my brown corduroy Norfolk jacket, which I'd bought at a cool store called Man at Ease in Chicago's Old Town, and I thought, "Okay, well, it must be cool"—it had a flap in back of it, a flap like Sherlock Holmes's. And I wore this with great pride the first night, when Alan Arkin took me to Mike Nichols's house on Central Park West, to a party where you recognize everybody. I smoked cigars at that time. One of the guys says, "David Steinberg smokes cigars," and this very Jewish-looking guy, who looked like a little rabbi, came over to me and said, "I understand you smoke cigars." I said I did. He asked, "Would you like one?" "I would love one," I replied.

He went and he brought back a cigar and lit it for me. That's when Arkin came over to me and said, "You got Isaac Stern to light your cigar?" I was dumbfounded. He lived right next door to Mike.

I then sat down next to a woman who looked like someone's grandma, but stubborn and unhappy, bad-mouthing everyone. She liked to hear herself talk, and she had a low voice. She liked me, for some reason. And what she was saying was interesting, not the conversation I was expecting. "What plays have you seen?" she asked me. I had just seen *Luv* because of Alan Arkin. So I gave her my opinions about that one, and then about everything on Broadway, because I felt like I was talking to a friend of mine from Winnipeg. She sat with me all night and wouldn't leave me alone, until finally I just had to get away from her. And then Alan comes over and says, "Wow, you made friends again—this time with Lillian. I said, "Yeah, Lillian, you look familiar." She said something like, "Tell the putz he is with Lillian Hellman." By the time Alan had walked to the other side across the room, I had withdrawn everything that I had said to her. I tried to apologize for every opinion I had. That's how green I was to all of this. Finally she left. Alan Arkin comes over and says, "I don't know the last time Lillian Hellman has been so engaged. I think she has a crush."

I should mention that before I left, Alan said to me, "Burn the fucking Norfolk suit!"

When I first got the audition for the original Broadway production of *Little Murders* in 1967, I was making a salary of $150 a week and only had enough money for a one-way ticket to get to the audition. When it was time to go home, Elliott Gould bought me my return ticket back to Chicago.

When I auditioned for the original production of *Little Murders* on Broadway (and also when I performed in the actual show itself), I reversed the attitude that everyone else had auditioned with. My role in the play was gay, but I didn't want to play gay the way that every comedian had done their cliché gay impression. Not because of a political point of view, but just because I couldn't play flamboyant the way other comedians could, so I chose to take the opposite approach. I worked with Jules Feiffer, who wrote the play, and I reversed it so that in the first act, when my character wasn't out at all, I was outrageous. And in the second act, when I had come out but no one knew it yet, I became very calm and just sat there onstage with sunglasses on, listening to Elliott Gould and Barbara Cook.

Barbra Streisand, who was married to Elliott Gould at the time, told Cis Corman, one of her closest friends, and also one of the most well-known casting directors of the time, to come see me in *Little Murders*. I met Barbra when Elliott brought me home. She was already a star at the time, and she's always treated me the same way—very loving, friendly, never snubbing me, ever. As Isaac Bashevis Singer was a friend

Backstage with Steven Vinaver and my great friend Jon Voight, circa 1967. Both Jon and I were starring on Broadway at the time, Jon in *That Summer—That Fall,* and me in the original production of *Little Murders.* They both lasted about ten days, but we had a great time.

Again backstage, this time with Severn Darden (*center*), an original member of Second City in Chicago. Severn was very intellectual, but very funny and light at the same time. Always getting laughs. He gave me a few tips for the show (*Little Murders*); it only lasted ten days. I obviously wasn't listening.

of mine, I introduced Barbra to his books. Remember, I had been in every one of Philip Roth's classes at the University of Chicago (Philip Roth, who knew everything about literature). He always talked about Isaac Bashevis Singer, so I had read everything he had written and gave his books to everybody.

So this time, several years later, when I was at Elliott Gould's, Elliott told Barbra that I was a fan of Isaac Bashevis Singer, and she responded that she had never paid attention to his work because she didn't feel she was in his league, yet now she had been asked to do an adaptation of his. So yes, it was me who introduced Barbra to *Yentl*. I had read it and told her it was incredible. At first, she wasn't buying it, because she didn't want to be a girl playing a boy. I told her that Singer would never let her change the whole substance of the irony of what the story was (as I said to Barbra, God is the best writer of irony), but to be Barbra Streisand, you have to believe in yourself 1,000 percent when most actors only believe in themselves 100 percent.

When Barbra was doing *Yentl,* I would have lunch with Isaac Bashevis Singer. He would introduce me to everyone, very prestigious people such as producers. I never got over that kind of generosity from a brilliant talent and wonderful man.

I returned to the Bitter End in New York City. That night, there were six people in the audience. Then I saw Sidney Poitier come in with Diahann Carroll. He was a huge star on Broadway at the time, also a good friend and mentor. If he hadn't come, I am not sure I would have continued to play full-out for those six people. Turns out that one of those six people was Dan Sullivan, THE theater reviewer for *The New York Times.* The next morning, the phone woke me up. Carly Simon and her sisters lived above me. I lived with my girlfriend Mary Ellen Mark, the extraordinary photographer who was addressing political and social issues, photographing Vietnam War protestors and urban poverty. She was a star. I was crazy about her. She was so smart and beautiful and taught me so much during the three years we were together. She always carried the same camera with her. Happily, we remained friends throughout the years. Me? I'd go to the coffee shop to read the newspapers before I started the day. That morning Carly called me, very early, and said, "Duddy, Duddy, have you read *The New York Times* today?"

I said, "No, Carly, I worked last night. I'm tired."

"Go read the fuckin' *New York Times*."

"I don't have *The New York Times*."

"Well, come up. I'm gonna give it to you."

It was Dan Sullivan's review:

"David Steinberg, a cross between Woody Allen and Lenny Bruce, is something else." You can imagine what it did for me.

My agent was Harry Kalcheim. He was a big agent and handled Alan Arkin, too. Down the hall from Harry's office was the junior agent, David Geffen, who had started working in the William Morris mailroom, notorious for its mail clerks going on to great things. By this time, he was on the nineteenth floor, and I talked to him all the time. He was just great: super-smart, super-motivated, super-focused—and a mensch. One day, Geffen asked me where was I going because I was rushing out, and I explained that Cis Corman asked me to come in to read for this movie that Mike Nichols was doing. Geffen said, "Oh, that one. They're not going to go with a little Jew like you; they're going to go with a tall guy like Tony Bill. So don't even bother." That was *The Graduate.* And, of course, they did it with a little Jew named Dustin Hoffman.

The other Broadway play I did was *Carry Me Back to Morningside Heights,* directed by Sidney Poitier and written by Robert Alan Aurthur. They became advocates of mine forever, and when Sidney did a movie called *The Lost Man* in 1969, he gave me a key role as a photographer wanting to capture the moment of someone dying. Sidney and I remained close friends, and a classier man you could not find.

You know who else came to see me at the Bitter End? Walter Matthau and his very funny wife, Carol. I didn't know them very well, but I will always remember the story Walter told after the show, still one of my favorites. It is true that Walter and Carol were always bickering, in a funny, good-natured sort of way, since they were married for forty-one years. They would fight and make up, fight and make up, and everyone who knew them knew this. So they got into a fight just as they were

With one of the great loves of my life, Mary Ellen Mark, when we were just starting out. Yes, the iconic photographer, in New York City, circa 1966.

going on a tour of Auschwitz. They were carrying on all through the tour. When they finished the tour and got back on the bus, hardly talking to each other, Walter said to Carol, "You ruined Auschwitz for me!"

In the fall of 1969, I had a show on ABC Television called *Music Scene,* featuring rock and pop music stars—Tom Jones was on the initial program, and Janis Joplin, James Brown, Crosby, Stills, Nash & Young, Three Dog Night, Isaac Hayes, Bo Diddley, Stevie Wonder. The show had many co-hosts, including Lily Tomlin. Mama Cass, with the Mamas and the Papas, performed on the show, and we became good friends. I really liked her. She had a wonderful sense of humor and was always ready to help anyone. When she died suddenly, at only thirty-two, we were so shocked and sad. Judy (my ex) and I went to the funeral. I couldn't get it together, and we were late, which embarrassed Judy. We got there, and the usher recognized me and proceeded to take me to the area where the family was sitting, and seated me with the Cass family on the stage, facing out to the hundreds of mourners. The family didn't think I was that close to her, so they were surprised to see me, let alone onstage with them. Everyone was wailing, and Judy said, "We are late, everyone is wailing, we're sitting with the family, so you had better start now." I overwailed, as a bad actor would. And as I remember that day, I really do miss Cass. She was a special person.

Mary Ellen Mark taking a candid shot of us in our New York City bathroom when we were just starting our careers, circa 1966. She went nowhere without her camera, and we are all lucky for that.

Ruth Buzzi, Madeline Kahn, the JFK-impersonator Vaughn Meader, Mort Sahl, and Joan Rivers all appeared on *The Ed Sullivan Show*. *Ed Sullivan* also brought nightclub comedians steady work in places like Vegas and in nightclubs throughout the country. The show ran on CBS from 1948 to 1971 and made stars out of people like Rodney Dangerfield, Totie Fields, Alan King, and Joan Rivers.

And you know who was my soul mate doing *Music Scene* with me? Lily Tomlin, who already had a cast of comedic characters she'd developed at the split-level Upstairs at the Downstairs nightclub on West Fifty-Sixth Street in Manhattan. What is it about these women who are so multitalented that their multiple titles don't even fit on one line on a cue card? Talent, ingenuity, originality, bravery, mind-blowing character creation, and hard, hard work. That was Lily's comedy. Like so many of us, Lily Tomlin started as a stand-up in the 1960s in her hometown of Detroit, and then moved to New York off-Broadway. In 1969, a mir-

Smoking a cigar and doing my best Groucho
impression, which was of course captured by Mary
Ellen, circa 1966.

acle happened, and the road that meandered between super-successful
Broadway, television, and films began to make its mark.

The facts:

Lily grew up in Detroit, so when we had lunch to catch up, I went
back to those days and wondered if she was funny then, if she had been
interested in comedy?

"I made up shows all the time, from the time I was five. I took ballet and tap at the Department of Parks and Recreation across the street
from our house—you know, they had programs to keep kids off the
street. What I loved was performance. I didn't know what show business was because first I listened to radio, which makes your imagination
soar, and then I went to the movies—because we didn't get a TV until
I was ten, which I think had a big impact on me. I was blue-collar,
Southern Baptist, grew up in an apartment house. And we lived in an
incredible little pool of humanity. Not just in the apartment house, but
going out block after block, as the houses would get bigger and bigger all the way to Chicago and Boston Boulevard. You know—the big
and ritzy streets. I went to school with many of those kids, and what I
watched, what I really saw, were the people in the building. They were
all so interesting. I used to hang out with my father a lot, like at the

What a beautiful picture of Lily Tomlin. We've known each other since the beginning of our careers. She actually once told me when we were in our twenties how tired she was of being single, and I told her, "Don't worry; you'll meet a wonderful guy." That's how naive I was.

bookie joint, and the track and the bars, and that broadened my world. My mother, a nice Christian woman who stayed at home, a very good wife and mother, would take me to church with her on Sunday. And then the rest of the weekend I'd go to the bars and the track. What a combination, right? That was great because those places were full of eccentric characters."

When Lily hit Broadway, the word spread quickly. People had never seen anything like it. No one had ever done a character show like the first show she did, *Appearing Nitely*, at the Biltmore Theatre in March 1977, which showcased her odd characters who captured the audience with their combination of humor—which, at its core, was based on eccentricity—intelligence, courage, and a ton of chutzpah. The same month, Lily made the cover of *Time* magazine with the headline "America's New Queen of Comedy." Her solo show then toured the country and was made into the record album *On Stage*. Fast-forward a few years, to 1985, and Tomlin starred in another one-woman Broadway show, the incomparable and unforgettable *The Search for Signs of Intelligent Life in the Universe*, written by her longtime life partner, writer/director Jane Wagner. The show won her a Tony Award

A joyful Lily Tomlin.

and was made into a feature film in 1991. Tomlin revived the show for a run on Broadway in 2000, which then toured the country through mid-2002.

When you know how observant Lily's eye is, and how courageously she watches and notes people's behaviors, you know that her environment has a lot to do with her comedy. Turns out there is more to it.

"I was very influenced by a woman who was dead by the time I discovered her, Ruth Draper, who was a great monologue artist. And I mean she became the watermark for a monologue. And she would often say, 'A monologue's not worth doing unless you've worked on it for seven or eight years.' I could really identify with that. Turns out I worked for years on each of my monologues."

Lily was discovered by Rowan and Martin in what were her break-out roles on the variety show *Rowan & Martin's Laugh-In,* which ran from 1967 until 1973. She was actually cast as a replacement in 1969 for Judy Carne, appearing in sketches with other comedians, when, suddenly, she began spotlighting characters that she created, which exploded into the public's imagination. You, of course, remember my two favorites—Ernestine, the condescending, very nosy telephone operator with that unforgettable snort and the opening line "One ringy dingy . . . two ringy dingys," and the line "Have I reached the party to whom I am speaking?" I loved it. I loved that she never had any empathy for the caller—she was a narcissist. She was the most unique character and became iconic right out of the gate, blasting out into the public as the most unusual, hysterical, on-point character that anyone had invented. But as with all of Lily's creations, Ernestine was touching while almost obnoxious, hysterically tough and yet tender—and she still remains absolutely unforgettable today.

You think it was just the ingenious creation of Ernestine that made the world stand up and notice Lily Tomlin? She was followed by Edith Ann, the precocious five-year-old girl who sat on that huge oversized rocking chair and waxed rhapsodic about everything philosophical, which, of course, was hysterical coming from a little girl. Her final line after every bit was, "And that's the truth," followed by a loud raspberry. Edith Ann, too, became iconic right out of the gate. She was a genius creation, and remains so all these years later.

In the 1990s, Lily created a prime-time series of animated specials, and her life partner, by then of more than forty years, Jane Wagner, wrote a book called *Edith Ann: My Life, So Far.*

In 1974, Tomlin was cast by Robert Altman in her first film; her performance as Linnea Reese in *Nashville* won her several awards and nominations for the Golden Globe and Academy Award for Best Supporting Actress. Other big roles in hugely acclaimed films followed, including such classics as *9 to 5* (1980), *All of Me* (1984), *Big Business* (1988), *Flirting with Disaster* (1996), *Tea with Mussolini* (1999), *I Heart Huckabees* (2004), and *Grandma* (2015).

Lily currently stars on the Netflix series *Grace and Frankie* (with Jane Fonda, just renewed for a seventh season) as Frankie Bergstein and has received four consecutive Emmy nominations for this role since 2015.

Lily and I did that show together in 1969 (*Music Scene,* which I mentioned earlier) that no one remembers, except that the guest stars and co-hosts are legend. With her usual humility, remembers Lily, "It was amazing. It was kind of a contemporary hit parade with a tie in to

Billboard. 'Cause we had concerts with the hippest people." I would call it a precursor to *The Midnight Special* and *Saturday Night Live,* because Billboard would have the hit music of the week, and then we would do satire on that hit music of the week.

And then came the identification and acknowledgment of gay rights and gay life. The night of the Star Spangled Night for Rights (1977), for the Human Rights Campaign, which was a gay rights organization, and the first big benefit for anything gay rights ever. At the Hollywood Bowl. What does Lily remember? That surprised me.

"I remember that Elaine May was sitting near the front row 'cause I could hear her laugh, and I remember that you were one of the first acts up, and you killed. And you did some material about masturbation. And how, with masturbation, you not having to dress for the date, you don't have to look your best."

I remember that night well. Let me back up a little, to the complicated talent and man that was Richard Pryor. Richard and I started out doing stand-up at the same time, in the Village in New York, in the early '70s. Back then, stand-up comedians didn't really have that much credibility. No one around us wanted to be stand-up comedians, as it was considered a silly thing to want to do. The Jewish kids mostly wanted to be doctors, or at least their parents wanted them to be, and the African American community folks were in music, not comedy.

There was a club in New York called Cafe Au Go Go—the rock group Blood, Sweat & Tears sort of owned that place. When they moved on, this new guy came in—and that was Richard Pryor. He and I worked at these clubs for about five months, saw each other's shows, and had dinner every night. Some nights he would have seventeen people in the audience, and I would have twelve, and so we'd signal each other to come watch. It was our ritual. He would say, "Son of a bitch, David, how come the Jews don't get pissed at you?" (Not quite true. They were pissed at me.) "My guys don't like a word of what I'm doing." We would both sit there, puzzled by it. I was puzzled by the Jews who *were* proud of what I was doing. Richie (Richard Franklin

Lennox Thomas Pryor) emulated Bill Cosby in the beginning, and worshipped Redd Foxx, Godfrey Cambridge. The odd thing about standup comedy is that you have to be a good writer. But you don't write comedy by putting it on a page and then reciting it. You let an audience shape it. You put yourself out on a limb, and they will tell you what's good and what's bad. And that's what we did.

Richie was different. He was always great with the audience, especially at doing impressions, and he was charming—a very boyish charm. And, like Cosby, he, too, was a writer, but only for himself. Richie was vulnerable as a person, which was obvious onstage, no matter how aggressive he would get about his ideas and about politics. He wasn't a big politics guy, but his writing was about Blacks and whites, and that was volatile in those days. He became a big shot, fast. He moved from the Cafe Au Go Go to the Village Gate, the biggest jazz place in New

Hosting *Movies, Movies, Movies* with my guests Richie (Richard Pryor),
Paula Kelly, and Roscoe Lee Browne, January 17, 1974. Richie and I took any
opportunity to be together. Just a few years later, Richie's daughter Rain came
to stay with my family for a while. She was adorable and smart, and Richie
adored her.

York. That transition, between two clubs literally half a block apart, was everything. The Village Gate had great jazz musicians—like Herbie Mann, who was there all the time. And unknown actors like Dustin Hoffman, who waited tables there before his career took off.

One day, the owner, Art D'Lugoff, felt there might be an audience for Richie. And, within days, there was a line around the block. The people who were around at that time—the jazz musicians, myself, the managers of the clubs—all were already seeing how advanced and unbelievable Richie was. He was absolutely charming and so bold, and the material was very aggressive, and some of it was anti-white, pushing the envelope. But he never did something *just* to push the envelope. He only did something because it was funny to him. Something ironic or offbeat. And, most of all, he was a writer. Wrote all his own material and then improvised. Many years later, in the 1970s, Richie wrote for such television shows as *Sanford and Son, The Flip Wilson Show,* and the 1973 Lily Tomlin special, for which he shared an Emmy Award.

Richie was a whole other level of genius, drawing from some authentic part of himself beyond what most comics were doing. He wasn't quite the Richard Pryor that he was going to be, but he was certainly heading there. After a while, though, people cautioned him. "You can't keep on doing this 'nig**r/white' stuff material!" It was shocking beyond belief, even in the hippest place in town. (By the way, it's still shocking today, although we hear the N-word all the time in rap lyrics. They're the only ones who can use that word—they own it.)

Richie didn't heed any words of caution, and he really made an impact. Somehow the word spread (oddly, it wasn't like the press wrote about it, because they thought of him as being sort of crude). When I went to the Village Gate to see him, the audience must have been five hundred, six hundred people, whites and Blacks (unusual at that time). He had penetrated in a way that no one had ever seen before. There, he had his own audience. And he could get away with a lot. At the time, you couldn't swear or people would leave, and, in the beginning, even *his* audience would leave. But after a while, they knew what to expect. Playing to that audience, which was not an audience that he needed to win over, was a huge success. After that, he just got better and better. He took stand-up farther than anyone else. The characters Richie created onstage were so real that you could actually see them on his shoulders talking to you. He was just a master of stand-up comedy in every way, because he was as charming as could be, even with all the irreverence. He was never afraid of anybody, not afraid of losing his job. And people stayed!

Richie became a huge success. He had overcome a brutal child-hood—was brought up in his grandmother's brothel, beaten by a care-giver, expelled from school when he was fourteen, served two years in the army (he spent them in prison due to beating up a soldier who had insulted Blacks). After his success, he toured, performed in con-certs, recorded his acts, starred in films and television. Later, he won an Emmy, five Grammy Awards, two American Academy of Humor Awards, the Writers Guild of America Award, and the first-ever Ken-nedy Center Mark Twain Prize for American Humor.

Then came that night, September 18, 1977. Richie and I—and Lily Tomlin and Bette Midler and others—did a big benefit concert at the Hollywood Bowl in Los Angeles, a venue seating seventeen thousand, and there was not an empty seat. It made headlines and went down in Hollywood history (but not because we were all so talented). The Star Spangled Night for Rights benefit, produced by Aaron Russo, who was Bette Midler's manager, starred Bette, Helen Reddy, Lily Tomlin, Los Angeles Ballet dancers John Clifford and Johnna Kirkland, Richard Pryor, and me, and it was the first benefit supporting the gay commu-nity, at a time when Anita Bryant and her anti-gay campaign were mak-ing headlines. At the time, "human rights" became the safe euphemism for "gay rights."

It was a huge event. It seemed like everyone in show business was in that audience, and it was a very liberal group. Lily Tomlin and I were the first acts, and mine was trashing Nixon. (I remember Paul Newman was there, and he came backstage and said, "David! That is great! But you're going to get in a lot of trouble with all this Nixon stuff!") I also did a big piece on prejudice. Ironically, I said, "You know, some Jews are good with money, some Blacks have rhythm, and some Orientals all look alike." And when I did that line, to a big white crowd, they started

The Star Spangled Night for Rights at the Hollywood Bowl, 1977. The first event ever of its time for gay rights, which we were so excited and proud to be part of. *Left to right:* David Steinberg, Lily Tomlin, Bette Midler, Johnna Kirkland and John Clifford (Los Angeles Ballet dancers).

to boo me. I had offended them terribly! Lily got her laughs by expressing her longing for "the 1950s when sex was dirty . . . and, of course, no one was gay, only shy."

It was a packed house. At that time, you couldn't say "gay," as it was a pejorative term. When Richie came out, he took all the negative, pejorative terms about homosexuals and started to work them. Now, any comedian knows that you never do a big concert like that and try out new stuff. But Richie didn't care. He was angry, and sort of hostile. My guess is, truthfully, that some bad substance was taken that night—at that time, cocaine was very popular, and performers who used it were proud to wear a necklace that had a spoon on it. Richie offended the audience, and then he started to attack them even more. He was always controversial, and he should probably have danced more on eggshells, but his biting wit combined with anger addressed it all head-on.

"I came here for human rights," he began, "and I found out what it was really about was about not getting caught with a dick in your mouth." And he was off. "You don't want the police to kick your ass if you're sucking the dick, and that's fair. You've got the right to suck anything you want." So much for "human rights." He was only beginning.

"I sucked one dick back in 1952. Sucked Wilbur Harp's dick. It was beautiful . . . because Wilbur had the best booty in the world . . . I'm talking about asshole . . ." And with one swoop, Richie became the huge star who spoke about gay sex in open, graphic words—in front of seventeen thousand people. And it went downhill from there. He was high, he was mad, and by the time he chastised the audience for not standing up for the Blacks during the Watts Riots, he was being booed mercilessly, so much so that he ended up by pulling down his pants, sticking his naked rear toward the crowd, and yelling, "Kiss my happy, rich black ass." He had lost his humor and was out of control because I think he was so high. The crowd, which had loved him, now threw chairs at him, got up, and left. He had alienated them and went too far.

In some ways it was unforgettable. *The Guardian* called it vintage Pryor, artful and impulsive. Richie had grown "increasingly allergic to the atmosphere of moral superiority" at the benefit's opening, was offended when he had seen a group of Black dancers being treated badly by the stagehands, and decided to just let it all out.

Bette Midler followed him, and she didn't know what had happened (she had not heard his set; it's not a big secret that most performers don't like to hear another performer, because you could be influenced by that performance). She heard something going on in the audience, but she didn't know why the audience was so irate. I wasn't watching her at the time, as I was backstage, but suddenly, as she started to sing, you could feel that the audience was still hostile. They weren't booing her at all, but they were still stunned by Richard's attack, which was not funny. It was kind of tragic. The night was so important to all the performers, and to the gay community, which was something Richie would have stood up for, but some say he was so out of it. And the truth is—it seemed that was the beginning of the downside of Richard doing drugs. It wasn't his personality, it wasn't society. It seemed like it was just drugs.

Amazing how people were trying to get by with it, not realizing that the FBI was probably listening in. But for someone like Richard Pryor, drugs got the best of him. It was tragic. In 1980, during the making of the film *Stir Crazy*, and after days of freebasing cocaine, it was said that Pryor poured 150-proof rum all over himself and lit himself on fire. While ablaze, he ran down Parthenia Street from his home in LA, until he was subdued by police. He was taken to a hospital, where he was treated for second- and third-degree burns covering more than half of his body. Richie spent six weeks recovering. His life continued on a road veering from success to tragedy. In 1986, he was diagnosed with multiple sclerosis. In 2000, Rhino Records released a box set of Richie's albums. In 2005, a few days after his sixty-fifth birthday, Richie died from a heart attack.

Richard Pryor was as good as you get, probably one of the best stand-up comedians I'd ever seen. (Jerry Seinfeld has called him "the Picasso of our profession.") Since his death, he's become a martyr to comedy, which I don't think is how he'd like to be remembered. He was the practitioner of an art, and a genius at it. When I close my eyes, I can still see his long fingers fluttering in the air, his whole body buzzing with the electricity of *being there*. He took the pain of his own life and made us laugh.

There's a term called "presentism," and it's about trying to describe the past, separated from the present. It's very hard to do. The best thing that a comedian can do for an audience, especially when you have a big house like Richie did, is to create pictures for them so that they're seeing out of your dialogue, and you, the comedian, disappear, and the pictures are what they get.

At that time, coke and heroin, all that stuff, was already there, and Richie had exploited it, and this audience was probably themselves high. What was so sad about that night is that Richie had as much charm as any person onstage; he was a generous guy and so, so talented. But he was vulnerable as a person, and that was obvious onstage. No matter how aggressive he would get about his ideas and about politics, and even though he knew how to put himself out on a limb, how to listen to an audience so they tell you what's good and what's bad, that night, he lost it.

To this day, no one remembers anything that happened that night before or after Richie. But Lily does. "It was intense. And I thought I should probably go out there, 'cause I felt that even though I wasn't Richard's best friend, we had our history together. Everybody's backstage going crazy, and I'm thinking, 'Just let it ride, you'll see, it'll be an epiphanies thing.' And everyone was just frantic, and the booing and the screaming was overwhelming. And finally, Richard said, 'You can kiss my rich black ass,'" and walked off.

"And then Bette," continues Lily, with much sadness and disbelief all these years later, "who was closing, who is the best one-woman show you could ever see, music and whatever, couldn't get the audience settled down. She didn't know what had happened. And I remember that somebody started to rush the stage, and it terrified her. She thought something wacky was going on. She couldn't understand the turmoil. So she came out and said, 'You can kiss my rich white ass.' Bette was brave. She never finished her act. She couldn't, because the audience did not know how to deal with what they'd just heard from Richie. But there was big applause when she left the stage, because they loved her."

As for Lily, this was her first experience with such a public catastrophe, and the issue of being gay before a crowd of tens of thousands who were gay, or at the very least there to raise money for gay rights. At that time, being gay was not something we had a lot of experience with. For me, with Lily, I always thought Jane Wagner was her manager. It never occurred to me until then that Jane was her lover, her partner, and that they shared a true love, which lasted more than forty years.

Times, they are still a-changin'. But Lily? She always had, and still has, that special thing that Bette Midler has . . . that special glow, encouraging to others, and always fun to be around. And she is still, always, uniquely Lily, still original, still brave, still brilliant, still enchanting, still working, still making people laugh, uproariously. And with love.

CHAPTER 5

THE COMEDIANS' COMEDIANS

Sid Caesar, Don Rickles, Mel Brooks, Jackie Mason,
Carl Reiner, Jack Carter, Shecky Greene, Flip Wilson,
Carol Burnett, Tim Conway, Harvey Korman,
Jonathan Winters, Robin Williams

They started in the Borscht Belt. Some of the biggest and best comedians of all time began their careers in the Catskills, the mountains that from the 1920s to the 1960s were known for their vacation bungalows, that were refuge from the humid Brooklyn summers but are actually part of Appalachia in southeast New York. Their training ground was the Butler Lodge in Hurleyville. And many of them played jazz. (Sid Caesar played the sax—he was terrific, joined the musicians' union, audited classes at the Juilliard School of Music, and played with the likes of Benny Goodman.) The big shift happened when the Catskills comedians came and started showing up on television shows like *The Ed Sullivan Show,* and eventually *The Tonight Show Starring Johnny Carson*—comics like Milton Berle, Sid Caesar, Mel Brooks, Shelley Berman, Don Rickles, Jack Carter, Jackie Mason. That shift eliminated comedians who had only a little bit of material, because once they ran out, they couldn't say it over and over again.

Mel Brooks remembers, "You're waiting, late at night, you do your show, you walk past the tea room with old ladies with their sponge cake, and they'd say, 'Melvin, you stink, but we love you,' and I would respond, 'Thank you very much, you stink, but we love you.'

"You know, David," remembers Mel. "The Jews were very strict at the Borscht Belt. They were a tough audience. If you said, 'Ladies and

With my old friend Mel Brooks after performing onstage together at the Wallis Annenberg Center for the Performing Arts in Beverly Hills, October 2015. It was a wild night. Mel actually did some push-ups while telling a story, and I jumped up on a chair with him and started to sing. The audience loved it.

gentlemen, here he is, the man of a thousand faces.' And you did one [he makes a face] and the band would laugh, and then you would make another face, that's two [makes face], and the band was still laughing. You did three. But those Jews are waiting for a thousand faces. Nothing less was good enough."

I always ask my friends the comedians, who made you laugh? Who were your influences? For many, it included Sid Caesar, Jerry Lewis, Jan Murray. For Mel, "it was the never subtle Harry Ritz. The Ritz Brothers were called the 'tumult comedians,' and really had me clutching my stomach. That was around 1934. They were nifty dancers who did slapstick musical numbers. Harry Ritz was in the center, Al and Jimmy on the sides. And they usually were the comedy relief in Sonja Henie pictures, but, unlike the Marx Brothers, they never really became stars in comedy. But they were incredibly funny [just ask Pauline Kael, the toughest film critic of all time, who was their great fan]. There was also an old Jewish comic from Russia or from Poland, Aaron Lebedeff. And he did a song, a brilliantly comic onomatopoetic song called 'Rumania, Rumania' in gibberish Russian—brilliant. That was in 1947, and it is on YouTube!"

Mel, who was close friends with Carl Reiner, and remained so for seventy years, remembers, "When we first met, we were with all these

On the set of *Inside Comedy*. These are all people I love. They light up a room. Mel Brooks and Tim Conway are always buoyant, Jon Lovitz is so smart and just finished doing a perfect imitation of Woody Allen's moose story, which he said inspired him into comedy. And my good friend Alan Zweibel, who is every comedy writer's matzo brei. (*Left to right:* Brooks, Lovitz, Zweibel, me, Conway.)

geniuses: Mel Tolkin, Lucille Kallen, Larry Gelbart. There was competition, but there was also respect. Carl Reiner was always there, as was Sid Caesar, a genius."

Every comedian on earth cites Sid Caesar as the best of all time. There were those who were just brave with their stand-up (Lenny Bruce); there were those who were the best writers (Steve Martin and Neil Simon and Mel Brooks); but Sid was above and beyond them all. Sid was actually all of those, but he was not a stand-up comedian. He was a comedic actor, a sketch comic, an idea genius, a master mime. Sid was a great mimic—he could imitate a Prussian general or an English fop or a pinball machine, it didn't matter. He could do it all, but he depended on his writers for his dialogue. He was a genius at panto-mime (imagine being a telephone, an elevator, a train, or a piano), at dialects (I dare you to differentiate between a real language and one of Sid's), and, according to Carl Reiner, "his ability to double-talk every language you have ever heard was absolutely flawless—never using one real word, although you would never know that." (And, by the way, Sid only spoke English and Yiddish.) His monologues were absolutely mesmerizing—he could make up double-talk that sounded just like real languages. He was just brilliant. He once told me, "Every language has its own music, David—if you listen to a language for fifteen min-utes, you know the rhythm and the song. You don't have to understand it or use those words."

Sometimes, appearances on *The Ed Sullivan Show* led to comedi-ans getting their own TV shows, like Sid Caesar and Jack Carter. Max Liebman, the producer of Sid Caesar's *Your Show of Shows,* was the Lorne Michaels of his era. He put together an original ninety-minute comedy-variety show for Caesar every single week and made stars out of unknowns. *Your Show of Shows* had a writers' room that became leg-endary, and was even the subject of a Broadway play by one of its writ-ers, Neil Simon, called *Laughter on the 23rd Floor. Your Show of Shows* premiered in 1950, was a huge hit, and ran for five seasons. Nominated for eleven Emmys, it won two, and was watched by about sixty million people (remember, this was the 1950s). *Caesar's Hour,* which followed it, ran another four years. Sid's shows were the crème de la crème of fifties' television, the gold standard for television satire comedy, their sketches sharper, edgier, more sophisticated than the other variety shows, by far. His comedy team on air included Imogene Coca, Carl Reiner, Bea Arthur, Howard Morris . . .

Caesar's writers were the very best, and all writers aspired to write for his show. These shows were not slapstick comedy, which was more common on TV. Sid hired writers who went on to make history in film, TV, and theater—Mel Brooks, Neil Simon, Larry Gelbart, Carl Reiner, Michael Stewart, Mel Tolkin, Selma Diamond, and Woody Allen. Put together the credits of all these writers who started with Sid, and, yes, you have the history of the best comedy in television, theater, and film. His TV shows' subjects included satires of real-life

Knowing Carl Reiner was to know one of life's blessings. We shared many laughs for over fifty years. Here we are spending the afternoon at his house. The world has lost one of its best.

events and people—and parodies of popular film genres, theater, television shows, and opera. But unlike other comedy shows at the time, the dialogue was considered sharper, funnier, and more adult-oriented. He was "best known as one of the most intelligent and provocative innovators of television comedy," who some critics called "Television's Charlie Chaplin"; *The New York Times* referred to him as the "comedian of comedians from TV's early days." And he was a comic actor as well—with credits like *It's a Mad, Mad, Mad, Mad World* (1963), *Silent Movie* (1976), and more.

Those who wrote for *Your Show of Shows* were the highest-paid comedy writers on television, and they all wanted to make Sid happy. It might've been Mel Brooks who compared the writers on *Your Show of Shows* to a litter of pups fighting for Sid's tit (though the original remark was probably not as classy). If Sid liked a sketch, that's all that mattered to the writers. They lived for his approval. Before Sid, Milton

Berle was considered the king of television, but he was dated compared to some of what Sid and Imogene Coca and Howie Morris were doing on *Your Show of Shows*.

To someone like Mel Brooks, and even Carl Reiner, Sid was a god. Curiously, at first blush, when Sid introduced Mel Brooks to Max Liebman, it didn't go all that well. Liebman's first impression of Mel was that he was a hanger-on who wasn't really all that funny, and Liebman even refused to hire him. Sid believed in him—Mel made him laugh—so after Max refused to hire Mel, Sid began paying him under the table, but his stuff was so good, he eventually moved out of the shadows and became one of Sid's yelping pups.

Says Neil Simon, "We called the writing on the show 'organized chaos.' Watching the writers create in a room was truly a religious experience. . . . I thought I was funny. . . . I would give him a sketch, and Sid would make it a hundred times funnier than we wrote it. When he acted it out, it was like watching the master create little plays. And this was years before those sketches on SNL." Actually, "I would say that we were competitive, the way a family is competitive to get Dad's attention," remembers Neil.

Mel Brooks calls it "a zoo. Sid would sit there, and we would all pitch him lines. Honestly, jokes would change fifty times." On Sid: "Caesar was our instrument that we could all play, and we played it very well." Continues Mel, "He was our idea man, and his bravery allowed us to take more risks than we would have. I know of no other comedian, including Chaplin, who could have done nearly ten years of live television!"

To Woody Allen, what was so different about writing for Sid was that the writers wrote situations, scenarios, not jokes. His favorite is also mine—"This Is Your Story," written with Carl Reiner, which was a parody of the hugely popular television show *This Is Your Life,* and which Sid considered his favorite as well. Contemporary and foreign movies, theater, other TV shows, and even opera were targets of satire by the writing team. And often the publicity generated by the sketches on these shows boosted the box office of the original productions. Some notable sketches included: "From Here to Obscurity" (*From Here to Eternity*), "Aggravation Boulevard" (*Sunset Boulevard*), "Hat Basterson"

(*Bat Masterson*), and "No West for the Wicked" (*Stagecoach*). Remembers Carol Burnett (who later had her own huge hit TV show for many years) about winning tickets to see *My Fair Lady* on Broadway: "I gave the tickets to my roommate because I thought *My Fair Lady* was going to be running for a hundred years, but Sid Caesar is live, and I will never see that again."

Sid's sketches were long (ten to fifteen minutes), and the cameramen knew to keep their lenses close-up on Sid's face at all times, because his expressions were priceless. His body language and facial contortions were unequaled—whereas slapstick was the rule on TV, he was in the forefront of writing. "Physical poetry," says Steve Martin, himself a genius at that form, which was the mark of silent screen comedians, as with no sound, the facial expressions, that pantomime (people compared him to Charlie Chaplin) was the format. Sid took that and brought those incredible dialects and jokes that changed comedy. If you ask his writers, like Neil Simon and Howard Morris and Mel Tolkin, they would tell you that Sid dismissed one-liners, which were everywhere on television, emphasizing the longer sketches and storytelling at which he excelled.

Just ask Larry Gelbart, one of the best comedy writers then and ever. Larry called Sid "a pure television comedian, with total control of the medium. That let us be 'urbane'—remember, David, between us we had read every book! Between us, we had seen every movie! Between us, we had seen every play on Broadway. If someone made a joke about Kafka or Tennessee Williams, we got it! And, by the way, we did everything together. We had dinner together. We went to the movies together. We were all friends—and that was so important because we appreciated each other. We loved each other a lot."

I directed Sid in many sitcoms, two of which were pilots that never went anywhere. Sid was not happy with the material. He wasn't a negative guy, but he worked from an energy that was just unbelievably powerful, and if something didn't bring him that energy, it didn't feel funny enough to him. And then I directed Sid in *Mad About You* (I directed about eight years of *Mad About You*). That was a treat beyond words.

Paul Reiser and Helen Hunt, the stars and producers, had been strategizing to get me in front of the camera, so they had me play a

Reform rabbi who was giving the sermon about someone who had died and who got every name wrong. "We're here to bury the beloved Tessi." And someone would yell out, "Esther!" "Yeah. Esther. And here to sit shiva for Esther is Uncle Ari." And Sid Caesar had to follow that, and had no trouble doing that. He'd watch me in rehearsal, so sweetly, and say, "David! That's wonderful! That's so funny that you got every name wrong."

Woody and Neil sum it up best. Says Woody, "Writing for Sid was the highest thing you could aspire to as a TV comedy writer. Only the presidency is above that." And Neil: "The first time I met Sid, it was like meeting a new country. All other comics were basically doing situations with all kinds of farcical characters. Sid was doing life."

And then there was Don. Don Rickles. Mr. Potato Head. Oh, yes, also stand-up comic, actor, author, and the ultimate insult comic. Went to the American Academy of Dramatic Arts. Yes, he did. Most of you may think of Don as the most popular guest on talk shows who spends his time insulting everyone. And I mean *everyone*. And you would be right—"Mr. Warmth," as he was fondly called, was omnipresent on *The Dean Martin Show*, *The Tonight Show Starring Johnny Carson* (he was a guest there over one hundred times!), and the *Late Show with David Letterman*. Hosts loved him, and laughed as hard as the audience even when he was insulting them—and I mean really insulting them. He appeared as a guest on many sitcoms, including *The Dick Van Dyke Show*, *The Munsters*, *Gilligan's Island*, *Get Smart*, *The Andy Griffith Show*, and more. But at stand-up, he was really the master, because the audience would heckle him, and he would insult the hell out of them—and leave them roaring.

And guess who really pushed to make Don a star? It wasn't his very best friend, Bob Newhart. It was Frank Sinatra. While working in Murray Franklin's nightclub in Miami Beach, Florida, early in his career, Rickles spotted Frank Sinatra and remarked to him, "I just saw your movie *The Pride and the Passion,* and I want to tell you, the cannon's acting was great." He added, "Make yourself at home, Frank. Hit somebody." Sinatra, whose pet name for Rickles was "Bullet-head," enjoyed him so much that he encouraged other celebrities to see Rickles's act and be insulted by him. Sinatra's support helped Rickles become a popular headline performer in Las Vegas. During a *Dean Martin Celebrity Roast* special, Rickles was among those who took part in roasting Sinatra, and Rickles himself was also roasted during another show in the series in 1985. When Frank Sinatra was asked to perform at Ronald Reagan's second inaugural ball, he insisted that Rickles be allowed to perform and do it unrehearsed. Rickles considered this performance the highlight of his career.

But what was Don's kids' and grandkids' favorite comedy routine? Why, the voice of Mr. Potato Head, first done in 1995, in the *Toy Story* franchise. "Mr. Potato Head is a great deal of fun because it gives you a great deal of money," says Don. "And my grandchildren only know Mr. Potato Head. I broke my neck in this business, and they only know 'Pop-Pop's Mr. Potato Head'—anything else they don't know about. But it's a fun thing to do, ya know, because there's no makeup. You sit in the booth like a moron. Not like with Scorsese, you know? I did a picture called *Casino*. Scorsese and De Niro. Now there's a duo. De Niro whispers, and Scorsese whispers, and I become a

Don Rickles and I spent the last fifty years wanting to sit next to each other at dinner parties and made sure it happened as much as possible. There's never a better seat than next to Don, anywhere. Here we are at the *Vanity Fair* Oscar Party, happy together yet again, 2015. I loved this man.

One of my favorite birthdays with Don Rickles, Marty Short, Bob Newhart, and of course my wife, Robyn, who threw the party at E. Baldi restaurant in Beverly Hills, August 9, 2014.

whisperer. Now De Niro mumbles. And Scorsese mumbles. Finally, I just say, 'Scorsese, I'm walking. I don't need this. I make tons of money in Vegas. I'm walking.' The man is a mumbler, and I don't understand what the hell he's talking about, and I don't need this.

"And they say, 'You can't say nothing to De Niro. You can't do any jokes.'

"But I figure, 'What can he do to me? I'm eighty-three—what is he gonna do, take my name and deport me? What is he gonna do? Ya know?'

"And the third day we were drinking tequila in the trailer, and he was going [De Niro impression], 'You know, Don, it's so great to be with you.' So he's got me."

Don is not finished. "You know, De Niro mumbles in real life. And when you go to a restaurant with him, he wants to eat under the table. So nobody sees him. Now I got a career—I'm trying to get hot in this business. I want people to see me. De Niro? He's under the table whispering, 'Pass the butter.' I said, 'Bob, what the hell is the matter with you?' But that's why he is the greatest actor—but you know, he's got a problem."

Don explains, "When I started in this business, in the lounges, I immediately started to talk to the audience. I used to do impressions badly, like a million other stand-up guys. I could never tell a joke. I really couldn't. That's why I started talking to the audience. Everyone wanted to see me at the shows. It was different in those days. Nobody else ever did what I do. And to this day there are some guys that try to do that, but it's not something you rehearse, it's by personality. To be sarcastic and not mean—that is my art. To be spirited, but not mean-spirited. I've never been mean-spirited.

"My opening show, there's always a basic middle, beginning, and ending. And every time I open, I never really know what I'm gonna exactly say. I know that the framework is there, and how I walk out, and how I walk to a certain place, and how I turn to the band and begin, but I never really know what I am going to say, which makes it kind of exciting for me."

For Don, it always worked. And he was always improvising more than most people. For example, the inauguration in Washington. "That was really one of the highlights of my life," Don says quietly. "What happened was that Sinatra said, 'Listen, Don, I want you to come to Washington to perform at Ronald Reagan's inaugural.'

"I said, 'Frank, ya had a little bit of the scotch again. C'mon.'

" 'Oh no, no, don't gimme the jokes,' said Frank. 'There's no scotch. You're doin' the show with me. You, me, and Dean.'

"I said, 'Geez!'

"Frank emphasizes again, 'Just pack a bag and come.'

"Fast-forward. I get to Washington, and he gets a call from the various people in the cabinet.

" 'Well, Frank, what are you gonna have?'

" 'Well, I have Don Rickles.'

" 'Oh, Don Rickles! What, are you crazy—Don Rickles?'

" 'Well, if you don't have Rickles, you don't have me.'

"I'll never forget him for that. That touched me. I couldn't believe it.

"'So, what is he gonna say?' asked that doubter.

"'He will say whatever he wants.' 'Cuz Frank trusted me, he did.

"So now we go in the dressing room, we're ready to do the show. Frank says to everyone, 'No drinking till after the show.'

"Dean says, 'You got it, pally. Don and I are not gonna touch it, don't you worry.' Frank walked out of the room, and Dean had a pocketful of scotch, vodka, like a bar inside his coat. Anyway, I did the show and it really went great for me. I had the cabinet fall down laughing. And Reagan's sitting there laughing like crazy.

"And that was the first time I played big theaters. And after that, big arenas with Frank. It changed everything for me. 'Cuz I was with Frank for the last two years of his working life. I used to walk out and say, 'You're gonna see him in a little while. [Indicates Frank's voice is gone.] Gone. Yeah, he doesn't have anything. So, I gotta kill time. It's over.' For some reason, I was the only guy who could say that.

"Once we're sitting in the Loews Hotel in Monte Carlo. Just Jilly, myself, and Frank having a couple of drinks. It's five in the morning and we're sitting there. A storm comes, big bay windows. KABOOM!—lightning—BABOOM! And we're in tuxedos and we're drinking. Frank looks over and he says, 'You see those guys outside taking my picture?' I asked, 'What picture?' He said, 'Well, you see the cameras going.' BABOOM! 'It's the lightning, Frank!'

"He says, 'I want you and Jilly to go out there and tell those sons of bitches I'm going to send some guys out there and beat the crap out of them. I want it stopped now.'

"I said, 'Frank—'

"'GET OUT THERE!' So Jilly and I, we're out there in the soaking rain talking to nobody, 'All right, you guys back up; don't take any more pictures.' True story, David."

Great story. They all were.

The first time I met the writer, director, stand-up comedian, actor, producer, and all-around insanely funny good guy Mel Brooks was in November 1970. We were going to meet at the Russian Tea Room, which was next door to Carnegie Hall. Mel stops short when he sees a poster on the door announcing the Stuttgart Ballet, which was performing. And he says, "David, what is it they're not saying? . . . Nazis!"

Then he goes on, "David, I made a fine living from Nazis. *The Producers,* David. Seriously, the only way to get even with anybody is to ridicule them. The only real way I could get even with Hitler and company was to bring them down with laughter. Kind of like that Yiddish expression 'Dancing on Hitler's grave.'"

Mel is on. Mel is always on. So it is November 1970. We walk into the Russian Tea Room—famous, elegant, full of that upper-class crowd. He immediately goes from table to table shaking everyone's hands—you'd think that they were all his best friends, since he is kissing and hugging everybody—like he is the Russian hero, as if he was the king. There are these two women sitting there, and they tell us they are going to see a Broadway show. He asks, "What show are you going to see?" and they tell him *Two by Two,* and he starts to sing the entire song, word for word, "I do not know a day I did not love you . . ."—and then the next thing we know, he is standing on the table, yes, in the Russian Tea Room, singing at the top of his voice. It was unforgettable, for the women, for every guest in the place, and for me.

So after his performance, Mel says, "David, I have to make one stop at that building across the street. It will only take a minute." We take the elevator, we get out and walk into a studio, and there, sitting on a stage, on chairs, surrounded by cameras, are George Segal, Dan Greenburg (writer and then husband of Nora Ephron), Stan Herman (fashion designer), Larry Goldberg (the Pizza King), and the host of what is obviously his show, David Susskind. David Susskind waves us on, and Mel and I are seated in the two chairs left for us. Mel had arranged for me to do the show without my knowing it. The subject was "How to Be a Jewish Son." Watch it on YouTube—it's very funny. It became one of the classics. Suddenly, and for ninety minutes, we discuss, with absolute hilarity, the Jewish mother as manipulator and instiller of guilt: Segal's 1970 film *Where's Poppa?,* with Ruth Gordon stories galore; my recollections of growing up in a religious household in Canada; the panelists' Freudian dreams about their mothers; Greenburg's recollection of introducing Nora to his mother; Yiddish- and Russian-speaking Jewish mothers' versions of American show business jargon; Mel's memory of introducing his wife, Anne Bancroft, a Catholic, to his mother and his memories of when he began doing stand-up in the Catskills ("They liked nothing . . .")—you get the idea. At the end, Susskind turns to me and asks me how was I able to bring an Italian girl (who would later be my first wife, Judy Marcione) home to my Jewish parents. I quickly answered, "You bring a Black girl home first." There was quite a bit of controversy over that after the show aired, but I explained that these were my parents' prejudices, not mine at all. Everyone who knew me or my work knew that.

Mel was, and is, priceless. And brave. He was ahead of his time with his films (written and directed by Mel) *Blazing Saddles* and *Young Frankenstein* (both released in 1974), *Spaceballs* (1987), *Robin Hood: Men in Tights* (1993), *High Anxiety* (1977), *Silent Movie* (1976), *The Twelve Chairs* (1970), *Get Smart* (1965–70 TV series), *The Muppet Movie* (1979), *2000 Year Old Man* (1975), and especially his show of shows, *The Producers* (the film was in 1967, and it later ran for many years and won buckets of awards on Broadway). The film starred Zero Mostel, Gene Wilder, Renée Taylor, Dick Shawn, and, of course, Mel, with the classic showstopper, "Springtime for Hitler" (which was actually Mel's original title for the film). It got mixed reviews at first, but Mel's bravery in tackling Nazis made it a cult favorite for decades to follow.

Truly, to this day, Mel Brooks has me laughing all the time. We have done interviews in public many times at large venues with five hundred people and more. Here is one of my favorite stories, which tells you so much about Mel's comedy, and about his sense of himself.

"I was working writing on the lot at Universal Studios. I looked out of my window, across the way, and there was a sign on the building that said 'Granart.' Turns out that was Cary Grant's company, Granart. I asked a guard, 'Wow, Cary Grant, does he ever come there?'

"He says, 'Yeah, almost every day.'

"So I'm walking to the commissary and I hear, 'I don't believe it!'

"CARY GRANT!!!!! It's his voice!

"He says, 'I don't believe it. Mel Brooks, I know you. You made a record with Carl Reiner, my favorite record!'

"I said, 'Are you imitating Cary Grant? A lot of guys do Cary Grant; you do him very well. You do him better than anybody!'

"Anyway, I knew it was him, so then I said, 'I'm very excited. I'm a kid from Brooklyn. I've seen so many of your movies.'

"He said, 'Where are you going?'

"I said, 'The commissary.'

"He said, 'Well, I'm eating alone, let's have lunch,' and we had lunch. And we talked. I said that I liked to go to the races. He said, 'I loved the races.'

"Next day, the phone rings. 'Mel, it's Cary Grant. The two of us! Lunch!'

"Wednesday: 'Mel, it's for you, Cary Grant.' We're best friends. Thursday, we're skipping to the commissary!

"Finally, it's Friday. Phone rings. I say, 'Who is it? Cary Grant? Tell him I'm not in.' I'd run out of what to say. I didn't know what to talk about."

As Mel would say, for nightclub comedians, *The Ed Sullivan Show* brought them steady work in places like Vegas and in nightclubs throughout the country. The Sullivan show ran from 1948 to 1971 and made stars out of people like Rodney Dangerfield, Flip Wilson, Totie Fields, Alan King, Joan Rivers, Richard Pryor, Phyllis Diller, Jackie Gleason. Comics bent down and kissed the hem of Ed's garment on the air or in person, but they made endless fun of him behind his back. The pianist and wit Oscar Levant once quipped, "Ed Sullivan will have a career for as long as other people have talent."

Sullivan became de rigueur for impressionists, Will Jordan being the first and probably the best of the Sullivan imitators. He was the one who exaggerated the hunched shoulders, turning his whole body instead of his head from side to side, and got big laughs with the signature phrase "really big shoe" for "show." (Ed never said "really big shoe"—that was pure Will Jordan.) Jordan even made a popular novelty record of the Everly Brothers song "Bye Bye Love," done in Ed Sullivan's voice. Ed tried to stop the record from ever coming out, and when Jordan asked him why, Ed replied, "Because of all those lewd things you have me say in the song."

"Bye Bye Love"? Lewd? Ed thought it was in bad taste.

The subtle shift was the talk shows on television. Something else was happening that never had before, and Newhart was one of the early champions of a style where you don't have to holler and scream at the audience, and you don't have to shout and be crude. That's the kind of history that I like. Not detailed, not pedantic.

If you go back and look at the comedians on *The Ed Sullivan Show,* they were good, although, by today's standards, they could have been cut by a few minutes. But the show allowed live comedy to explode around the country. Little clubs, big clubs. Vegas wasn't necessarily a good place for comedians. It was for singers, but then, when comedians started to hit Las Vegas, that's when the money came into it, and a whole change occurred, and it still goes on. I opened for Frankie Valli and would always try to get in my car to go home by the time I heard him sing "Big Girls Don't Cry," which was such a relief for me because I didn't have to do another show, but the money was great. Vegas helped the comedians by giving them a living and stardom, but in terms of their work, it didn't help them, because they repeated the same things over and over and over again, and it didn't grow into something other than that, until the culture started to change with comedy albums.

I saw Jackie Mason at his peak in his later years, and he was as funny and as interesting a comedian as you'd ever see onstage. He exaggerated his own Jewish accent to make his point. He was on *The Ed Sullivan Show* all the time, and because Sullivan was so popular, if you appeared on his show, it didn't matter if you were good or bad (you couldn't tell in those days because Ed couldn't absorb the comedy himself, being probably the most humorless person ever to host a variety show). If you were on his show, then you had a career the next day. It was even bigger than *The Tonight Show* because it wasn't competing with other variety or talk shows at the time. Ed Sullivan gave you a career.

But some, like Jackie Mason, didn't last long on TV. Once, when Jackie was performing on the show, a phone rang backstage, and he gave the finger to whoever screwed up. He started to rant. He has a temper, which, as I said, is not a bad thing if you're a stand-up comedian. (In fact, if you don't have a temper, you're probably going to be a mediocre stand-up comedian.) But as the story goes, when Jackie Mason gave the finger, Ed Sullivan thought it was directed at him, so Jackie was never allowed on the show again. And after that, no one would hire him. He went back to the Catskills, but that was pretty much over by then. So Jackie went on the road to little clubs, roadside music places, restaurants that would hire him for half an hour. He'd walk from table to table like a singing waiter. He did that for ten to twelve years, in near obscurity. Finally, he was playing right outside of Los Angeles, and it just so happened that Carl Reiner and Mel Brooks noticed that he was there.

"Let's see what the guy's doing." So they went to this little nothing restaurant—people eating, not really listening—and they couldn't get over how funny he was. All that time he had been doing nothing but developing material and creating his own metaphorical thumbprint as a comedian. And they couldn't get over it.

Carl said to Mel, "We gotta help him! The guy's great!"

And Mel said, "But no one's really laughing."

So Carl said, "It doesn't matter, it's really great! We gotta get him an audience." So they rented out a little theater in Los Angeles, and they brought in all their show business friends. It spread like wildfire, and Jackie became, in my estimation, one of the best stand-up acts I'd ever seen. Some called him an irascible, sometimes unpleasant human being—but that DNA helps you in stand-up. Nonstop audience laughter. Mostly Jewish audiences, but Middle America loved him, too. Even when the era of the Jewish comedian was over, Jackie had a way of talking in an exaggerated Jewish accent, but you didn't have to be Jewish to really like him. I've always believed that the more personal you are, the wider the audience. Eventually, Jackie would appear on Broadway in a series of one-man shows in the late '80s and early '90s. In fact, that turned out to be the summit of his career. They were wildly successful, and they led to a short-lived TV sitcom with the actress Lynn Redgrave, but something about Mason and TV didn't mix. That sense of danger—even meanness—worked for a hot medium like the stage, but he was too hot for the cool medium of television.

The lead-in for *Your Show of Shows* was *The Jack Carter Show*. But almost from the beginning, Jack's show was doomed. He couldn't book guests or submit scripts until *Your Show of Shows* had first dibs. Even many years later, at Jack Carter's dinner table, you could hear him complain, "It was always Sid Caesar, Sid Caesar, everything Sid Caesar!" (Jack was a great complainer. The best was when we were at his house in Beverly Hills for Passover Seder—myself, Sid Caesar, Jan Murray, and, of course, Jack. Jack was once again complaining about one of his surgeries. We were all shaking our heads, so to kind of change the subject, I said to Sid, "It's your turn to read the Haggadah. Sid—Japanese?" And, of course, Sid did—in his own version of Japanese.)

But, in fact, Jack was his own worst enemy. He turned down everything the writers came up with, and he insulted the crew—the guys with the tool belts—so they'd stand around until the last minute to build a set. It was all a shame really, because Jack Carter was a terrific comic with boundless energy. But once his show didn't get the ratings, he started to perform at the condos in Florida, where all the Jews just wanted to hear other Jews talking Yiddish. You only had to say "mazel tov" to get a laugh. When he lost his show, Jack Carter was bitter, but then he didn't need a reason to be bitter. He wasn't easy—he was bitter about the food that came for lunch that day, and he would holler at people for no reason. But, still, if you talk to Sid Caesar or Mel Brooks, they will tell you that at his peak he was one of the best stand-up comedians.

There was a whole Miami version of comedy, which Jack Carter connected with. Florida had the condo circuit, which kept alive Buddy Hackett, Shecky Greene, Red Buttons—all those guys. Jan Murray—real name Murray Janofsky—was in that group, too. That's where eventually the old Jewish comedians, who didn't have an act for the Catskills anymore, would perform in apartments, in cellars—they would just put chairs down and the Jews would come. Like Shecky Greene at the time. I wouldn't say that Shecky was elegant. He would fall into the meshuggana category more than the elegant category. And he was a hypochondriac. But that was a plus, too—the more diseases you think you've got, the better your material will be. Shecky had cameos in a few Frank Sinatra movies, where he was often hounded by the mob. Once, he actually was attacked by hoodlums (but at least he got a joke out of it). He would tell the audience, "Frank Sinatra saved my life once. One night when I was walking home, I was jumped by two guys who started to beat the living crap out of me, when suddenly Frank Sinatra showed up and said, 'Ok, that's enough.'"

Shecky appeared in one of Sinatra's movies—it was *Tony Rome*—with bandages. Who really beat him up? Rumor has it that he had drinking and gambling problems, so it could have been that. Or Sinatra's cronies. But everyone loved him because his spirit was generous, he was funny, and he worked hard.

So did my dear friend Flip Wilson, who hosted his own show, *The Flip Wilson Show*, from 1970 to 1974. He was the first African American to host a very successful variety show, which won two Emmys. I was a guest on his show half a dozen times. He had a lot of friends, but when he went onstage, it seemed like the entire audience was made up of friends of Flip. We were good friends, and if you thought we joked around, we didn't, because Flip was a serious guy, street-smart, and, believe it or not, as the hottest star of television in those years, Flip had the use of a private jet. Here is how I know that.

While shooting one of his shows, Flip asked me to have dinner, which we would do quite a lot. I told him I had to be at a benefit in St. Louis for the United Jewish Appeal, and I would do my stand-up. Flip asked how I was getting there. I said I had a flight out after rehearsal. Flip then told me that instead of me "schlepping to the airport," he had access to a private plane and would be happy to fly me to St. Louis—and would keep me company. So we flew to St. Louis, and as I went onstage to a packed audience, Flip said, "If you want to bring me out and introduce me to the audience, I would be happy to do it." Now, remember, Flip was a huge star. So I did my act, and then I said, "I am so glad to be here, and I have a friend who would like to come out and say hello." Flip came out, the audience went crazy, and he went into his beloved Geraldine act, even without wardrobe, and started with his famous line, "The devil made me do it."

Flip was such a good friend, an immense talent, and I miss him to this day.

Is the description of someone as a "classic" overused? Not here. You will find it attributed to Carol Burnett in every part of her career. Carol Burnett has been a classic in the theater, on television, in films, for nearly seventy years. And she is the best at all—comedian, writer, actor, singer. This classic was most often in the forefront of humor, of no-holds-barred, fun comedy, of parodies and characters, of taking her guests and turning their duets into award-winning classics. And Carol and Tim Conway, a regular on *The Carol Burnett Show* for eleven years, who has been called the funniest human on earth, by me, have given us the gift of their memorable skits that are truly comedy classics.

As is often the case for actors, Carol's childhood was tough. Born in Texas, to parents who were involved with movie theaters, and were alcoholics, she was left with her grandmother, a musician, who moved with her to Hollywood. Hollywood High School and UCLA followed, as did the playwright program and an appearance where she made her audience roar. "I had always been a quiet, shy, and sad young girl. Everything changed for me when I heard that laughter," she says. Carol was raised by her grandmother in the 1940s. Together, they saw umpteen double features a week. Carol remembers, "That was a kinder time for the movies, as you know. The bad guys got it, the good guys made it. And so there was no cynicism really, and I grew up with that imprint. That everything was going to turn out like 'Mickey and Judy.' So with that kind of optimism, when I went to New York, I had never been further east than Texas. I wasn't scared, because I realized that if I was turned down for a part, I would think to myself, 'Okay, it's her turn, it's not my turn.'"

Fast-forward to New York, where, in 1957, she sang what became a hit parody—"I Made a Fool of Myself over John Foster Dulles"—on *The Tonight Show Starring Jack Paar* and on *The Ed Sullivan Show*. Then everything fell into place, one hit after another. Carol started as a regular performer on *The Garry Moore Show*. "And Tim came on as a guest a few times," she says. "Years later, when he got on *McHale's Navy*, I thought he was so funny. But he had all these shows on that got canceled after thirteen weeks. In those days, thirteen weeks was the cutoff. His license plate was 13 WEEKS. So we hired him to be a guest on our show, and he was such an important part that he became a semi-regular on our show. And how smart were we, or how dumb were we—we didn't make him a regular weekly performer until the ninth year. But he was on just about every other week." And then Harvey Korman, who Carol always reminds us "was one of the best comedic actors you could find. He could do everything, he looked like the people he was playing. He could do any accent, and his timing was that of Jack Benny."

New York brought Carol her first Broadway show, *Once upon a Mattress* (for which she was nominated for a Tony), and a regular gig on *The Garry Moore Show* (until 1962), which gave her an Emmy. And then she became a headliner with her friend Julie Andrews in *Julie and Carol at Carnegie Hall*, which was created by later award-winning talents Bob Banner and Joe Hamilton (whom Carol later married), and written by Mike Nichols and Ken Welch. That brought two more Emmys. And, in 1967, *The Carol Burnett Show* became a television classic, winning twenty-three Emmys. Other huge talents came into her personal and professional lives. Lucille Ball became a friend, Jim Nabors was both a friend and an annual guest star on *The Carol Burnett Show*, along with Harvey Korman, Vicki Lawrence, Lyle Waggoner, and, of course, Tim Conway—but more on him later. Carol's classic features, besides the musical numbers and parodies, included her trademark Tarzan yell, her impromptu Q&As with the audience, and her tugging at her left ear (a sign to her grandmother) as she closed each show.

Carol remembers, smiling, "I had auditioned for *Babes in Arms*, and they were all very encouraging. I was raising my kid sister in New York, and I went back to the apartment and said, 'I think I got it.' And the phone rang, and they were going with a name. I started to cry. When I left UCLA to go to New York, and my classmates gave me a party, they said, 'Carol, what's gonna be the first thing you will do?' And I said, 'I will work for George Abbott. That'll be my first show. The wonderful musical comedy director, the daddy of them all.' So I've just lost this, and minutes later the phone rang, and it was Bill and Jean Eckart, who were producing a little show off-Broadway called *Once upon a Mattress,* being directed by George Abbott."

Suddenly Carol had two jobs of a lifetime in the same year. And in both, she honed and perfected and finally came to personify comedy at its most sincere, with her enchanting honesty that was able to mock but never denigrate, her fearlessness of being just plain silly, her courage even to make people cry—and, finally, to make the audience love her.

Yet two shows in the same year had its challenges. "I would rehearse for Garry's show during the day. We'd tape the show Friday nights, and then I would do the show every night. On Friday, we would finish right at eight, I'd get on the subway and head for *Once upon a Mattress* downtown, get to sing my favorite, 'I'm in Love with a Girl Named Fred.' So there were times when I didn't have a day off. I was in *Mattress* for a year, and Garry Moore was so terrific, he plugged the show all the time. And at one point, we did the whole first scene on *The Garry Moore Show.*

"It worked out just right. I was not really into doing movies. I'm really a workhorse. I like knowing that the curtain is gonna go up, you go out, you do it, the curtain comes down. But the sitting around and the waiting, and the lighting and the this, the that—not for me. We did our show like it was a live show, as fast as we could go. A Broadway revue every Friday. I was really spoiled doing that. There are no real regrets. I'm really happy. My time, and a lot of people's time, happened in the golden age of variety. Which doesn't exist anymore. Because when we were on, there were sometimes as many as nine variety shows. *Smothers Brothers* and *Sonny & Cher* and *Laugh-In* and *Flip Wilson* and *Dean Martin.* It was wonderful. And, of course, *I Love Lucy.* But doing the sitcom wasn't my thing. Although Lucy became a very,

very close friend of mine, a mentor, and she called me 'kid,' and would give me advice, and I just loved the way she could clown around and do things like that, the musical comedy revues, the variety—that was *my* deal. And I remember the wonderful old comedian Ed Wynn came on Garry's show once as a guest, and we were all sitting around the table, and he defined the difference between comics and comedic actors. He said, 'Comics say funny things, comedic actors say things funny.'"

And then there was Tim. Tim Conway, also known as the funniest human on earth. Says Carol, "There may be people almost as funny, but I don't know anyone funnier. I was a regular performer on *The Garry Moore Show,* and Tim came on as a guest a few times. We didn't bond at that time. But it was years later, when he got on *McHale's Navy,* that I thought he was really funny. And you know the craziest thing? Then we hired him to be a guest on our show, and he became a semi-regular!"

Tim remembers it this way. "I didn't want to be in this business. I was in Cleveland, horsing around at a local television station, and I wanted to be a jockey. I only weighed ninety-seven pounds when I graduated, and even though I was terrified of horses, and I didn't know how to ride that well, my dad was training them, so I thought, 'Well, this is an opening here.' And he'd let me gallop around the track at Randall Park and never really race or anything. But one day, the starter called me into the gate. Now, with a horse racing, they go from standing to forty miles an hour, immediately. There's no—'Uh, you ready, here we go.' No. there's no gliding out of the gate. The gates open, and I was sitting there on the ground thinking, 'Hmmm, I wish I were *on* that horse.' Because people get annoyed when they bet, and you're not on the horse. There's no refund on that. So then I went in the army. Ours."

I want to laugh, because Tim always makes me laugh, but then, out of his mouth comes "And two court-martials. They had no sense of humor at all in the army. They really didn't. 'You can't handle the truth!' I had guard duty. It was peacetime. I was in Seattle. What am I guarding in Seattle? So, I go to meet this lieutenant, and I realize I forgot my rifle. It's in the car. The army is touchy about that. They give you a rifle, and they want you to clean it, to hang onto it. I don't have it. Court-martial.

"I would call that a failure. I've had so many. I've been canceled by everybody. As Carol knows—my personalized license plate was 13 WEEKS. And then I got one that said 6 WEEKS. Because they were cutting them down. And you know what, David? All my shows were . . . hold it . . . gone."

Tim did have a big hit—*McHale's Navy*, with Ernie Borgnine. Lasted three years. And then came Carol. "All my shows were failures— except for anything to do with Carol. She was the best, and she still is. It was great. And eleven years of working with Harvey, a very poor performer, always laughing. I don't know if you noticed, no control."

I disagree. "Tim, Harvey and Carol were always laughing at every-thing that you did!"

Tim: "I thought they were professional, but you know . . . Well, I was a writer on the show, too. So, I'd write one thing and then never say it. And Harvey was always going, 'Hmmm, where are we going?' With the dentist sketch that we did on the *Burnett* show, I had never shown Harvey the part about the Novocain. And we were rehearsing all week. And he said, 'This sketch really stinks.' And I said, 'I'm gonna try something.' And he said, 'There's nothing that can save this.' And so, we did it on air. And it exploded."

I always wonder, and ask, which other comedians influenced a comedian.

Tim remembers, with great fondness: "Steve Allen was big-time. I loved Louie Nye, Tom Poston, those guys. I just couldn't wait at night to see Jonathan Winters. Don Knotts became a very close friend. We spent forty-five years knowing each other. We did a movie one time, Don and I, for Disney. We were supposed to be at Dancehall Dandy's; the Apple Dumpling Girls. We were dressed as dancehall girls with little tutus, skirt, the wigs . . . And Don used to say, 'Tim, I can't get dressed like that in the morning; it's freezing out there.'

"I said, 'Don, why don't you have the wardrobe guy bring the outfit to you and then get dressed in your room and then drive?'

" 'Well, that's a good idea. I'll try that.'

"So, they bring him the outfit, he gets dressed, does the makeup, gets in the car. One night we're coming home. And the motel is across the street and I say, 'Don, I'm gonna go get a beer. I'll see you later.'

"And in Stockton, there are cowboys. I mean real cowboys who don't like performers. So I walk in the bar and go, 'Whoa, it's rough in here.' I'm sitting at the bar, I look up, and here comes Don, with this girl's wig on—the skirt, the whole thing.

"'Uh, Tim, you got the key to that room?'

"I said, 'Well, don't you think we oughta talk about price first?'"

You probably remember the memorable times on the *Carol Burnett Show*—especially those breakups.

I told Carol, "You know one reason why I watched the show? To watch the breakups." Carol remembers the breakups—those hysterical times when the comedians would break themselves up during a skit— this way: "We've been criticized a few times about that. Not one of us ever planned to break up. But you get Conway on a roll—it's that delicious feeling you get when you're a kid in Sunday school or in a library—and you couldn't repress whatever made you laugh. Most people have said that they are always waiting for those moments to see if we would laugh. And, of course, we did. Remember, we were all in on it!"

Carol, Jerry Seinfeld, Robin Williams—ask any and all of them, and the name Jonathan Winters comes up universally. As Robin said, "I would not have a career without Jonathan Winters." Replies Jonathan, "What he actually said was, 'Jonathan Winters is my mentor.' And I corrected him. I said, 'That's a nice thing to say, Robin, but I am from Ohio, and they think Mentor is a city. It's better to say "idol."'" They get that right away. 'Mentor' is something else. It's a little too cute. It's like private school." Continues Jonathan, "I don't see Robin as often as I'd like to. He's busy making a fortune. I'm surprised that he's not up against somebody like Wells Fargo because he should have his own bank."

Why do all comedians worship Jonathan? What is it about this brilliantly funny curmudgeon that changed people's—comedians' and the

Jonathan Winters on the set of *Inside Comedy,* 2011. He was brilliant, yet you could feel his fragility. What a great mind.

audience's—experience with comedy? I have always thought that Jonathan was universally loved because his comedy was no-holds-barred, honest and direct humor that crossed all boundaries. He invited the audience in, and no matter how edgy the comedy was, he was able to connect with his audience and make them roar—and repeat his words to every one of their friends.

And he was just funny to the core. Everyone laughed at Jonathan. Everyone embraced his talents, which spanned every part of entertainment—he was a comic, he was an actor, he was an author, a television host, and later in his life, a very fine artist. He recorded his comedy, over fifty years of albums, got eleven Grammy nominations (eight of which were for Best Comedy Album). And like so many of us, Jonathan found his comedic passion in school.

"In the fourth grade," he remembers, "I played Old King Cole, but nobody came to see me. Even my relatives didn't come. Then I did two plays in high school, when I was fairly good-looking—not pretty, but I was cute. I didn't have this sunken kind of look. I had chiseled features, and when I smiled, people went, 'Ohh.' Both girls and boys. At any rate, I didn't get the lead role. But I did get to be a DJ in Dayton, Ohio. My mother was on WIZE in Springfield, so I got to be their

DJ—Johnnie Winters Show, six to eight. Basically I played records, mostly Nat King Cole and Stan Kenton music. But my mistake was that I interviewed myself. See, in Dayton, it was not easy to book interviews with Neil Armstrong or Groucho Marx, or anybody. You just get guests with agricultural equipment, who tell you, 'Hey listen, these really work well out here. We're with International Harvester and the weather's been so bad I've been unable to do any alfalfa work.' So, obviously, you lose the audience, in droves. So I'd interview myself.

"I'd say, 'Here's Wing Commander Louis Brighton, who flew a secret aircraft into Dayton airport. What was it like coming in over Dayton, Wing Commander?'

" 'It was fantastic. I've flown over India, Cairo, Germany—of course I couldn't stay there long—and I've flown over London. Flying over Dayton at night is like flying over millions of diamonds on a black velvet carpet.'

"The station's switchboard lit up like a thousand Christmases. Who the hell was this? And then the manager of the station, Ed Carnes, wearing a polo coat over his shoulders, came up and said, 'Who is this guy that you interviewed?' I said, 'It's me.' 'Don't do that anymore. Stay with Nat Cole.' That was a beginning of rejection.

"So I went to college—Kenyon College. For one year. That was something else. The GI Bill paid for my year at Kenyon, which people think is in Africa. Paul Newman went there, and Rutherford B. Hayes, but when I tell people I went to Kenyon, they ask, 'What was it like in the Congo?' And I say, 'A lot of drums and strange homes.'

"I thought I would date, and even though I was good-looking (then), women were only attracted to me until they found out I rode the bus. I was always broke. And I would say things to my dates like, 'I thought we'd go to the graveyard.'

" 'Why?'

" 'People don't talk out there. We can just lie down on a slab and have a good time.' And that frightened the women. Then I failed medieval history. I thought Charlemagne was a drink, so the teacher flunked me. So, of course, I went to New York. Had fifty-six bucks. I did a lot of voice-overs—radio, commercial stuff. I didn't even have an agent. I even tried to get on *The Ed Sullivan Show* on my own. I showed up, and the head of casting was at a desk with one piece of paper in front of him. He said, 'Kid, name?'

"'Jonathan Winters.'

"'What do you do? Sing, skate, what?'

"'No, I do comedy.'

"'Let's do it quickly.'

"So I put together the best five minutes I could, and his reaction was 'Wonderful . . .' I knew I was in the toilet. And when he said, 'I don't think Mr. Sullivan will understand you,' I went across the street and got drunk to kill the pain.

"By 1961, I had just had a breakdown, and not because of booze or drugs, just stress. And the doctor wouldn't give me a label—bipolar, manic-depressive—so it was a long stay in the hospital. When I got out, I was back at home with the kids and my wife, Eileen, when the phone rang, and Eileen says, 'Stanley Kramer, a producer doing a big picture, is on the phone. He wants to talk to you.'

"Stanley Kramer, my God, this is a big name! I got on the horn.

"'Mr. Kramer!'

"'Jonathan, I want you for a picture—*Mad, Mad, Mad World*. We've got Spencer Tracy, Buddy Hackett, Mickey Rooney—a whole bunch of people. I want you for one of the leads. Could you come out here pretty soon?'

"You can imagine. I don't think I'd ever been more scared in my life. I'd been inside the hospital for eight months. I said into the phone, 'Mr. Kramer,' exact words, 'give me a chance here. Don't go away.'

"I hung up and said to Eileen, 'I don't think I can do it, Eileen. I'm scared. I never had to learn any lines. I've been up there for eight months.'

"And she said, 'Jon, if you don't take this, you'll never work again.' She was right.

"So I went to work for Stanley Kramer (who remained my friend all my life). I was just on a natural high. I mean, I didn't know what Lithium or Prozac was, I only knew about aspirin. But I took on a character, began my new life. Filming was, and still is, a highlight of my life. Stanley was my guiding light. Filming *Mad* took me on a trajectory I never imagined. Gave me a new life, a new way to use my talents, such as they are, and his faith in me gave me confidence that I truly had never had.

"One time during a break, I said to Stanley, 'Did you know I was in a mental institution for eight months?'

"'Sure,' he answered quietly. 'Meet Marvin Kaplan, drunk. Vivien Leigh, Judy Garland, Montgomery Clift, drinking and drugs. You want some more?' My relationship with this guy was unique because he'd taken a chance on me, and I never forgot that. Never."

Jonathan lived in Montecito, California, until he died, when he was eighty-seven. Tributes flooded the web, from comedians and from fans, for many months. I spoke to Jonathan a few months before he died, catching up. He loved living in Montecito, where he had carved out a new career for himself as a painter, and his works sold worldwide. The last time I had seen him was when we taped an episode of my show *Inside Comedy*. On the phone that last time, I reminded him that all the comedians I interviewed over the last few years called him "their idol," except Robin Williams, who called him "my Buddha." Jonathan chuckled, quietly. "Of course he did," said the icon to all. "What does he know?"

Jonathan, the shining light to almost all other comedians, was that beacon because Jonathan was genius in his fearlessness while still being vulnerable, never afraid to go all-out outrageous and end up magical, outlandishly funny, which was awe-inspiring in that the result was always the most uncanny and oddball, absolutely unforgettable humor. It is really not a surprise, even predictable, that Jonathan Winters was Robin Williams's idol. If you have seen them both perform, if you consider every single adjective ever applied to either one, you surely see the obvious parallels between these two geniuses. And why they so loved each other.

I first saw Robin Williams perform in 1976 in San Francisco, at the Boarding House, a big, sort of offbeat club. We didn't know each other. I had finished a show at the hungry i, and I didn't see him at first, so I just stood in the back. Suddenly a man grabbed the mic, turned around,

Two of my best years on the road were spent with Robin Williams (here on our plane on tour in 2014). We traveled the country and had dinner together after every show. He never stopped asking me questions. We never stopped laughing. But I remember every morning he would go out by himself and explore the new town we were in. He would walk into local shops and shock people in the stores. He was so casual about it. He was loving, unique, funny (the funniest). There will never be anyone like him.

and it was Robin, and he was instantly mesmerizing. As a comedian, you know when you're spontaneous and are creating something. It's the best moment. It was obvious that Robin was just purely spontaneous. He was brilliantly improvising and able to change in an instant, never repeating anything. After his bit, I went backstage to see him, and I gave him a warm hug, and he hugged me back, and it was like we had known each other forever.

Seeing that genius, so early on, was astonishing. Hearing his stories? More astonishing. And toward the end of Robin's life, I was lucky enough to spend two years touring the country with him. To say that was unforgettable is an understatement (more about that tour later). Meanwhile, here is Robin in his own words from all the times we were together. Actually, the minute the conversation starts, you might as well just lean back and go, "Okay, this is the last thing I am going to say for a while. Go, Robin!"

"I was born in Chicago," he says. "My dad was in the automobile industry, worked with Lincoln Mercury for years, so we moved back and forth between Detroit and Chicago. My mother—a very interesting woman. Broke the rules. Her idea of natural childbirth was without makeup. She was a Christian Scientist (I used to call her a Christian Dior Scientist) who had plastic surgery. But she was very sweet, really funny, and I think that's where I got the comedy.

"My dad was an amazing guy. He was in the navy and got hit by a kamikaze aircraft carrier in World War II, so his view of the world was a little less rosy. His philosophy was, the world's going to shit on you sometime, so get ready to duck. The beginning of my whole comedy relationship with him was the two of us watching the old *Tonight Show* with Jack Paar.

"I was an only child. Well, actually, I'm not an only child. I have two half brothers. And the weird thing about that is that, for a long time, I was told that one of my half brothers was my cousin. My mother had a kid after World War II and dropped him off in Memphis with her mother, who raised him, and when I got to be eleven years old, we had this weird conversation where she sat me down and explained, 'You know, Robin, Mac is not your cousin. He's your brother.'

"I was really kind of quiet, but spending a lot of time alone, and I had this wild imagination. I collected toy soldiers, and I used to give them standing armies and a lot of different voices. It got me through the loneliness of being that only child. And I watched television. The greatest thing that I watched, and the first time I realized comedy, was *The Tonight Show,* the night I saw Jonathan Winters. I remember it exactly to this day. He came on dressed as a great white hunter with a helmet, and Jack Paar said, 'What do you hunt?'

"And Jonathan said, 'I'm a great white hunter and I hunt mainly squirrels.'

"And then Jack said, 'Well, how do you do it?'

"And Jonathan replied, 'I aim for their little nuts.'

"And at that point my father lost his shit, and I went, 'YES! I LOVE THIS MAN!' And that's when I realized, that's the way to go for me.

"I didn't really start acting till I went away to college, at Claremont Men's College in California. I started taking poli-sci courses, but the only place where the women were was in the improvisational theater course at Scripps, a nearby school. So, naturally, I took an improvisational theater class, and all of a sudden I went, WOAH! This is fun! And that was the beginning of me studying improv. We started off with a thirty-seat audience, and by the end of the semester, we were performing for two hundred or three hundred people. And it was like Second City, the beginning of the idea that, wait a minute, this is insane fun."

Robin started studying acting and doing plays at the theater, and that eventually parlayed itself into going to Juilliard for two years, which was an amazing accomplishment for a young boy from Chicago with limited theater experience. At Juilliard, Robin was only one of two students accepted by John Houseman in his advanced program. The other was Christopher Reeve, who remained a close friend of Robin's until Reeve's death in 2004. By the way, Robin paid many of Reeve's medical bills after the horrific accident that left him a quadriplegic. Robin was as devoted a friend to Chris as was possible. "I got a scholarship to Juilliard, and Christopher Reeve and I were both master's students in this two-year program," remembered Robin. "They picked Chris because, obviously, he's a handsome leading man, and I was the character. 'Hey, little hairy boy, you, too, come along.' Juilliard was great, with really great acting teachers. I had a terrific method-acting teacher, who said things like, 'You know, a lot of times method acting is like urinating in brown corduroy pants. You feel wonderful, we see nothing.' And Marlon Brando taught an acting class, which was kind of wonderful."

Christopher remembered, "Robin wore tie-dyed shirts with track suit bottoms and talked a mile a minute. I'd never seen so much energy contained in one person. He was like an untied balloon that had been inflated and immediately released. I watched in awe as he virtually caromed off the walls of the classrooms and hallways. To say that he was 'on' would be a major understatement!"

The two were masters in a class of dialects, and Robin blew everyone away, including the teacher, Edith Skinner, who had no idea what to make of Robin, as he had multiple, perfect dialects at his fingertips—including Spanish, Irish, British English, Russian, and Italian.

Robin stayed at Juilliard for two years—left when Houseman told him that there was nothing more he could teach him. He went back to live in San Francisco (okay, followed a girl) and worked the late shift in an ice-cream parlor, where everyone was stoned. While there, he saw a flyer for an improv night in a Lutheran church. At that time, in the many clubs in San Francisco, comedy started to build into being a real comedy scene. It was Robin, Dana Carvey, Paula Poundstone, all trying weird stuff, and then eventually the idea was to go down to the Comedy Store in LA and, eventually, get on *The Tonight Show.*

Robin was so great on television, such a great guest. He made many appearances on *The Tonight Show* and other late-night shows. Johnny Carson loved him, had him on many times. And I would say that, if the host is secure, Robin is that host's best guest. If the host is insecure, he's going to be holding on to his chair for dear life, because Robin's going to take off into another universe. All Robin had to do was feel good with the person he was talking to—that listener was more important to him than the whole audience. On Johnny's last show, after thirty years, Robin was the last guest Johnny wanted to have on. Bette Midler, who was one of Johnny's favorites, and Robin, who Johnny loved most because of his spontaneity—remember, Johnny was a really good improviser for many years, and he knew how great Robin was.

What was also rare about Robin is that he was a gifted actor. It's hard to be an actor who's good and also a great comedian. Those things do not go together naturally, because you have to devote yourself to one or the other, just in terms of time and experience. When you look at Robin's films and television shows, he was just as spontaneous on film as he was in front of an audience in a character, so he was naturally an actor. It was a long way from comedy clubs to starring in a sitcom by Garry Marshall called *Mork & Mindy.*

Mork & Mindy was a fluke. The only reason that they did the first episode, in 1978, was that Garry Marshall's son, Scott, had seen *Star Wars.* He went to his dad and said he wanted to see an alien on *Happy Days,* which was a huge hit. Garry loved the idea and went to every comic in LA to audition for the part.

Robin remembers: "Richard Lewis was coming out of the audition as I was coming in, and I thought, 'Ooops!' I walk in and go, 'I got nothing,' so I start doing this weird helium voice, sitting on my head in a chair. And I mooned them. And they said, 'You've got the part!'

"I thought, that's just a one-off, they'll never do anything with this." All of a sudden Paramount, which had a commitment to ABC to put a series on the air, needed a show. No pilot. They had scheduled twelve episodes with Pam Dawber, who they had playing a nun. After Robin's audition, they did a split screen of the two of them, Robin as an alien and Pam as a nun, and taped the first show. Robin remembers, "It was amazing, because the audience was laughing at everything! Then suddenly my hero, Jonathan Winters, is cast as my son, and he was amazing! (I loved that man. One of my favorite vintage Jonathan moments: he wanted to park in a handicapped parking spot, and this woman came up to him and said, 'Mr. Winters, you're not handicapped,' and he said, 'Madam, do you see inside my mind?') Jonathan was such an important part of the show, and he was one of a kind.

"And some people just got him, and others went, 'What the hell?' The stories! Every day it would take Jonathan forty minutes to get from his car to the set as people stopped him to hear a story, and he would just be doing routine after routine the entire way. As they would shoot us on the set, they'd run out of film because he was the king of improvisation like I had never seen—it would basically be like a machine gun in an old movie . . . boom . . . boom . . . boom . . . He was always about just trying anything. He made sounds based on a lot of people he grew up with, a lot of people he was with in the marines—he literally could morph into a hundred different people. He was living on a different planet." Robin admired him, even worshipped him, and was so sweet to him. He made sure that, when it was Jonathan's birthday, he would go to Montecito and spend time with Jonathan.

The show just took off. No one at the time could have imagined that kind of success for any of that cast. And it was really Robin who was out there—he would take a chance, talk to the audience, not be afraid of what he was saying, be bold and courageous.

Mork & Mindy ran for four years. It was a huge hit in the beginning; then ratings dropped. In 1982, the show got canceled, which

Robin said he found out in an article in *Variety.* Kind of like opening *The New York Times* and reading your own obituary and going, "You're dead!" But by then, in 1980, he had his first film role, in *Popeye.* It was an unusual roster, and the combination of behind-the-scenes power was also unexpected—Robert Altman directed, Jules Feiffer wrote the script, and Robert Evans was the producer. Big names!

Robin loved to reminisce about *Popeye.* "We shot in Malta—the Mediterranean, blue skies, blue water—and all of a sudden, after shooting for a month, the weather craps out, so we basically wait for the weather to clear up, and it turns out that we can't shoot for a whole month. And the studio goes, 'Fuck off, we're not paying for this anymore.' This is new to me, but the studio starts bringing people home. The special-effects people left first (Huh? Right). And we don't know how to end the movie! We don't have an ending!

"Bob Evans says, 'How do we end the movie?'

"And I jokingly say, 'I can walk on the water like Jesus . . .'

"And he says, 'Yes!'

"And that's the scene you'll see in the movie—me dancing and falling in the water! And, at that point, I thought that even my manager was on coke because I called home and said, 'Charlie, how do you like the dailies?'

"And he said, 'Oh, Rob, the dailies are okay, but could you open your other eye?'

"I went, 'Charlie, you fucking idiot, he's only got one eye! It's POP-EYE.' "

The movie opened and didn't do that well, although over many years it became a classic. Robin figured that his dreams of being a big movie star would disappear, and he had no other plans. And then, in 1982, George Roy Hill produced and directed *The World According to Garp,* from the huge novel by John Irving. Supporting actors were John Lithgow and Glenn Close (later nominated for Oscars), and Robin was offered the starring role. He remembers:

"After *Popeye,* I thought I was never going to work again! And here I am with Glenn Close! The first day, I'm working with the director, George Roy Hill. Glenn Close is my mother, and we do the first scene, and I do the scripted lines, but it's me, so I start to improvise. George makes a face like a weasel and says, 'Just say the lines, Robin. You know, the ones that are written?'

"And I go, 'Oh, you mean like acting?'

"And he goes, 'Yeah.'

"And that was the beginning of a director actually teaching me stuff. And the roles kept coming. And then, in 1987, my moment. *Good Morning, Vietnam.* I had done *Moscow on the Hudson* (1984) after *Garp*—but *Vietnam* was an amazing experience. I started improvising and trying different characters, and then I asked Barry [Levinson, the director] if we had enough of the radio shots, and he said, 'Yeah, we have eighteen hours. I think we're okay.'

"Here I thought my career was in comedy, yet my movie career kept going. And I always learned from the director. In *Dead Poets Society* (1989), Peter Weir told me, 'You know, you can be a very powerful listener.' In *Mrs. Doubtfire* (1993), Chris Columbus told me, 'The hardest thing is finding the voice.'"

A rule for almost any actor with a director is that you have to trust that director, and vice versa. Directing comedy is making the actors feel comfortable and letting them take chances. I told that to Robin early on, but he was already there. Robin was a very smart actor, but if someone challenged him in some way, he wouldn't necessarily have a confrontation; he would think and then protect himself. He followed the Second City philosophy without even knowing it—work from the top of your intelligence, understanding that if you care about being good and moving on, the more you know, the better you are. Honestly, he knew it. And he loved making movies. He made seventy-two films in thirty-five years. Who does that? Not many actors, and no other comic actors.

Robin loved the work, and at first, that's why he worked so much and so hard, doing four films each in 1991, 1995, 1997, and five in 1996. That is unheard of—if an actor works in one film a year that's pretty great. Many make a film every few years. Robin, again, was exceptional in every way.

Robin and I stayed in touch over the years. In March 2009, Robin had open heart surgery at the Cleveland Clinic. Doctors replaced his aortic valve, fixed his mitral valve, and corrected an irregular heartbeat. As always, Robin had his own take on the life-saving surgery.

"The 'new heart'? It's nice to have one. I was at the Cleveland Clinic, a well-known hospital, a great hospital. So they give you choices. 'Here's some options for a new valve. Porcelain? A pig valve? And then they offered me a mechanical heart, but it clicks, and I thought of people being near me, and there will be tick, tick, tick, like you have a little Morse code going (it was saying, 'Don't get that heart, don't get that heart!'). I went with a bovine heart, which is made from cow, which sounds like a Mel Gibson movie, 'Cow Heart!' The really weird thing is that it felt different to perform onstage after that. It was a bit like, uh, I'm back, kind of. You kind of pace yourself, and I would back off it a little because I would do something that's so physical and feel like I was dying, and at that point, the method actor in me goes, that's all fear. Use it."

So when Robin was asked to do a benefit for the Cleveland Clinic, David Steinberg, his manager (we call him "the other David Steinberg," and, ironically, my wife is a Robyn and I'm a David. I had to check who was in bed with me), told Robin, "We have to get David Steinberg, the comedian, for the benefit." Robin approached me and said, "David, I've got the perfect thing. It's a benefit for the Cleveland Clinic, and you could interview me, but I have no material." Robin was always worried that he didn't have enough material. He then said, "Incidentally, you're a Jew. You're going to have a heart attack somewhere along the way, so why not get to the Cleveland Clinic now! We could do this together!"

And we did.

The genius of Robin the comedian was so complex. He was a great actor. He had an unbelievable sense of what is funny, and his mind went so fast! But his real genius was his improvisation—brilliant, sometimes scary, because you never knew where he was going. We would walk onstage, sit down, and I would say, "Ladies and gentlemen, Robin Williams."

And he was off. All I had to do was one line at a time.

I asked, "You are amazing with your impressions. Did you ever do your mother?"

"I loved doing my *grandmother*, who lived in Memphis. You know, 'I'm watching wrestling, having another mint julep!' It's that whole thing about Southern women, who always say, 'Bless your heart,' rather than, 'Back off, bitch.' Most comics do comedy for their mother. I used to have a pillow that drove my mother nuts. It said, 'If it's not one thing, it's your mother.'"

And so we went on tour. It was 2012. Two years.

The first show of the tour was in Montréal, and, as you well know, I am Canadian. Canadians love other Canadians. It was the first time we got onstage together, and they were in love—with Robin. Robin and I always talked about that show together, that first show that mattered so much, because, after, you're going to grow and change, and then the goal becomes not to get stale, not to repeat what you're doing. That was second nature to Robin, because he always wanted to change. In fact, if he could do a new show every night, he would, and he mostly did. The audience loved it. For us, once we went onstage, it was so natural. I'm the kind of comedian who is, in my own way, secure, so I didn't need to be getting the laughs all the time. Having come from Second City, you know that when you're onstage with another person getting laughs, the audience doesn't remember which one got the laugh.

We tried not to meet and talk too much before the show. We tried to surprise each other, because you don't want to fall into a pattern. Then what he read that day, and what I read, would come out together. It was a totally spontaneous show. Many comedians work really hard to get their material to feel spontaneous, but with Robin, it was natural. He was always on fire, instantly and constantly changing and challenging himself and his audience. For me, having spent years at Second City, it was so reassuring to have someone totally spontaneous, very much in my style. Robin wanted to know everything about Second City. I said to him: "You *are* everything about it. You don't need to know one thing. What you're doing is what we did there."

Robin was out there, taking chances, talking to the audience, not afraid of what he was saying. He was always bold and courageous. As he has said many times, Jonathan Winters was his mentor as a comedian. Now, Jonathan Winters, if you gave him a script, wasn't that interesting. If you took away the script, you would get an instantly brilliant person, and that of course is what attracted Robin to him. Robin was more famous in those years than Jonathan Winters, and he really loved him. He liked to look after people. That was the personal, incredible thing about Robin Williams—he had the biggest heart.

We never walked offstage once, never once, in two years of touring, without his arm around me, us walking offstage together and Robin saying, "I'm so proud to be with you." This is who he was. He was an empathetic person who would put himself aside to help anybody. His comedy was just getting better and better, and every night I could see it. He was braver and braver—he liked me to move him around, change the subject, do something new, which was very unusual in comedy. People think stand-up comedians are doing the same show every time they see it. ("You've seen it before—he's been doing that, or she's been doing that, for years.") Well, with Robin, you had never seen it before. That was his genius spontaneity. He could just take off on a subject, and I let him go, and it would sometimes be three minutes, sometimes ten minutes. His thumbprint was truly his own. The audience was always mesmerized. And it was phenomenal.

I would suggest things to talk about, and he got more and more spontaneous. He was such a generous performer—he refused to let me not talk and just interview. He always kept pushing it back to me a little bit, and that started our relationship. When we laughed onstage, we were genuinely laughing, because I didn't know what he was going to say, and he never knew what I was going to say. We both had such a good time improvising for the audience, and they adored him. He was so beloved. Which is why the tragedy of his death is all the more devastating. I thought he knew how much he was loved, how much support he had from his fans, his audiences, his friends.

People call people "great" all the time. Johnny was truly great. So was Robin. Robin, since he is gone (in 2014 when he was sixty-three), I can call him anything I want, and he's probably up there hearing me and saying, "Why didn't you say I did this, and why didn't you say I did that?" I'm not going to take that chance, but I would say, unequivocally, that Robin Williams was a genius, and also, Robin was a mensch, a special, generous person who never stepped on people's lives. And, as for the work, as I have said before, every comedian has a thumbprint, and Robin's is a big one out there in the comedy world.

CHAPTER 6

THE HILLCREST COUNTRY CLUB

It's Not the Golf, It's the Comedy

Groucho Marx, the Marx Brothers, George Burns,
Jack Benny, Danny Kaye, and Danny Thomas,
who at least looked Jewish

As I mentioned previously, in the fall of 1969, I had a show on ABC called *Music Scene,* which aired from 7:30 to 8:15 p.m. and featured rock and pop music stars, such as Tom Jones, Janis Joplin, James Brown, Crosby, Stills, Nash & Young, Three Dog Night, Isaac Hayes, Bo Diddly, and Stevie Wonder. The show showcased a handful of talented co-hosts, including Lily Tomlin. In the '70s, advertisers weren't as interested in the youth audience, and they targeted most of their ads to the middle-aged crowd. It's funny, because that's almost entirely flipped now. Lily Tomlin already had a cast of comedic characters she'd developed at the split-level Upstairs at the Downstairs nightclub on West Fifty-Sixth Street in Manhattan. Ruth Buzzi, Madeline Kahn, the JFK-impersonator Vaughn Meader, Mort Sahl, and Joan Rivers all appeared there. Tomlin had been on *The Garry Moore Show* and *The Merv Griffin Show.* She was actually let go from *Music Scene* early on, but that wasn't the end of her career, it was just the beginning. The producer George Schlatter hired her on *Laugh-In,* and the rest is history. It wasn't long before Tomlin had a hit comedy record and two hugely popular TV specials.

Ken Fritz and Stan Harris produced *Music Scene.* We didn't last too long—just one season—but that's how I got to spend more time

I invited Groucho Marx, who was my close friend, and whom I worshipped, to come on *Music Scene* and co-host it with me in 1970. There we sang "Father's Day":

"Today, Father, is Father's Day
And we're giving you a tie . . .
You say it was nice of us to bother
But it really was a pleasure to fuss
For according to our mother you're our father
And that's good enough for us!"

with Groucho Marx. Producer Arthur Whitelaw knew that Groucho was looking for a writer to do *Minnie's Boys,* the story of the Marx Brothers. Arthur set up an appointment for me to meet Groucho. He warned me that Groucho was very difficult, that "it won't be easy—but if it works, you will have fun with him." I walked in, very nervous, introduced myself, and told him I would like to write *Minnie's Boys.* Groucho quickly responded, "Got a pencil?" And we had a deal.

Groucho Marx was the last co-host I had on the show. On the air, I thanked him for "coming on a show that's failing." Without missing a beat, he said, "They don't call me the kiss of death for nothing."

One day, Groucho asked me to walk with him. We walked from Hillcrest to the Brown Derby, a real Hollywood hangout for major stars. (I was twenty-eight, Groucho was in his late seventies, and I was more tired than he was walking ten blocks.) Groucho and I sat at the

Sharing a cigar with Groucho, as we always did. He was reluctant to come on as my co-host, but I'm so glad he did; it really meant everything to me, and the audience loved him.

back of the restaurant and talked. People would spot Groucho and stop. Groucho would ignore them and keep on talking. And then two priests came in to get seated for lunch. It was very unusual to see priests in that particular restaurant, but there they were. And they walked past us, and I saw them notice Groucho. One of the priests broke away from the other one and went up to Groucho and said, "Mr. Marx, I'm so glad to see you! I want to thank you for bringing so much joy in the world."

And Groucho, without looking up, said, "And I want to thank you for taking so much out."

Groucho would just regale me with stories, such as the time Charlie Chaplin's name came up, and I asked what this genius of talk thought of Chaplin's silent movies. Groucho said, "He was the best in his day. He once told me, 'I wish I could talk on the screen, like you can.' He couldn't talk on-screen because his character was too famous."

Groucho said to me on one of our walks, "Let's meet at Hillcrest. All the guys want to see you." Surely you must remember Groucho's famous edict: "I would not want to belong to a club who would have me as a member." We had lunch at Hillcrest every Tuesday for a year.

Hillcrest Country Club is located across the street from 20th Century Fox Studios, in Los Angeles. It was the first Los Angeles country club for Jews. For the price of a small house, you could play eighteen holes of golf there, or a game of tennis, but the real action was at the comedians' table, set back in a corner of the main dining room. The country's most famous comedians were there, some at a daily get-together.

Milton Berle (he was a member of Hillcrest for seventy years; when he joined, the membership fee was $275; when he died, it was $150,000 or so, depending on how much money you had given to the United Jewish Appeal). "Uncle Miltie," as he was known from his show that ran for years and as Groucho loved to call him, was a true vaudevillian with that huge personality. His unbridled joy at entertaining was obvious every single minute he was performing, often dressed as a woman, which Groucho also loved to tease him about and which audiences just relished. Milton and I go back to when I was starting out in comedy. The memories are omnipresent, as they were so important to my craft, and so outrageous. Milton and I were once guests on a Dick Clark special. We were a twosome for the first time—and hadn't really worked together before. Milton, before we went on camera, said to me, "When we are doing the scene, I'm going to grab your arm at a certain point, squeeze it, and hold it, and I don't want you to do anything, David—not to walk, not to speak, until I let go of your arm, so we can hold for all of my laughs."

When I was doing my show, *The David Steinberg Show*, in Canada, we flew Milton up to be a guest star. Ziggy Steinberg (who was a writer on the show, my best friend, and no relation) and I went to Milton's hotel room with the revised script. We knocked on the door, and he asked, "Who is it?" We said, "It's David and Ziggy." He opened the door and was standing there, stark naked, with the "Do Not Disturb" sign hanging from his legendary enormous penis (not as large as he would have liked people to think), singing "Thanks for the Mammories."

Danny Kaye (who was Jewish despite the changed name—he was born David Daniel Kaminsky) was what we now call a "renaissance man," a brave comic who constantly took chances all over the entertainment map. His expertise included stand-up comedy, of course (he got his early "training" in the Catskills Borscht Belt); he was a comic actor with huge physical comedy talent and antics—over-the-top "clowning" with very strange pantomimes, a lot of singing of silly parodies, and onomatopoetic sounds. Which leads us to his talent and passion for music. Although he couldn't read notes, he ended up recording actual songs without his known comedy antics, but he also recorded musical tongue twisters and conducted orchestras all over the world, most of it for charity, raising money for the musicians' pension fund, and never taking a fee for his work. But his obsessive and extraordinary passion was for UNICEF, becoming its first goodwill ambassador in 1954, and on whose behalf he once piloted a jet to sixty-five cities in five days.

There was universal amazement for Danny and his unending talents and passions, which were always included in his comedy sketches and portraits of characters. He had a decades-long obsession with cooking—not for Jewish food, but Chinese; he installed a full Chinese kitchen in his home, which he called Ying's (his daughter, famed journalist Dena Kaye, remembers that, nevertheless, he had no food prejudices, enjoying good caviar as much as he loved Kentucky Fried Chicken). He was also a passionate pilot, who loved flying (he had a commercial pilot's license). And the "funny" in his life is memorialized at his gravesite, which seems to be a tribute to the comedy he so loved and is still known years after his death. On a bench, there are sculptures of a baseball and bat, an aircraft, a piano, a flowerpot, musical notes, and a chef's toque.

When Dena Kaye wrote about her dad in *Her Heart Belongs to Daddy,* she eloquently described the man I revered, saying, "Imagine

Robin Williams, Tommy Tune and Tony Bennett all on the same stage, at the same time, and you'll have an idea of what it was like to see Danny Kaye perform solo." Dena continued, "Walter Winchell once wrote about my father in a movie review, 'Ushers might be knocked to the ground by people rolling in the aisles.' He was an actor who danced (just think, he performed Fred Astaire's role in 'White Christmas'), a dancer who sang, and a mimic who brought tears to your eyes. He had style and grace. He was elegant even when he was zany. His gymnastic face expressed every emotion. The great pianist Arthur Rubinstein noted, 'As with Chaplin, I am not so much amused as I am moved.' A fitting tribute to Danny Kaye is what Harry Belafonte said: 'Danny accepted no boundaries, and that's the highest form of creative energy.'"

George Burns (born Nathan Birnbaum, the "ever see him without a cigar?" comic), who showed up every single day, from noon to 3 p.m., for his bridge game at Hillcrest, and, two days before he died in 1996, showed up to play in a wheelchair, was the "driest" comedian around. You never saw him laugh. He was that sardonic person even in films. I hope you saw him in Neil Simon's film of his play *The Sunshine Boys,* for which George won a Best Supporting Actor Oscar, about which, as he told me, "Who would have known?" I don't think I saw a smile when he won the Kennedy Center Honors in 1988, either.

By the time I was with Groucho at Hillcrest, Gracie had died, so George always came to Hillcrest alone. I missed seeing them together in person, but on film, they were magic. George would be the silent straight man, cynical, wry but with a sweet smile, hands always folded with the cigar in his hand or in his mouth (with his mouth open)— you know, that smirking but sweet guy—while Gracie, who was an absolutely lovable, hysterical part of their act, was the silly, daffy, exuberantly happy and giggly sidekick. Together they made a comedy act that stood out from the crowd for decades in vaudeville, in stand-up, on radio, in television (they received eleven Emmy nominations for their show), and in films.

Jack Benny, his longtime manager, Irving Fine, and George Burns had known each other for years and years, and they still loved being together. They were in their seventies and eighties when I spent time with them at Hillcrest, and someone would mention a name like "Higgins from Philadelphia," and these *alte cockers* would say, "That cocksucker!" You know why? He was a critic who'd given them a bad review a million years ago, and they never forgot him. George would say, "That son of a bitch gave Fink's Mules [a vaudeville act] a better review than Gracie and me!" And then they'd rattle off everyone who they hated, and be funny about their hostilities.

The truth is—they loved each other. George, at Hillcrest, always had a great story and was funny through and through, but he did seem like kind of a half person without Gracie by his side. To make up for it—in the most sensitive manner that belied those who didn't know him—it was Jack Benny who, though he would say, "I am a sucker for George," was actually always there by George's side. We would say, "If someone sneezed and George Burns said 'gesundheit,' Jack Benny would laugh for two days." They were close friends and great support for each other. That kind of friendship, between two of the greatest comedic talents ever, was so special to be around. Much like Mel Brooks and Carl Reiner were—until recently, sadly. Carl Reiner left us as I was writing this. We spent wonderful times together over the years, always a kind, caring, and brilliantly funny man. He was such a mensch.

On any given day, you could see many of them sitting together for lunch and talking shop, trying out new material, and reminiscing. Danny Thomas was actually Hillcrest's first non-Jewish member, in 1987, about which Jack Benny quipped, "The least they could've done was admit someone who *looked* like a gentile." A funny aside: Danny, who was Lebanese, learned Yiddish as a nightclub comedian and from living in a poor immigrant melting-pot neighborhood in Toledo, Ohio. And when he was a client of the William Morris Agency, his agent, Abe Lastfogel, who spoke Yiddish, taught Danny more Yiddish, and that is the only language Danny ever spoke to me—because no one on set ever understood it, and he loved that we had that kind of secret com-

With Jack Benny at the Johnny Carson tribute dinner, circa 1971. I love Jack Benny, and he recently had come on *The Tonight Show* to surprise me while I was guest hosting for the first time. He came out and just stared at me for the longest time and said what he always subsequently repeated every time he saw me since, "You are sooo young."

munication. As Marlo Thomas recently told me, when her dad starred in *The Jazz Singer,* he learned to sing the "Kol Nidre" and other songs in Yiddish. That's because, says Marlo, those songs were very much like the songs in Arabic that he learned in his youth. So you can imagine the conversation when, in the 1950s, oil was discovered on the country club grounds, and members (including Groucho) began to collect tax shelter dividends, which became so valuable the members left them in their wills.

I was eager to know more about vaudeville, and the Marx Brothers' vaudeville background was unrivaled. When they were a vaudeville team, they were called the Four Nightingales—Groucho, Gummo, and Harpo (along with Lou Levy); eventually Chico and Zeppo joined, and they were *all* musical. Chico played the piano, Harpo played the harp, and Groucho was the fast-talking one. He told me that vaudeville was just terrible and that the audiences mostly came in drunk and always heckled everybody. But when people started to talk badly to them, Groucho, who became hostile easily, could put anyone down.

At Hillcrest and elsewhere, Groucho wasn't really a storyteller as much as a wit. He was one of the greatest put-down artists I've ever seen, not that you'd want to see too many of them. Don Rickles was certainly influenced by Groucho. But if you had to be around one, Groucho Marx was the one. He was a knockout counterpuncher. His zingers always had a kernel of truth about them, even a lieutenant colonel of truth about them, but there were a few stories he enjoyed telling. One was about how, in 1941, as Hitler's deputy Rudolf Hess was parachuting into Britain with his so-called peace plan, Winston Churchill was informed of it while in the middle of watching *Horse Feathers,* a Marx Brothers' movie.

I spent a lot of time asking Groucho for tips about comedy. I once asked him how he'd know if a piece of material was working or not. He said, "If the audience is a little bored and they're yawning and talking to each other, then that material's nothing. If they're looking at their watches, that's okay," he said, "but if they're shaking their watches to see if they're still working, then we'd immediately change the material."

One of my favorite "Groucho at Hillcrest" stories concerns Groucho and the poet T. S. Eliot. Eliot was a great Marx Brothers fan and was particularly crazy about Groucho. He even wrote Groucho a somewhat fawning fan letter that timidly asked for an autographed picture, which of course Groucho, flattered beyond belief, was happy to send along. When the two men eventually met in London, where Eliot lived for much of his life, Groucho had brushed up on his Shakespeare, so to speak, by reading Eliot's famous verse play *Murder in the Cathedral.* But "all he wanted to do," Groucho recalled, "was ask me about the Marx Brothers and how we did certain things, like the mortar shell coming through the window in *Duck Soup.*" (That's the kind of detail that makes history bearable.)

When the Nobel Prize–winning poet died in 1965, Eliot's widow, Valerie, invited Groucho to the memorial service. Groucho was reluctant to speak, but, when encouraged by Laurence Olivier, he did manage to say a few words. When Groucho returned to Hillcrest, his pals around the table—Jack Benny, Milton Berle, and George Burns—gave him a hard time. "How could you, Groucho?" they said. "You know that son of a bitch was anti-Semitic!"

"Well," Groucho replied, "there are a lot of Jews I don't like, either." That was Groucho.

One day, at one of our Hillcrest lunches, Groucho looked over and saw Adolph Zukor at another table. He asked if I knew him. I said no. (Zukor was a hundred years old and was the head of Paramount before Paramount was Paramount. He'd financed a movie starring Sarah Bernhardt, that's how old he was.) All I saw was a cap in a chair.

Groucho said, "Come with me and I'll introduce you to him." Jack Benny was behind Groucho motioning, "Don't do it, say no," waving with his hands. We walked over. Groucho lifted up Adolph's cap and said, gesturing to me, "You remember Chico, don't you?"

My mouth was open. I didn't know what to say. I still don't. He smiled and I smiled.

It didn't occur to me that I would still be visiting Groucho regularly when he was that old. One day, I brought my friend Elliott Gould, who worshipped Groucho. They exchanged stories (Groucho wanted to know if Barbra sang at home), and Elliott wanted to shave Groucho because he felt he needed a shave. It was such a sweet gesture on his part. Just unforgettable.

Then there was the time that I was at a party at Lucille Ball's house with Groucho. You can imagine the fanfare with familiar faces just hanging around. I was watching from the sidelines. Groucho was sitting quietly, in the corner, alone. I remember someone walked up to him and said, "I am just wondering how do you know Lucille Ball, because . . ."

And Groucho quickly said, "Zeppo fucked her."

I dined out on that story forever.

One thing I noticed hanging around these legendary comics is that actors like being around comedians more than comedians like to be around actors. And being a comic actor is not the same thing as being a comedian. Case in point:

To be a guest at that table at Hillcrest was ecstasy for someone like me. It made me remember my first fourteen years of life in Canada, when I loved radio, when I listened to *The Jack Benny Show* and *Burns and Allen,* which were great for a kid who'd grow up to be a comedian. It was kind of like the British rock stars of the 1960s, with kids staying awake at night listening to the early rock and blues American stations coming through Radio Luxembourg. And listening to Jack Benny, you realize that he didn't need a line, he didn't need anything to get a laugh.

After the longest pause, he could look at the audience and say, "You're young," and the audience would laugh. Radio paints pictures, because you have to visualize what you are hearing.

I noticed at Hillcrest that comedians are different when they're together. They don't talk that much about comedy. If you're hanging out with older comedians, they'll keep you engrossed just by telling their stories. Basically, I was seeing a bunch of guys who'd worked through the history of twentieth-century entertainment—vaudeville into radio, radio into television, television into movies. For me, it was like being let into a magic kingdom. I was like a bar mitzvah kid with these guys. I was so young and they'd always talk about that. "Young, young, David, you're too young!"

Now, when I go on the set of whatever show I'm working on, I'll hear from a young comedian, "It's so exciting to meet you." It's come full circle.

CHAPTER 7

COMEDY IN THE AGE OF NIXON . . . WHAT COMEDY?

I first became aware of Richard Nixon (and who knows? Maybe he became aware of me then, too) in 1960, when he ran for president against John F. Kennedy. He lost the all-important televised debate with JFK, and then the election, mostly because of the same dense five o'clock shadow that's plagued me, too, since puberty. And when it was time to go on television myself, I knew to slather on enough pancake makeup so I didn't look like a werewolf in training. Thanks, Dick.

My other big debt to Nixon was his famous "Checkers" speech of 1952. Since the Steinberg family didn't have television back in those Winnipeg days, I didn't see this amazing performance in its entirety until 1962, when they replayed it during his run for California governor. I was enthralled. I was mesmerized. It was the best awful television performance I'd ever seen. While watching Nixon whine on and on about his wife's "Republican cloth coat" and Alger Hiss's pumpkin and Tricia and Julie's little liver-spotted dog, while sticking in mean little jabs at the Democrats *and* kissing Ike's ass, I wondered: Was it really possible for a potential leader of the free world to talk with such a Queegish mixture of naked venom, treachery, and self-pity? Actually, in the era of Trump, it doesn't seem all that crazy, does it?

I continued to be cocky in my regular comedy life. At the first New York Film Festival in 1971, at Lincoln Center, after the premiere

of Henry Jaglom's *A Safe Place,* starring Tuesday Weld, there was a dinner, and I was the MC. On the dais were major faces like Peter Fonda,
Otto Preminger, and my friend Jack Nicholson. Jack and I arrived
together—late. Why? We were a little high from smoking weed, and
then the elevator got stuck. So as the film ended, everyone was clapping
and looking around for me and Jack. They were really getting restless
as we walked in. Jack goes right to the dais. I grab the microphone
and introduce everyone sitting on the dais, one by one. As I start to
introduce Otto, he looks at me and says, "We, here, are all very accomplished. But you, Mr. Steinberg, have done nothing."

Before I could stop myself, I reply, "Better to have done nothing
than *Hurry Sundown.*"

My only excuse for that comeback was that I was a little high, that I
was a very young up-and-coming comedian, and Preminger was a huge
star, an incredibly talented director, and very full of himself, deservedly
so. The result: half the audience was in shock that I, the young kid,
went up against the icon, and the other half laughed, albeit nervously.
When the evening was over, Otto came up to me, hugged me, and said,
"We need to get together." And we were friends ever since.

Then Nixon beat Hubert Humphrey. I watched the new president
with some horror but a *lot* more fascination and delight. The most fas-
cinating part to me, as an observer of human behavior, which made up
my comedy, was that in a job where you had to be loose, extroverted,
and communicative—communicating with politicians, world leaders,
and the public is most of what a president does all day—he was the
most uptight and introverted person possible. I knew some comedians
who were shy and uptight offstage, yet able to express themselves in
front of an audience, but Red Skelton and Imogene Coca didn't negoti-
ate with Mao or have access to nuclear weapons.

This led to the most delicious comic and satirical possibilities for
me. It was as if a funny, invisible friend was constantly whispering great
material into my ear. By 1970, Nixon's secret plan was revealed to be the
carpet bombing of Cambodia, making him public enemy number one,
especially on college campuses. I couldn't have been more delighted
because colleges were where a lot of my audience was.

"You know I don't do political satire," I told the thousands of students in the audience. "But that's because I am not as good as the people who are really terrific at it, and also because I don't feel you could even remotely top the political events of the day so far as satire is concerned. But I will tell you something about President Nixon. And once I have told it to you, you are never going to see him the same way again. Because what I am going to tell you is the truth, and the strange mystical thing about the truth is—once you have heard it, it remains lodged in your memory forever. And the truth is: President Nixon has a face that looks like a foot."

This stuff really went over big at Bowdoin and SUNY New Paltz. *The Tonight Show Starring Johnny Carson* was another matter.

In 1971 and 1972, when the anti-Nixon movement was really heating up, so was my guest-hosting career. Johnny being Johnny, he was all for me to push the boundaries, but there were a few things—maybe because I'm Canadian, probably also because I was a cocky, fairly insensitive young putz—that I never really realized at the time. One was that much of the audience didn't like these jokes.

The first thing I didn't realize was that *The Tonight Show* wasn't Second City or the hungry i or even the John Jay College of Criminal Justice. Back then, there was no cable, only three networks, no Letterman and no *Nightline,* and everyone—I mean *everyone*—watched *The Tonight Show.* And when you're talking about everyone, you're talking about a lot of people who weren't crazy about me and my material. And they especially weren't crazy about my making fun—not gentle Bob Hope fun, but serious fun—of the president of the United States. Remember, this was before *Saturday Night Live, Spy* magazine, and Monica Lewinsky. Richard Nixon had executive privileges, one of which was to never, ever be mocked or, God forbid, have his wisdom or sanity doubted.

But, me? In front of millions of people watching *The Tonight Show,* I said: "President Nixon has a face that looks like a foot—he is having face-to-foot confrontations with Mao Tse-tung."

I got a few sacks of hate mail and some nasty looks from the NBC suits, who would have loved to have gotten rid of me, but couldn't, because Carson liked watching me say what he couldn't. And I got a big new fan base of people who were just beginning to wake up to Richard Nixon's incompetence and the real danger their democracy was in. They thought I was a sensitive, politically astute entertainer slash activist.

Wrong again. Actually, I was still just a cocky, insensitive young putz. Since I didn't realize how many people I was alienating, all I felt I was doing was tapping into a vein of golden comedy. After all, I'd made fun of the Bible—and gotten away with it. I would have made fun of Pete Seeger or Daniel Berrigan if I could have gotten laughs with it. Sure, I thought Nixon was a dimwit. And that the Vietnam War was an abomination. But, though nobody admits this anymore, back then my feelings about the Vietnam War itself were so superficial that it never occurred to me that the soldiers who were over there—the ones who couldn't stay in college or get a teaching job or make it to Canada or fail their physical by faking pedophilia or a bone spur—should be respected. I thought the soldiers were doing a terrible thing propagating a war against defenseless people. Basically, I thought pretty much what Jane Fonda thought. With much less research and a much worse complexion.

By the time I got the gig to open the Persian Room at the Plaza Hotel in Manhattan in 1972, they wanted to show how hip they were, so they opened starring me. About five days before my opening, they started running quarter-page ads in *The New York Times*. So in my mind the whole thing was like a gala Broadway opening. And in real life, the opening was a big PR event, with everyone—except me, of course—wearing tuxedos and evening gowns. In the audience were celebrities like Lauren Bacall, Neil Simon, Paddy Chayefsky, Jerry Orbach, and Barbra Streisand. Even my sister Tammy and my brother-in-law Harry flew in from Beverly Hills. Just for that one night!

I'm scheduled to go on at 8:30. At about seven o'clock, my then wife, Judy, and I are in my dressing room. I'm fairly nervous but still plenty cocky. There's a knock at the door:

"Who is it?" I say.

"Mr. Steinberg, could you please open up?" says a deep voice. "This is the FBI."

"The FBI?" I say, my voice rising a couple of octaves.

"The Federal Bureau of Investigation. Could you please open up, Mr. Steinberg?"

"Just a minute!" I say.

My life and career, not necessarily in that order, flash before my eyes. I rattle around the dressing room for a few minutes. I pull myself together in my best "John Gielgudian" manner and welcome the G-men as public-spiritedly as possible.

"What's the problem, uh, agents?" I say.

The FBI men are two tall, nondescript guys in identical nondescript suits. They glance around the room. At the floor. The ceiling. Judy. Me. The tallest one steps forward:

"Mr. Steinberg," he says politely, "a call has come into the switchboard. Somebody out there says he'll be in the audience and he'll shoot you if you do your Nixon material. But don't worry. You go ahead and say whatever you want. Because we'll be here to protect you."

Protect *me*?

The *FBI*?

Wild thoughts raced through my brain so fast that they almost caught up with my stark raving terror, which was running the race of its life. It's easy in hindsight to realize that something fishy was going on, but remember: it's 1972. Even though I'm still too naive to realize exactly what effect my political bon mots are having on the Establishment, I'm a pretty fast learner. Plus, the idea that these FBI guys might be pulling my chain never even crosses my mind. Because, again, remember: it's 1972.

It's still pre-Watergate, pre-Irangate, pre-Waco, pre-special-agents-leaving-their-top-secret-laptops-behind-in-the-DC-subway-system. The idea that an FBI special agent would actually lie to me—to anyone—was as if Jimmy Stewart had joined the Black Panther Party.

"So what are you going to do, Mr. Steinberg?" asks the FBI man, kindly.

"What am I going to do?" I say. "I'm going to go out there and do my act."

Did I actually say that? Yes, I did.

To my surprise, and Judy's horror, my mind sprints to the conclusion that if I back off and cancel or censor myself in any way, my career as a comedian is over. Mockery and being a smart-ass are mostly all I have going for me. If I give them up, if the audience senses that I'm holding back anything, I'm dead. Onstage. And offstage. No more routines, no more magazine articles, no more comedy records, no more *Tonight Show,* no more fame, no more limousines, no more money.

Not exactly *Profiles in Courage,* but as close as I'll ever get, I guess.

So even though Judy and all the friends around me beg me to reconsider, I selfishly decide to go on with the show. The tall FBI man asks me nicely if I wouldn't rather leave out the Nixon material.

"Nope," I say, and open the dressing room door, where fourteen FBI guys wait to escort me to the stage. Most of us pile into this tiny elevator and ride down to the stage level. Then a really strange thing happens. When the door opens, I'm greeted by a nattily dressed guy holding a tape recorder. He says he's a reporter for some magazine—*America* or *American Weekly* or something—that sounds vaguely familiar but which, in retrospect, I've never heard of and doesn't really exist.

"I've just got one question," he says, walking backward in front of me with his little microphone in my face.

"Shoot," I say.

"What is your attitude toward Nixon and the presidency, David?" he asks. "Do you think it's okay, do you think it's safe to make fun of them?"

I say, "You know, Nixon is no different to me than Johnson or Humphrey. In my mind, my job is to be edgy. If it's an 'attack' on these politicians, then it's just me being who I am, doing my job. Just me doing 'my' humor. So all I am doing is dealing with Nixon in a funny way—same way that I deal with any Democrat or Republican politician."

The reporter smiles and turns off his tape recorder. And for some reason, I think, maybe he knows that what I've just said is nonsense, because in truth, back then, my kneejerk liberal side automatically hated Nixon and thought he was the biggest asshole who ever lived.

So I'm introduced, I walk onstage, and the beginning of my first appearance at the Plaza Hotel doesn't go all that great. I do the edgy material first, the Nixon stuff. And a bit making fun of Bebe Rebozo, and my joke about Governor John Connally switching parties from Democrat to Republican, which, I point out, is the rare instance of a rat swimming *toward* a sinking ship.

And I get some laughs, but they're hesitant, delayed laughs—like the people in the audience are a little shocked by the material. Or maybe it's because there are fourteen FBI agents standing six feet apart along the side and back walls of the theater, keeping an eye on everyone in the audience while I'm onstage. But the fact is that the FBI guys are laughing louder and more freely than anyone.

Things get better when I revert to my older non-Nixon routines. I get a nice hand when I say good night. And to top it all off, the first two FBI guys are waiting for me. They shake my hand and congratulate me on a great show. Then they escort me into my dressing room and tell Judy and me that they'll be driving us home "for our protection."

And we would gladly have gone with them, when there's a knock on the door. An FBI guy opens it, and me not knowing that a huge surprising new friendship was about to start, I smile as my old friend, the actor Jerry Orbach, his wife, Marta, walk in, with two other men. The first is a short, slim, extremely well-dressed guy whom Jerry introduces as his good friend Joey Gallo, and the second is a taller, more powerfully built man, whom Jerry introduces only as "Punchy." In other words, the notorious Mafia kingpin Joey "Crazy Joe" Gallo (just released from prison)—and his henchman slash bodyguard by his side, right back here in my Plaza Hotel dressing room.

"Hey, great show, David!" says Joey, shaking my hand before throwing himself on me and giving me a big hug. Joey then says something to me that I knew I'd remember for the rest of my life.

"At Attica you were everyone's favorite."

"Well, thanks, Joey," I reply, kind of surprised at the news.

Joey looks over my shoulder and spots the two G-men.

"Hey, guys!" he says, as if they're both old acquaintances.

"Hey, Joey! Nice to see *you*!" say the FBI guys, and both shake his hand.

And he winks at the FBI guys, who, to my—let's call it "surprise"— laugh and nod and walk out the door. And Marta and Jerry, and Judy and I, and Crazy Joe and Punchy all drive home together, and I don't just have a new fan, I have a new "family friend." As for my Plaza debut, the next morning all the conservative geezer columnists like Earl Wilson and Leonard Lyons pan my performance and call me a "sick" comic and anti-American.

A little backstory: Joey Gallo was about forty years old when we met and about as famous in his own high-visibility field as I was in mine. Born in Brooklyn, tight with his brothers and fellow juvenile delinquents, Larry and Albert "Kid Blast" Gallo, by the time he was in his teens he was working as an all-around enforcer for the Profaci mob. In 1957, Joey might have committed the "unsolved" killing of Albert "Murder Incorporated" Anastasia, after which he was a "made man." And I ended up being best man at Joey Gallo's wedding, but hold on for that story and its shattering ending . . .

The late '50s and '60s were a blur of bloody, frankly-too-complicated-for-a-layman-to-follow gang wars between the Gallos and the Profacis, and the Gambinos and the up-and-coming Colombos. Luckily, Joey was out of the line of fire, having been locked up for extortion in 1961. In prison, he became a kind of underworld integrationist, mixing with and befriending Black and Puerto Rican convicts and inviting them to stay in touch when they got out. Another eccentricity: he also supposedly wrote poetry, read the great philosophers (they say Sartre, Kafka, Camus, Proust, Tolstoy), and took up watercolor painting, all while upstate. He was released on March 11, 1971. At that time, his sworn enemy, Joseph Colombo, who was the boss of bosses, started the Italian-American Civil Rights League, a group devoted to claiming that the Mafia—or the Cosa Nostra, the mob, or whatever you wanted to call it—didn't exist. The league also tried to reason with Francis Ford Coppola to stop him from making his "slanderous fairy tale," *The Godfather.*

Joe Colombo was shot and declared brain-dead—he slept slightly above the fishes in a deep coma for seven more years—on June 28, 1971. Several of Joe's civil rights–oriented associates killed the shooter on the spot. Many figured Joey was responsible. None of this had any effect on Jerry Orbach, who kind of adopted Joey after he got out of prison. These days, people know Jerry as one of the stars of *Law & Order,* but back then he was a Broadway musical star with lead roles in big hits like *The Fantasticks, Promises, Promises,* and *Carnival.* He'd also had a role in the 1971 movie comedy *The Gang That Couldn't Shoot Straight*, based on Jimmy Breslin's book, in which he played Kid Sally Palumbo, a character obviously based on Joey Gallo.

Joey assured the Orbachs he'd gone straight, and every Sunday night, the Orbachs had Joey and his fiancée, Sina, over to their apartment for a big pasta dinner, to which they also invited their friends from show business, the arts, and journalism. Joey's other regular hangout was Elaine's, the famous literary haunt, where he mixed with writers like Breslin, Pete Hamill, Tom Wolfe, Peter Maas, Nick Pileggi, and other actors and writers who were as fascinated with Crazy Joe as their predecessors were with Bugsy Siegel and Mickey Cohen, and the current generation is with John Gotti and the whole *Sopranos* phenomenon.

There was a sort of Damon Runyon–esque quality to Joey that everybody liked, including me. And I was thrilled to mix with this crowd. But unlike Jerry and Marta and most of the other people in Joey's new world, I didn't buy into this "going straight" business.

And Joey, being even a better liar and judge of fellow liars than I was—it was how he made his living, after all—he knew that I knew. So when I called him on it one day, he didn't get mad but smiled, hugged me, complimented me on my street smarts—the polite Canadian variety—and opened the door a crack so I could get a quick peek into his part-time job as a ruthless sociopath. Joey confided to me that no, he didn't spend *all* his days at the Forty-Second Street library writing his memoirs for Marta to sell to a book publisher or the movies. When not in the literary mode, he was muscling in on the Columbo family's territory, using some of the hoodlums he'd met in prison. And no, he didn't always carry a gun—but Punchy (whom I cleverly figured out had gotten his nickname because he'd punched a few people in his life) did. I could feel it against my chest every time the friendly bodyguard gave me a heartfelt hug of greeting or farewell.

We had long talks, Joey and I. Naturally, I wondered what the future would bring for Crazy Joe, but not even I imagined the twists and turns it so quickly took. One day in February 1972, I get a call from Marta Orbach. "We're going to have a cocktail party for Joey and Sina at our apartment tomorrow. It's going to be just close friends, informal. He wants you, and we want you to be there." I show up a little late, just after 6 p.m., and to my horror, everybody's waiting for me. Joey isn't angry that I'm late. In fact, just the opposite.

"Hey, I need a best man!" says Joey. Looking straight at me. "I want David to be my best man." That was terrifying to me.

As uneager as I was to be Crazy Joe Gallo's best man, it's not the kind of offer . . . I think you know the rest. So I go up and sign the wedding license, inscribing my name for organized crime historians to copy down for all time, and then we all go uptown to Broadway, tickets reserved and paid for by Joey, to see Lauren Bacall star in her hit musical *Applause*. On April 6, we all go to see Don Rickles perform at the Copa (Copacabana)—another Colombo-run place, although I didn't know it then—and when Rickles, in the middle of his act, spots Joey with me, he drops to the floor and makes machine-gun noises. For Joey, the

I hadn't known Joey Gallo that long, maybe a year or so, but I arrived at Jerry and Marta Orbach's house for a party, and when I got there, I was told that Joey and Sina (*center*) were getting married right then. When Joey insisted I be his best man, the priest was so excited. I froze, surprised and shocked, as you can imagine (I thought it should have been Jerry, who had known him for many, many years). And here I am right after the "I do's" with the happy couple, March 1, 1972.

night is young, and he wants Judy and me to join everyone for something to eat. For no other reason than the fact that my night owl days are just about over, and my 'in-my-jammies-by-eight-p.m. period' (which continues to this day) is beginning, I beg off. I hug Joey goodbye. And for the first time since I've met him, I feel a gun under his coat.

Judy and I take a cab home, and we're asleep by midnight. The rest of the group decides to take in Rickles's second show, then heads downtown to Little Italy to a restaurant owned by a friend of Joey's. It's called Umberto's Clam House.

At around 5 a.m., Joey is finishing his shrimp and scungilli. Two Colombo goons enter the restaurant and shoot him five times. Although the cops say later that the first shot should have killed him, Joey stands up, pushes Sina and Lisa out of the line of fire, staggers out of the restaurant and onto the sidewalk, falls down, and dies. He is exactly forty-three years old. Happy birthday.

The next morning, I turn on the radio and get the shock, though not exactly the surprise, of my life. Judy and I are both sad and terrified in a nasty combination I don't wish on my worst enemies. Not even Nixon, whom we still did have to kick around. And he continued to seriously affect my life. Seriously.

Back guest hosting *The Tonight Show,* my first guest that night was Charles Bronson, a people's movie star if there ever was one, and after I savaged Tricky Dick in my monologue, Charles came out and sat on the couch.

"You know," said Bronson, not smiling as only Charles Bronson cannot smile, "I disagree with everything you just said out there."

"That's okay, Charles," I said, with a Marxist waggle of my eyebrows, "but you don't disagree with the idea of me being free to stand out there and say it, do you?"

"I'm not even sure of that," said Bronson, not smiling even harder.

It was a tense moment, and nobody laughed, and it polarized the audience even more. But I thought, "Hey, I wasn't afraid to go to that scary place. This is old-fashioned show business made new again."

Ironically, Charles and I became friends after that.

At first, *The Tonight Show* producers—not Johnny—told me that they were "trying out other guest hosts." Then they told me that the show's ratings went down further when I was on than with any other guest host. I didn't worry too much about it—not realizing, as I do now, that *The Tonight Show* was the engine powering the rest of my stand-up, recording, and front-of-the-camera television career.

For me, the Soaring Seventies were just about over.

But who could have predicted that, or even worried about it, when the country was in the middle of a revolution? And better still, all of it was televised! Like everybody else, I was absolutely hypnotized when the Watergate hearings began. Ehrlichman. Haldeman. Senator Sam Ervin. G. Gordon Liddy. The Saturday Night Massacre. The Pentagon Papers. Daniel Ellsberg's psychiatrist. It was a wonderful show, a combination *Caine Mutiny* and Marx Brothers movie marathon. And I watched it with my usual amused and bemused detachment.

Then, one day, a guy named Donald Segretti—the "dirty tricks" commander of CREEP, the Committee to Re-Elect the President—raised his right hand and swore to tell the whole truth. On either side of him sat two of his trickster flunkies: *the two FBI agents I'd first met backstage at the Plaza Hotel nearly two years earlier.* Do I have to spell it out for you? And it turns out that the Chief Trickster had one more kick in the ass left. For six months, a *Newsweek* writer named Art Cooper had been following me around for a cover story on America's "new breed" of bright, hip young comedians: Richie Pryor, Lily Tomlin, and David Steinberg.

The cover story was scheduled for the August 9, 1974, edition.

Richard M. Nixon resigned on August 8.

The presses were stopped, a new cover was chosen, and the piece with me in it was moved to the back and became the least-read entertainment story in *Newsweek*'s entire history.

Not even my show business friends—including the ones who *only* read articles about show business—ever saw it. And to make matters worse, August 9 was my birthday. Happy birthday.

CHAPTER 8

THE BRAVE HUMOR OF
THE SMOTHERS BROTHERS

I am not sure what it is about politics that makes people especially sensitive, opinionated, and enraged. But "political comedy," scathing in its observations about people, behavior, society's rules and expectations, and, of course, about politics, is often brilliant, always unforgettable and impactful. For me, "political comedy," whether in the form of stand-up routines, theater, or scathing commentary, traces back to my first experience hearing Lenny Bruce.

It is this humor that changed my life, and those of many other performing comedians and writers of comedy. Over the last thirty years, important commentators' life-changing truths, often in the form of satire, affected many lives, as writer David Bianculli (who also generously appears in the documentary of my life, *Quality Balls*) reminds us in his informative book, *Dangerously Funny: The Uncensored Story of "The Smothers Brothers Comedy Hour."* There was George Carlin, whose infamous "Seven Words You Can Never Say on Television" and "Filthy Words" comedy album routines sparked a free-speech battle that went all the way to the Supreme Court. Stand-up comic and civil rights advocate Dick Gregory not only challenged segregation by becoming the first Black comic to headline in all-white nightclubs, but also demonstrated alongside Martin Luther King Jr. and Medgar Evers in history-making confrontations in Montgomery and Selma. Bill Maher lost his ABC late-night talk show *Politically Incorrect* after saying, about the Al Qaeda terrorist hijackers who commandeered passenger airliners and steered them into the World Trade Center and the Pentagon, "Staying in the airplane when it hits the building—say what you want about it, it's not cowardly."

After all, do we still need reminding, after three hundred years, that freedom of speech is the backbone of our Constitution? These comedians were all brave men and deserve our respect. So were Dick and Tommy Smothers, which is why, when they received the US Comedy Arts Festival Freedom of Speech Award, from me, I said, "The most innovative variety show on television shut down because of political pressure. But the Smothers Brothers got their revenge. Never giving up, they sued CBS—and they won. And they forever became prominent symbols in the fight for free speech."

Let me start at their beginnings. The brothers were raised by their mother, since their dad, a major in the US Army, had died in World War II as he was being transported from a Japanese POW camp. They started as folk singers, musicians, and comedians in 1950s television. They grew up in Southern California, developing an act while students at San Jose State, an act they polished at North Beach nightclubs in the '50s. It was their 1961 album, *The Smothers Brothers at the Purple Onion,* which established them as leading entertainers on the folk music scene.

"We were famous before we were good," Tommy Smothers says. "Then we were good, not famous." The act changed little over the years. "We've been two feet apart for fifty years. He's always on my left. I'm always on his right. Same with our baby pictures. We've always been looking at each other that far away. We'll get offstage and he'll look at me and say, 'When are you going to have that cyst fixed?'" They not only mined the fascination of the day with folk songs, but also the passive-aggressive relationship between brothers—"Mom always liked you best"—a role that often spilled over into their offstage life.

Tommy, who played guitar and regularly spouted elaborate made-up stories and heated emotional outbursts, was obsessed with comedy. Dick, who played bass and acted as the grounded and kind of weary straight man, was obsessed with racing cars. Together, they have a history as a comedy team that covers more years than the Marx Brothers, Stan Laurel and Oliver Hardy, Bud Abbott and Lou Costello, Dean Martin and Jerry Lewis, Dan Rowan and Dick Martin, and even George Burns and Gracie Allen. They released many albums of their routines, performed together on television variety shows (the first one was on *The Jack Paar Show* in 1961), and recorded their stage performances in clubs nationwide. Their routines were never "routine"—while Tommy always played the "dumber" brother, who was very funny, Dick was the wiser, more serious brother who corrected and put Tommy in his place. Their first show, *The Smothers Brothers Show,* was scripted.

The Smothers Brothers Comedy Hour, which debuted in 1967, started out as a "hip" variety show, written by the likes of Steve Martin (he had a brilliant mind for writing what I call "abstract comedy," could make anything work in his unique style, was easy to work with, and was also visually oriented while playing his five-string banjo), Carl Gottlieb (who went on to be a successful writer, and wrote, among other things, the movie *Jaws*), Lorenzo Music, Pat Paulsen, Bob Einstein (amazing, one-of-a-kind voice and Albert Brooks's brother), and me. And let's not forget the great Rob Reiner, who, although well known as Carl Reiner's son, was a truly talented writer and went on to easily become one of the best directors and actors in comedy. Besides these brilliantly talented and courageous writers, the brothers also showcased new musical artists who found it hard to get airtime on other variety shows because of their political views (remember advertisers who objected to certain points of view?). These were no minor musicians; the list included George Harrison, Ringo Starr, Joan Baez, Buffalo Springfield, Cass Elliot, Harry Belafonte, Cream, Donovan, the Doors, Glen Campbell, Janis Ian, Jefferson Airplane, the Happenings, Peter, Paul and Mary, Spanky and Our Gang, Steppenwolf, Simon and Garfunkel, the Hollies, the Who, and even Pete Seeger—to mention just a few.

In this show, Dick developed a keen appreciation for the role the straight man plays in comedy teams. "The straight man in vaudeville was traditionally paid more than the comic," says Dick. "That was the skilled position. The straight man could introduce acts, and you could

With Steve Martin, Bob Einstein. and Carl Gottlieb. We were all starting out on *The Smothers Brothers Comedy Hour,* circa 1968. I'm wearing a towel around my neck because I was actually performing that night on the show. These were the state-of-the-art comedy guys, and I was fortunate to be included.

put him with a funny guy and have him control that. If you don't believe the straight man, you don't believe the comic. Look at Bud Abbott, Dean Martin, Dan Rowan. I learned this in fifty years in the business—the quality of the straight man defines how good the act is."

It was this show that became, and remains, one of the most controversial programs of that era, because Tommy and Dick's routines were critical of mainstream political thought and seemed to be sympathetic to the political views of the counterculture. That was dangerous at the time (remember, this was the Vietnam era). At a time when most families still watched television together, in the same room and on the same TV set, it was impressive that *The Smothers Brothers Comedy Hour* spoke to and attracted young viewers without alienating older ones. With its humor, guest list, and high caliber of entertainment, it bridged the generation gap at a time when that gap was only growing. As Dave Bianculli explains, *Comedy Hour* introduced new talent—from Pat Paulsen and Mason Williams to such emerging rock groups as Buffalo Springfield, Jefferson Airplane, and the Who—while making

This photo captures the mischief of Tommy Smothers as I have known him for all these years. Being on *The Smothers Brothers Comedy Hour* was one of my favorite things, and Tommy always rejoiced in taking me to the back room to show me my many duffel bags of hate mail.

room for veteran stars from movies, TV, even vaudeville. On one show, Kate Smith shared billing with Simon and Garfunkel. Another show featured Mel Tormé, Don Knotts, and Ravi Shankar. Musicians came on not to perform their old or current hits, but to unveil new ones—a bold departure from established practice. The Beatles even provided the brothers with a US exclusive—the videotaped premiere of "Hey Jude"—and in the middle of the Smothers Brothers' battles with the CBS censors in 1968, George Harrison showed up as a surprise guest to offer moral support. "Whether you can say it or not," Harrison urged them on the air, "keep *trying* to say it."

And they did. First, individual words and phrases that CBS found objectionable were cut from skits after rehearsals or edited out of the final master tape. Then entire segments were cut because of their political, social, or anti-establishment messages. The brothers soon found themselves in regular conflict with CBS's network censors. At the start of the 1968–69 season, the network ordered the Smothers Brothers to deliver their shows finished and ready to air ten days before airdate so that the censors could edit the shows as they wanted. In the season premiere, CBS deleted the entire segment of Harry Belafonte singing "Don't Stop the Carnival" shown against a backdrop of the riots during the 1968 Democratic National Convention.

And this is where I came in.

I met the Smothers Brothers when I was performing at the hungry i in San Francisco. Both of us were performing; I was also doing stand-up. Tommy immediately wanted me to be on the show they were creating because I was a different kind of comedian—not shouting, screaming, serious, not telling jokes, soft spoken, making the audience come to me (not trying to get the audience's attention, as I often turned my back to them). Then I met them again, in 1968, at the Bitter End in New York, the same year that they were working on their television show. When Tommy asked me to come on the show, my first appearance was a bit called "How to Win a Friend." In my next appearance, the sermon I gave was one of the first bits that raised the network's ire, and it involved nothing more flagrant than my giving the following sermon, basically saying that Moses burned his feet on the bush, and there are many Old Testament scholars who to this day believe it was the first mention of Christ in the Bible.

Here it is:

When Moses was a little child, he cast off a cherubic light from his face. So his father said to his mother (Yokheved), "Yoooooo! Let's take this little child and thrust him into the Nile so that we might have some decent lighting in here again."

Moses is raised in the palace of the Pharaoh—he is thirty years old; he goes wandering in the desert, chasing after a sheep. Moses was a prophet, not a pervert. In the distance, he saw a bush that was burning, yet it would not consume itself. A voice came out—

"Mooooses"—Moses, with the astute bearing of a prophet-to-be, runs to the sheep and looks in its mouth.

"Mooooses, take off your shoes from off of your feet," God says in His redundant way. "For the land that you are standing upon is holy land."

Moses takes the shoes off his feet, approaches the burning bush. Burns his feet.

God goes, "Aha! Third one today!"

Moses swore. We are not sure what he said. There are many Old

Here I am on *The Smothers Brothers Comedy Hour* with
Tommy, March 21. 1969. He suggested I do another
sermon, and we all know what happened after that.

*Testament scholars who believe that it was the first mention of
Christ in the Bible . . .*

*"MOOOses—go unto the Pharaoh and tell him—to—let—
your—people—go."*

Moses says, "Who shall I say sent me?"

God says, "Whom! Whom! I am that I am."

Moses answers, "Thanks for clearing that up."

*Moses goes up to Pharaoh, his staff in one hand, his little
brother Aaron in the other. "Phaaaaarah, let my people go."*

Pharaoh says to Moses, "Who sent you?"

Moses: "Whom!"

Moses: "You're not gonna believe this. . . ."

And the Pharaoh didn't believe him.

*So God destroyed all the land, with the mystical humor that
is only His.*

And that was the last straw for CBS.

There were many things that contributed to the Smothers Brothers
getting thrown off the air. My sermons were considered the last straw
by many. Was it my sermons? Was it the show hiding master tapes from

the affiliates? Was it CBS executives with personal vendettas? Or was Nixon threatening the network? Was it one thing, or did all of these do the show in? No one knows with certainty, but everyone agrees that the brothers were fired, not canceled. And I should point out that I have been giving these sermons in my act for fifty years, starting at Second City, where the ministers who came to hear them laughed hysterically and never threatened my livelihood or my life.

There's one thing that still bothers me. When I gave my sermons at Second City, there were people who thought I was ridiculing the Old Testament. That was never the case at all. The sermons are funny, and they're meant to be funny, but they're serious, too. I never think of jokes when I'm doing them. I think of the facts. Sometimes just repeating the facts will make the point.

With some local stations making their own deletions of controversial skits or comments, the continuing problems over the show came to a head after CBS broadcast a rerun on March 9, 1969. The network explained the decision by stating that because that week's episode did not arrive in time to be previewed, it would not be shown. But that was just not true. In that program, Joan Baez paid tribute to her then husband, David Harris, who was entering jail after refusing to serve in the army. When the show finally did air, two months later, the network allowed Baez to state that her husband was in prison but edited out the reason. Tommy and Dick were furious.

Then, surprisingly, despite the conflict, the show was picked up for the 1969–70 season on March 14, 1969, seemingly ending the debate over its status. However, and without any notice, network CEO and president William S. Paley then abruptly canceled the show on April 4, 1969, explaining that the Smothers refused to meet the pre-air delivery dates in order to accommodate review by the censors. This cancellation led the brothers to file their breach of contract suit against the network, which they won. But neither the brothers nor the show ever returned to the air. Despite the cancellation, the show went on to win the Emmy Award that year for best writing.

Remember the first lines of *A Tale of Two Cities* (yes, Dickens): "It was the best of times, it was the worst of times." The sixties fit into that painful sentiment as well. Also, remember that Nixon pushed for greater governmental control of broadcast media at the same time. His well-placed allies, from new CBS programming chief Robert D. Wood to *TV Guide* publisher Walter Annenberg, adopted hard-line stances against the sort of envelope-pushing content the Smothers Brothers were trying to present in prime time. The truth is, both sides got increasingly petulant and combative. Tommy fought fervently for every word and idea, and slipped obscenities into the scripts just to test the censors, who promptly removed them. Eventually, some say that Tommy lost his own sense of humor while railing against the network heads. All agree that CBS executives grew impatient and resentful of having to defend or discuss the Smothers Brothers everywhere they went, and they began to both change the rules and enforce them ruthlessly. Indeed, "it was the best of times, it was the worst of times."

I think it is undeniable, even all these years later, that CBS wanted Tommy and Dick Smothers off the air because of the ideas they presented on their show, and eventually removed them using the phony excuse that the brothers had violated the terms of their contract by not delivering a copy of that week's show in time. As David Bianculli says in his spot-on analysis (I love this analogy), "It was like the Feds busting Al Capone: the crime for which he was convicted was a mere technicality, but it got Capone off the streets." In the case of CBS and the Smothers Brothers, they got them off the air. Fired, not canceled, as Tommy Smothers invariably and repeatedly corrected people in an effort to set the record straight.

A few years later, in 1973, in the case *Tom Smothers et al. v. Columbia Broadcasting System, Inc.,* the US District Court in California ruled that CBS, not the Smothers Brothers, was the party in violation of its contract. I testified, they played my Jonah sermon, lots of laughs in the courtroom. The Smothers Brothers won. But by then their prime-time platform had long been torpedoed and their influence stolen from them. I take some comfort in their lasting influence on the brave creators, producers, and writers of the shows that followed. The attitude they reflected would continue to flourish on *Rowan & Martin's Laugh-In,* and in late-night programming on *Saturday Night Live,* which, you may remember, was right there in the 2008 presidential race as an invaluable and loud voice shouting out what was, and wasn't, funny about national politics and politicians. But in prime time, where the Smothers Brothers once dared to offer the same sort of probing and timely humor, the concept of relevance in entertainment shows would become an endangered species, if not completely extinct.

In September 2008, Tommy Smothers accepted a belated trophy for his contributions to the team that won the 1968 writing award for the show's final season; Smothers left his name off at the time, fearing the inclusion would draw controversy. When he accepted his Emmy, he was typically plainspoken and eloquent at the same time, a Smothers hallmark. (The speech is on YouTube.)

"Freedom of expression and freedom of speech aren't really important," he told the audience, "unless they're heard. The freedom of hearing is as important as the freedom of speaking. It's hard for me to stay silent when I keep hearing that peace is only attainable through war. There's nothing more scary than watching ignorance in action. So I dedicate this Emmy to all people who feel compelled to speak out, not afraid to speak to power, won't shut up and refuse to be silent." (By the way, the long-awaited release of the comedy show's third and final season on DVD is out, including the portions of the show CBS censored, which included Harry Belafonte singing "Don't Stop the Carnival.")

It is important to emphasize, I think, that the muzzling of the Smothers Brothers at the height of the Vietnam War and the era of student protest was an emblematic act of political repression that came three months after Richard Nixon was elected president. But the firing of the Smothers Brothers has echoed through the years, becoming a case study in mass media censorship. The brothers, who arrived on the small screen as clean-cut, wholesome folk-song parodists, stumbled into the turbulent times.

All these years later, Dick recounts, "Instead of vacuous comedy, we thought, 'Let's do something with some bite.' There was the Vietnam War, voters' rights—all sorts of issues that we thought we could reflect and develop a point of view. We didn't even know it was important until they said, 'You can't say this.' Forty years later, people are still talking about it. Isn't that amazing?" He and his brother went off separately, as Tommy struggled to find himself. "Everything was so serious," he says. "Then I saw Jane Fonda on *The Tonight Show* one night talking about burning babies. It was like an epiphany for me—there was no joy, no sense of humor, no laughter. It just turned me around. Now there is Howard Stern. What a way we have come."

To me, Tommy and Dick are, to this day, the epitome of bravery in the face of attacks by power, integrity in the face of corruption and harassment, and courage in tackling important issues in the face of those censors intent on stifling freedom of speech.

CHAPTER 9

THE TONIGHT SHOWS

Johnny Carson, and hosts before and after

A stand-up comedian in the '60s and '70s was very different from a stand-up comedian today. Now, everyone wants to do stand-up. This glut of comedy? I can't walk down the street in Beverly Hills without some older Jewish guy coming up to me and saying, "I was riffing with my son today . . ." But being a comedian in my earlier years was about being an outsider. People weren't accepting of comedy as a career, so you had to find your own way of doing it.

When the late-night talk shows started, they gave comedians an alternative to performing at small, intimate clubs. These shows, especially those helmed by hosts who changed the entertainment world—Steve Allen, Jack Paar, Dick Cavett, David Letterman, Conan O'Brien, and the king of them all, Johnny Carson—changed everything. Many were to follow, each making his or her own mark—Jay Leno, Stephen Colbert, Jimmy Kimmel, James Corden, Jimmy Fallon, Chelsea Handler, Carson Daly, Jon Stewart, Trevor Noah, and Samantha Bee.

Steve Allen is so often earmarked by other comedians as having been influential in their comedy. He was outrageously funny, a great wit, a truly gifted musician who played the piano (when he had jazz greats as guests, he played with them). But his genius on his late-night show was that he was the straight man who set up everyone—he did not play for laughs. He let the guests get the laughs, and they scored with the audience. Thus *The Steve Allen Show,* which was originally a variety show, evolved into the show that changed late-night television forever. It was Steve Allen who brought the first form of a sit-down conversation across the desk. The beginning half of the show was a variety as he invited those who had performed earlier to stay and talk, and then he added new guests who would chat with him about what they were doing. It was just like what Steve had done on the talk show he had on radio years before. This was the first incarnation of the talk show format. It is important to note that Steve was absolutely thrilled when his guests got laughs.

Jack Paar's was strictly a talk show—no variety, no acts. Jack (with that famous dimple on his chin) and a guest sat at a desk, and he and his guest would talk. But this was no ordinary conversation between a host and his guest, because Jack was no regular host—he was overwrought with emotion, almost crying at each show. Everything touched him deeply. A guest like Jonathan Winters would do an imitation of President Kennedy so right on that Jack would be just dumbfounded, screaming with laughter. His bit about bringing in Marlon Brando to solve the Cuban Missile Crisis (available on YouTube) is still priceless almost fifty years later.

And Jack would tear up—literally tear up, tears pouring down his cheeks, about something. It became such a shtick, but it was real for Jack, and mimics would parody him: they would always cry, and that became the universal imitation of Jack Paar. Jack introduced Jonathan Winters, and it was a phenomenon. It was the first time a comedian (especially on a late-night show) came out as a hundred different caricatures.

.   .   .

And then came Johnny. He changed television. And he changed my life.

It is no exaggeration to say that Johnny Carson was the king. His first show was on October 1, 1962, and he wore the crown of late night for the next thirty years, leaving only when he was ready.

He was something else, that Johnny Carson. He was smart, he was inflexible in his standards of excellence, he was a brilliant comedy writer, and he was on the money with his calm, measured, and intelligent delivery. He was supportive of the talent he admired and scathing to those he considered disrespectful or inconsiderate or sloppy in their work. If you crossed him with that disrespect or disregard for standards of excellence, you would not be invited back.

If you are looking for any scandalous or critical anecdotes about Johnny from me, you are not going to get them. I revered him because I learned from him, and because he appreciated my work, my humor,

Can you believe that's not earmuffs? That's my hair. On *The Tonight Show* with Johnny Carson, October 13, 1970. We were talking about me being in Chicago in the '60s and staying at Hefner's and doing a quaalude for the first and last time with my really, really close friends Max Lerner and Shel Silverstein (*The Giving Tree*), who later went on to write the song "Freaker's Ball," which I did in my act, and "The Cover of 'Rolling Stone'" for Dr. Hook.

and because we had a relationship based on mutual respect, honesty, and a lot of laughter. There was nothing like Johnny laughing at your work. Just ask Rodney Dangerfield, Don Rickles, Robin Williams, Eddie Murphy, Jerry Seinfeld, Jerry Lewis, David Brenner, Andy Kaufman, Jim Carrey—the endless list of the most talented comedians anywhere—and they will tell you that they lived for Johnny's approval.

Let me explain some of the ironies of being a comedian. When I performed at the Bitter End and there were, say, only six people in the audience, as a comedian, you still have to get up to do a show for these six people. You don't hate everyone who isn't there, you hate these six people, because you have to do a show for them. At one such show at the Bitter End, there were two guys in the front who knew all of my material. One of them started to talk with me, and I thought, "Wow, these guys are so excited to see me, they deserve a show." That night, I did two shows to a full house. Clearly, that Dan Sullivan review in *The New York Times* had drawn an audience, and they were receptive to everything. That's when Rudy Tellez, a talent coordinator for *The Tonight Show Starring Johnny Carson,* saw me. Apparently, Johnny had sent Rudy to check out my show, and when Rudy liked what he saw, he invited me to come on *The Tonight Show* with Carson.

Going on the road had been grueling, but I liked it—especially the comedy groupies. But suddenly, thanks to Johnny, in 1968, I had *The Tonight Show* instead of the road. That place beside Johnny was the coveted thing. Other comics have said to me that getting one laugh from Johnny was worth every struggle, every sparsely filled club. Besides, being on *The Tonight Show* gave a comedian an audience of millions, and, on a good night, a terrific and eager live audience in the studio as well. In some ways, the late-night talk shows—Jack Paar, Steve Allen, Johnny Carson—made the world safer for comedians.

Johnny was committed to me, wanted me to come back, like, immediately. I came back the second time soon after, and it went well; he was sweet about it, laughing and happy. And, after a commercial, he said, "You know, these shows are so hard to do. Next Monday, do you want to host for me?" So imagine, I'm twenty-eight years old, and it's next Monday, and you know the awful thing about being as young as I was, I thought, "Sure!" I thought it would be me, Chopin, and Groucho Marx who were going to be remembered for this at the end of our careers. Why wouldn't I host the show?

My popularity was surging at the time, so NBC wasn't that nervous about me guest hosting. That said, there were sometimes problems because guests didn't always want to be booked on the show when Johnny Carson wasn't there. Rudy once said, "David, you know, Bette Davis wants to do the show. Just call her and tell her it's you, and that you're hosting, and it'll be fine."

I said, "Okay," and I called up the number. I didn't really know what I was going to say, so when I heard Bette's voice on the line, I said, "Miss Davis, I'm hosting *The Tonight Show* this week. My name is David . . ."

I don't think I got out "Steinberg" before she demanded, "How did you get this number?" She shouted it out like she was a German Nazi and I was a Jew. I started to stutter and apologize, and I realized, you know, I can't do any better, so I just hung up on her.

On one of my first hosting gigs, I found out that the guest was Cassius Clay. This was in 1968, so he was still known as Cassius Clay. And he just killed, he wiped the floor with me. He was so funny and so sharp, with a very intuitive sense of humor. And then the next time I hosted it was Louis Armstrong, who talked about his favorite subject, laxatives. Then I am guest hosting my first show, at the last minute— I did not know that Johnny was upstairs in another studio, at the star-studded Kraft Music Theater charity benefit roast. I'll just tell you—all of a sudden I hear a roar from the audience, and first out is Milton Berle in a tuxedo. Milton always talked too much, he had to do that for the audience to laugh. And they did. And he leaves the stage, and I talk about him afterward for a while, and then I hear another roar from the audience, and Dean Martin walks out, also in a tuxedo. And this goes on. The longest laugh without a word said was when Jack Benny walked out (he had a look—he touched his chin and stared at me for a long time and said, "Young, you're so young"), also in a tuxedo. I was funny, but I didn't know what to do, so I tried to act like a big shot on purpose so the audience wouldn't see how I felt. Then Johnny came out at the end, and he said to the audience, "If you are wondering who the new comedy stars of the future are, you're looking at one of them," pointing at me. Unbelievable.

Johnny, his producer Peter Lassally, and I eventually got into a routine in which we'd have lunch every time I was scheduled to go on the show. I'd just hang out until it was time to go on, and inevitably something funny would come out of those lunches that I could use on the show. But what cracked us up over our Cobb salads didn't necessarily make the audience laugh, so Johnny—always devoted to whatever was best for *The Tonight Show*—put an end to the lunches. He wanted to keep the show as fresh as possible. I had no problem with that at all—I was an improviser. Johnny was, too, and he also had some terrific writers. But Johnny didn't want to read cue cards—it didn't give him the flexibility to make changes as he was reacting to the audience's reactions.

So there was a guy who used to appear on *The Tonight Show,* Harry Lorayne, a memory expert. And he would come on the show when it was still in New York. Outside, as people were lining up to come into the show, Harry would introduce himself to each person in the line, and they would tell him their name. Harry would then come out as a guest on the show and ask everyone to stand up. All five hundred people. And Harry would know every single name and point to a person and name them. By the time he went through the audience, every person was sitting down. It was remarkable, and everyone loved it. But he had a memory device, and Johnny knew this memory device. It was word association. One word, or an image, so you'd picture something in your mind. Johnny didn't want to use a teleprompter, because if the monologue was tanking, he'd be stuck reading the entire thing. And he didn't want to use cue cards for the same reason. So he'd memorize the entire monologue, like twenty-five jokes, using this Harry Lorayne system. Remember, on *The Tonight Show,* Johnny had an easel, which no one else had seen him do. The cue cards were stapled left to right, so he could edit them himself. He was great at reading the audience, which meant that he wasn't forced into a structure he didn't want. Then, if the audience wasn't responding to one joke, he knew how to move on to another joke.

Bob Hope did one of the shows that I was also a guest on. I was on first, sat on the couch, and then Bob Hope came out and sat down, and he did his little stories, and then he said to Johnny, "Well, John, I've gotta go," and there was another half hour of show, and he left—he actually never stayed. I didn't know that, and I said to Johnny, "Where does he have to go that's so important? He lives in Toluca Lake, you know, it's five minutes away, the president's not in town." And it was just that Hope felt that that was a cool thing to do. It made him look like he was bigger than Carson. I couldn't believe it.

There were other unconventional moments. There was always a coordinator of the show who would speak with the guests before going on and suggest topics. He never did that with me, because Johnny trusted me to discuss anything I wanted. But this one time, the coordinator said, "You can talk about anything you want, except marijuana or drugs."

Just to make sure, I asked, "Not at all?"

"No—unless it is for medicinal purposes."

It was around the time that Nancy Reagan had put out that wonderful edict of hers, "Just Say No" to drugs. That day, I was reading the newspaper and I happened to see an article that said that marijuana was being used to cure glaucoma. So when I started to talk to Johnny on the show, I said, "You know, Johnny, I was reading in *The Boston Globe* that they are doing some testing with marijuana as a potential cure for glaucoma. That would explain why, when I was at a party in Malibu just last week, it seemed that so many were suffering from the dreaded disease." Johnny put his head on his desk. He loved when I pushed the envelope. (For years after, people would yell out of their cars at me, "I have the dreaded disease.")

George Carlin had one disastrous guest appearance. For background: George Carlin was just starting to emerge at this time. When I was at Second City, Carlin and Jack Burns were a team, "Burns and Carlin." Jack Burns was outrageous, kind of an adorable Irishman—a drunk Irishman without having to drink. One of those. They were playing at the Pump Room in Chicago, which was a big fancy place, and they both came to Second City. Burns wanted to join, but Carlin wasn't sure—he was playing the straight man at the time. George and

I became friends, and then later when I started doing stand-up, he was also doing stand-up, and for a while we had parallel images as outsiders. George was just a bighearted, sweet person. He had his dark side of substance abuse, but that was mostly against himself.

So George came on *The Tonight Show* when he seemed high, and he went at Carson in an uncharacteristic way. They had to cut out most of it. Johnny seemed okay with it at the time, but then Carlin wrote a seemingly crazy, acid-freaked letter to Johnny, because he must've been doing more drugs at that point. Peter Lassally, the executive producer of *The Tonight Show* and *Late Night with David Letterman,* said, "We're not going to have George on for a long time because he was threatening, and Johnny's frightened." So for one long year or more, George Carlin didn't get on the show. Later, when I was directing *Designing Women* in the 1980s—I was at the studio all day and all night—I ran into George. He was doing a TV special. I hadn't seen him in years.

"David, how are you?" he asked. We hugged. He was the old George. I could just see it. I went back to *Designing Women,* and his manager said, "You know, David, George is not the same person who wrote that letter to Carson," and he asked me if there was anything I could do.

I let it sit in the back of my head. I did *The Tonight Show* two more times after that, and then, when I was hanging out with Johnny one night, I said to him, "I saw George on the lot. He's in great shape. He's doing a series." I asked Johnny if he'd ever have him on the show again.

"Well, I don't know," Johnny said. "It was scary, David." And he didn't give him a spot right away, but he didn't say no.

Maybe three months later, Johnny had George back on the show, and Lassally told me that the fact I'd talked to Johnny had made a difference. Someone must have told George, because years later he thanked me. "David," he said, "I know you got my back."

And then there was Orson Welles. Let me back up. There once was a restaurant in LA called Ma Maison on Melrose. It was famous because it was the first restaurant where Wolfgang Puck was the chef, and he introduced his now world-famous pizza with smoked salmon and caviar, later the staple of Wolf's Spago restaurant and his Oscar catered dinners. It was *the* hangout for the elite of LA, especially famous celebrities. And it was where *the* Orson Welles ate lunch almost every single day. He even received his mail there. And it was the place where, each Tuesday, Orson Welles and I had lunch. We met at 12:30 p.m. and ate and talked until almost 5 p.m. Orson wanted to know whom I was sleeping with, but before I could even tell him, he shared his love stories, which were much more interesting and famous than mine: Rita Hayworth (whom he married), Hedy Lamarr, Dolores del Rio, Geraldine Fitzgerald. In between the tales, each person who entered the restaurant walked up to us to shake Orson's hand—especially women, who were nuts about him, so it wasn't a surprise to see him greet every woman, famous or not, with great joy and enthusiasm, which made me always wonder if they'd become another one of his many paramours. And every now and then, between the women, there would be a stop by the likes of Andy Warhol and David Hockney. We also discussed Orson's having no discipline to write—strange to know about one of the most brilliant writers of all time. One day, Orson asked me to star in a film he had written, *The Cradle Will Rock,* which he could not get financed. The next night, I went on *The Tonight Show* and told Johnny, "Opie [Ron Howard] can get any film financed, but Orson Welles, the greatest, most prolific, excellent talent of all time, can't." Johnny couldn't believe it, either. Orson just loved that I told the story, and it cemented our friendship (he would bring up Johnny and the show at all his lunches after that night), until the day he died of a heart attack, on October 10, 1985. I was at the memorial at the Directors Guild of America that November. My head and heart were swarming with memories and feelings sadder than I thought possible.

And by the way, Orson never, ever, picked up the check at those lunches.

All in all, over about eighteen years, I guested and hosted *The Tonight Show* 140 times. Changed my life. And as Johnny became even larger than life, he expanded as well, hosting the Academy Awards five times, beginning in 1979. He never really enjoyed it. If you have a show on every night that everyone's watching, it's not that exciting. It was frustrating for him, but he was hugely popular. First of all, his genius was that he never made the Oscars about him. It was about the stars—about the audience. He was frustrated at the length of the show, because he knew ways to shorten it, but the producers wouldn't do it (cut the dance production numbers, the speeches, the special production awards, the award to the accountants). He wanted to talk—he was oratorical, sarcastic, biting, acerbic. He had written and hosted the Emmys twice, in the early '70s, and had been really sarcastic on those shows, to great acclaim. He went over big on those shows because he did a lot of inside industry stuff that normally people didn't do. I think he just pretended that the Oscars was the Emmys, and he hosted in the same style. He would basically turn the Oscars into a roast. It was not about himself, as the show had been with Bob Hope hosting.

The interesting thing about the Oscars, from a comedian's point of view (not that I've ever done it, but just knowing comedy), is that there's no other time when, as time goes on in the two to three hours of the show, you're playing to more and more losers. So by the end of the evening, no one wants to laugh—they want to go home, they're pissed that the other guy won. It's a progressively tougher show to do than the monologue. Johnny did keep them laughing, though. And he had the tools that his co-writers, Jim Mulholland and Mike Barrie, gave him. They remember:

"Johnny always did very well. He had a certain dignity about him, so he could get his zingers in without making it about himself. He was so good at reading the audience, he could modulate his performance throughout, and bring a sort of dignified wit to it, as opposed to doing comedy bits.

"He would want to be doing a soft shoe in a tuxedo, but he would come up with lines that were personal. He was going through a divorce, so he came up with using the titles of the films that year, all applying to his personal life. He used the names of the nominated films, and it was great. He wrote this himself. He wanted to do those just to get away from telling joke, joke, joke—he wanted to throw them a curve."

Here's what he said:

"My personal life has been exactly like this year's Academy Awards. It started off with *Terms of Endearment,* I thought I had *The Right Stuff* . . . then came *The Big Chill,* and for the last month, I have been begging for *Tender Mercies.*"

Obviously, Jim and Mike were prepared. "We tried to give Johnny the tools for every possible catastrophe and unexpected behavior. If the guy who won gave a long speech, or the guy didn't speak English, we would have five or six jokes and just give Johnny the card, and he would bring it out (you could probably see him on the tape bringing out that card), and he would say it, and everybody thought he was just making it up. If Raquel Welch's breast popped out, we were ready. And, sometimes, something would happen, and we'd have to come up with something on the spot."

Now, remember that Bob Hope, who had hosted the Oscars nineteen times, always read cue cards. Everyone who was on during those shows was reading. No one ever made eye contact, no one ever looked at another person, because they were looking out over the cameras. Johnny was a little more astute with the audience, about how the audience felt, than Bob Hope. Johnny was always reading the audience and he would edit as he would go along.

The writers, Mike and Jim, continue: "The last Oscar show that Johnny did was also great, this time because of the guests. Incredible people won, which made it really dramatic, and Johnny really got good laughs. People like Cary Grant, Laurence Olivier, Gregory Peck, George Burns, Natalie Wood, Ruby Keeler, Dean Martin, Steve Martin, Sammy Davis Jr., Raquel Welch, and Robin Williams, too, for Best Picture. And Johnny introduced them. Sometimes the writers of the Oscar show would provide Johnny with introductions to these people, but he would often want us because he wanted something he knew would be funny to say. For example, the second year Johnny hosted, Howard W. Koch, the producer, came over to the show, and he was all upset.

" 'Alan Splet's not showing up tonight. I just found out, he's having car trouble.'

"And Johnny goes, 'Who's Alan Splet?'

" 'He's getting a special award for sound editing.'

"And Johnny says, 'Well, there goes the show.'

"So we started doing jokes about it, trying to figure out what happened to him, why he wasn't going to show up, and Johnny made it into a big deal that night.

"Johnny: 'It happens every year. One year it was George C. Scott, next year it was Marlon Brando not showing up, this year it's Alan Splet.'

"Then, throughout the show, he would give Alan Splet updates.

" 'His car broke down in Barstow, he's hitching a ride.'

"It was so brilliant—and really was the first of the running gags they now do on award shows. Splet was gold for not showing up, and then we were afraid he was going to show up, and we were gonna send a couple of goons to push him into a hotel room and keep him, because we had all this material depending on him not showing up." (In Alan Splet's obituary, they mentioned that he was the talk of the Oscars, and what had really happened was that he had flown in from somewhere and was asleep the whole night, and when he woke up the next morning, he was a celebrity. Because for two hours, Carson kept saying his name over and over again.)

"We'd try to cover everything that happened in the movies over the course of the year, as well as stuff that was in the news that might be related, plus all those jokes about the show going long, stuff that you're preparing that you may never use, but just in case you need it. We worked just the two of us, and at some point, Johnny would just say, maybe two weeks before the show, 'Let me see what you've got,' because we wouldn't want any jokes to be stale. And we were writing *The Tonight Show* monologues as well. So after about six weeks of *Oscar* work, we had maybe two hundred jokes, which we would give to Johnny, and he would check off the ones he wanted, and that was it.

"And you know what? He never complained. Never asked for changes—just would make the changes he felt were needed as he was onstage, feeling the crowd's reactions. Remember, he never really liked doing the Oscars. He was nervous the first time—he came out of his dressing room in his full dress suit, with tails, looking like he just wanted to get into his car and go home. When you watch the show, you can see he's a little bit nervous at the beginning. Then he starts to get laughs and he's fine. I remember he came offstage and he said, 'Well, the rest is a cakewalk.' Because he went over big. And he was so brilliantly talented that he would come up with stuff on the spot. Every year. He would never share the opening monologue with anyone—the day of the show, he'd tell us. No one else was allowed to see his monologues (except the cue card guy). He would be super-secret about it because he wanted everyone to respond spontaneously.

"There was always a point, even though we had written a lot of stuff, when maybe an hour and a half into the show, he would say, 'They're restless, they're hungry, they're not listening to me, they're wondering whether they're gonna win an award or not—from now on I'm just an usher. Get them on and get them off,' because he knew that they were impatient. And the big awards were coming up in the last half hour, and everybody's nervous. And he was right.

"And then there was the show that went on the day President Reagan was shot. We called him up and said, 'You better turn on the TV. Reagan was shot.' Nobody knew if he was gonna live or not, or what was going on at that point. Then they said he was hit, and he was in the hospital. Half the monologue we had written was Ronald Reagan jokes. But then Reagan was okay, and he did a live feed from his hospital bed, and Johnny went out and did all the jokes anyway (as an aside, Bob Hope did the Oscars the Friday after Martin Luther King Jr. was shot. Hope was different—the Oscars were postponed a day, and Hope's attitude toward the whole thing was that he seemed more concerned about it affecting his jokes. His attitude: 'I can't believe they postponed it over this') because the audience knew by that time that Reagan was okay.

"And Johnny's joke was, 'He was gonna cut funding to the arts, and this is his biggest assault on the arts since he signed with Warner Brothers.' That got a big laugh, and then he sort of saved it by saying, 'That should get him up, that should get his blood going,' something like that. 'That should get him up and out of bed.'"

By the second Oscar show, Johnny had changed the style of what hosts did by being edgier and more topical, more acerbic and more inside. His philosophy was, if you don't make the studio audience in the theater laugh, it doesn't matter if they're not laughing at home. So Johnny did a lot of inside stuff, stuff out of the trades. And he got a little criticism on that, that you had to read the trades to get some of the jokes. But it was important to get the crowd laughing. And that criticism was underestimating the audience because the audience was smarter than people thought. On the other hand, Carson always used to say to me, especially when I was doing Nixon, "You know, you're way ahead of the audience on this." And I asked, "Does that bother you?" And he said, "No, not at all." It didn't, because it was his point of view as well. But later when he did the Nixon bits, it was precisely the right time to do it. (Remember, when I did it, the FBI followed me around for two years.) Johnny always had the sense of the audience, and respected it, whether it was at *The Tonight Show* or the Oscars.

For Johnny's last show on the air, he had two of his favorite guests: Robin Williams (if you want to see Johnny really enjoying himself, watch the first show Robin appears on—when he talks about his dyslexia and how in his neighborhood, at Halloween, he would say, "Trick or Trout" and people threw fish at him) and Bette Midler, in the fondest farewell ever seen on television. Suffice it to say that Robin was brilliant, and Bette, who sang Johnny's favorite song, "One More for My Baby (and One More for the Road)," right to him, tore down the house. As Johnny's tears ran down his face, the audience (I was sitting in it) was just awed in silence, and then blew up in totally affectionate, respectful, and nostalgic applause . . . so touching.

After Johnny retired, he and I would go out to lunch with his producer Peter Lassally at least once a month, just to have fun and to laugh. Incidentally, comedians bond over the people they hate, not the people they love. "It doesn't matter who you love, but if you want to talk about who you hate, come sit by me." That was our philosophy, and it gave us a lot of shared laughter. Eventually, when Johnny wasn't doing well, his nephew Jeff told me that Johnny really didn't want to see anyone because of the shape he was in, so I didn't see Johnny in the months before he died. But one day, to my incredible surprise and joy, before he went into the hospital, Johnny called me.

"David," he said, in the voice I truly loved. "I've got this yacht now and I'm going to Seattle, which is close to Vancouver, your country and all that. It's just me and the crew. Want to come?" But I was back East and couldn't get back in time as Johnny was admitted to the hospital. I was sad that I couldn't go. It made me think of how lonely he was as a person—he spent a lot of time alone, especially at the end.

And then he was gone. I miss him every day. Memories come to mind. Things happen and I wish I had him to share them with. He was the most important person in my career.

Conan O'Brien is such a playful person. Whenever I see Conan in a restaurant, or anywhere, he always pulls me over to say something loving and really funny. Here pensively sitting on the set of *Inside Comedy,* 2012.

I speak of Johnny not just with great affection, admiration, and respect, but with awe, and I am qualified to do so. He changed my career, my life, and I owe him everything. And, simply put, I loved him.

On the other hand, Conan O'Brien and I have nothing in common. He is taller than I am. He likes children more than I do. I believe in a free Israeli state—wait a minute, he is always insisting that he has controversial views that no one knows. And we are, truly, the two palest men in Los Angeles. You can see every vein in our bodies. I like the sun and he—well, in his own words: "I can't go in the sun because I'm genetically engineered to live in a bog in Ireland. You know, I'm 100 percent Irish, and suddenly I've moved near the Mexican border, but genetically I'm supposed to be under peat moss, you know, hibernating, so, yeah. I have no melanin in my skin. I have these freckles, and when I go outside, you can smell the smoke within thirty seconds."

Let's step back a little. Conan Christopher O'Brien, an Irish Catholic from Massachusetts, is a comedian, a writer, a producer, and a host of many late-night talk shows. He stands out from other comedians—the Jews, the Canadians, the guests on talk shows rather than the hosts (myself excluded). Oh yes, in 1985 he graduated Harvard (as did his dad, who is a physician and a professor of medicine there) and was president of the *Harvard Lampoon*—so we know the "writer" label is so true. (We also know that because Conan's senior thesis concerned the use of children as symbols in the works of William Faulkner and Flannery O'Connor. You know I could not make that up.)

Then Conan wrote for *Saturday Night Live, The Simpsons,* and, in 1993, late night found him, and he took over for David Letterman on *Late Night.* Lasted sixteen years. He then took over for Jay Leno. That lasted seven months. I have to say, when that fiasco happened, Conan put out a statement that showed what a classy man and performer he is. Part of what he said:

"Every comedian dreams of hosting *The Tonight Show* and—for seven months—I got to do it. I did it my way, with people I love, and I do not regret a second [of it]. . . . All I ask is one thing, and I'm asking this particularly of young people that watch: Please do not be cynical. I hate cynicism; for the record it's my least favorite quality. It doesn't lead anywhere. Nobody in life gets exactly what they thought they were going to get. But if you work really hard and you're kind, amazing things will happen."

For the last eight years he has hosted *Conan* (that makes his tenure of hosting late-night talk shows twenty-seven years) on TBS; he's also hosted the Emmy Awards and has been touring in stand-up. This past September, TBS decided that the show would become a thirty-minute format, and Conan's podcast (called *Conan O'Brien Needs a Friend*), interviewing celebrities who may or may not be his "friends," would be expanded. One of the casualties—his beloved band.

So back to having nothing in common. I imagined Conan had the big Irish anti-Semitic family. Ten siblings?

"Five. Siblings. Catholic. But I exclusively dated Jewish women for years. I was fascinated with the Jewish culture. I like that religion more than my own. There's something that seemed centered and calming to me about Judaism."

I find Judaism the opposite. Not calming. It's . . . you know, it's one war after another . . . one oppression after the other. But Conan persists.

"That's the history. I'm just saying that the religion itself is simpler. We have too much incense in the Catholic Church."

But I seem to remember that my dad felt that the Irish, though intelligent, sell their children for whiskey. But my girls don't want whiskey. I don't think they know how to spell it. Conan is excited. We agree on something.

"I'm already seeing the huge generation gap between the way I grew up and the way my children grow up. My lovely wife is constantly asking our two kids how they feel about what's going on and getting them to express themselves. She's taking care of their individual needs and making sure that each of them is really catered to emotionally, and I don't understand what the hell's going on, 'cause I was the middle of six, and both my parents were busy all the time."

My dad had a grocery store, and he worked all the time, and when he wasn't at the store, he was at the shul. That makes Conan remember.

"Let me tell you a story. And I'm name-dropping here, but it's organic name-dropping, which is the best kind. When I moved back to LA, one of the first people I made friends with was Lisa Kudrow. We were both starting out. This is years before she was on *Friends*. We're taking an improv class together. We start comparing notes. I went to Harvard. She went to Vassar. I studied history and literature. She was pre-med, and we were thinking, 'Isn't it strange that we both ended up here trying to get into show business?'

"Then I find out that her dad's a doctor, and I said, 'Lis, isn't it funny how, like, on the weekends, our dads would work all through the weekend at their lab?'

"And she says, 'I don't know what you're talking about,' and that's when I realized that my dad was probably in a tree in the backyard reading a *Penthouse* magazine and smoking."

I remind Conan that my dad was in shul. Remember what I said? Shul? That's a synagogue. No *Penthouse* magazine there. But maybe my siblings had *Penthouse*. I will ask my sister, Tammy, who is fifteen years older than I am. Where were you in the family order, Conan? Like, were you the second? Third?

"Heterosexual. I was third from the top. Fourth from the bottom. I once was interviewing Tony Randall, and he said, 'Where are you in the family?' And I said, 'I'm the middle of six,' and Tony Randall looked at me—this is on the air, and he said, 'There is no middle of six,' in a perfect Tony Randall way. Like I said—nobody nurtured anybody. My older brother Neil was quite large, so most of the time he tossed me around like a ragdoll and laughed at me. We loved each other, but it was a madhouse, and, you know—it's too many kids. I always tell my mother she went for quantity, not quality, and she does not laugh. My mother is Margaret Dumont from the old Marx Brothers movies. She was always at the table saying, 'Now I'd like if we all tried to behave with a certain modicum of . . . ,' and then we would just start throwing potatoes and smashing things. She'd say, 'Well, I'd like to think that we were the kind of people that—' Splat. Pie in the face. I mean that's what it was, pretty much."

So I guess he had to be into comedy . . .

"Had to be. We're a funny family, but they go through the checklist. Am I a good athlete? No. Am I the guy that all the girls want to sleep with? No. Am I the math whiz? No, and for me it was just a lot of empty boxes. And then we got to—do you make other people laugh? Yes. I doubled down on that."

I wondered if he was the class clown. I was. I was funny—on all the time. That shrink once told me it was because my brother died that I worked hard trying to make everyone around me laugh. Again, Conan's story is not mine.

"I was a serious student at Harvard, not the class clown. I always say, 'The class clown is the guy who gets up on the desk, the guy that sets the clock back, the guy who puts the explosive device in the teacher's desk . . . that guy always dies in a motel shootout. Steve Martin was not the class clown. You know, all the people that you and I admire in comedy were not the class clowns. They were quiet, in the back, and they were watching. And I was that guy. I was funny with my friends, but I was a hardworking, serious student, and I was going to go on to do big, important things. I was fascinated by comedy, but I did not think it was a career. I had no idea when I was a kid that you could make a living doing it."

Neither did I. We agree again. Not until I was at Second City did I realize that people do this for a living. And when I saw Lenny Bruce, I realized that I could be happy being my own true version of what he did.

"Yes. It took me a while, too. I got into Harvard, 'I'm gonna work hard. I'm going to go to the Kennedy School of Government. I'm going to be a mover and shaker. I'm going to save the world. I'm going to write great essays.' And one day, it was the classic 'my roommate is going'—John O'Connor was going to check out the *Harvard Lampoon* magazine, the oldest humor magazine in America, founded in 1876, and a lot of great writers wrote for it—John Updike was on the *Lampoon*, and Robert Benchley was on the *Harvard Lampoon*, and Fred Gwynne, TV's Herman Munster. I knew nothing about it. You know how I felt? Like the baby duck being put in water for the first time."

Again, the same for me. I walked into Second City and felt like I was home. Conan is excited. "Me, too! I had been a serious, anxious, hardworking guy, and then I walked into the *Lampoon*, and they said, 'Write something.' I did, and they said, 'Hey, that's really funny.' And then the next thing you know, I'm running it! Sleeping there. Everyone there was taking this comedy thing seriously. Some of them were going off to, you know, to actually write. Some of them had left to write for *Saturday Night Live*. I couldn't believe it. That was just a revelation."

We agree again. It's a great thing to find out what you want to do. I was at the University of Chicago, screwing up every scholarship program that I could, by accident, and Second City came through. And I saw them perform, and I just couldn't get over it. I said, "I'm not like them and not as good as them, but I can do that," and it changed my life. So what changed Conan's life?

"This is it. One day, the phone rang at the *Lampoon*, and it was the woman who headed the Harvard a cappella group. She said, 'We need someone to emcee our big show at the Sanders Theatre.' And since I'd answered the phone, they offered me the gig. Now, I had always been interested in performing for my friends, and that's all I had ever done. But I said, 'Yes. I'm the man for you.' Classic thing—always say yes. 'You bet. I'll be there in ten minutes,' and I hang up. And then I went crazy writing jokes on blue cards. I borrowed a friend's yachting cap, put on a blue blazer, got a cigar—an unlit cigar—and walked out there. I was the height I am now, but about a hundred pounds lighter and with questionable skin, and I went out and started telling jokes, and I actually won them over at the show, and got the bug. You get that laugh, and that's heroin."

Heroin for sure. Which is a natural jumping-off point to ask Conan which other comedians he admired.

"I was always fascinated by good comedic prose writers who also performed. Woody Allen was the first one. Then Steve Martin came along and wrote *Cruel Shoes* while he was also working on TV. The biggest influence on me as a kid was W. C. Fields, and I took the kind of muttering thing from him. But I think television is where I'm best used, because I can improvise and sometimes explore other sides of my personality. I think I could come up with some really funny ideas for a movie, but the minute someone would want me to construct the plot, I'd say, 'Oh, no, I don't know anything about that.'"

Conan understands the relationship between news and comedy, and remembers the process it took to write for television. "David, you were truly a part of changing history in terms of censorship in comedy," he tells me. "My first gig was kind of about the news. Greg Daniels and I worked together on a show called *Not Necessarily the News,* which was an early HBO show. After that, we worked on a few failed shows and did improv, and then Lorne Michaels hired us to work on *Saturday Night Live.* That was zero to one thousand miles an hour overnight. The first day, we were pitching to Robin Williams, Steve Martin, and Tom Hanks. I was twenty-four.

"Then I got burnt out. *The Simpsons* heard I was available and hired me. It was still the original writing staff. A big highlight for me was when I wrote an episode in 1991 that fans really liked, called 'Marge vs. the Monorail.' With the help of Jeff Martin, I wrote a song in it that's a parody of *The Music Man.* Years later, in 2014, *The Simpsons* called me up and said, 'We're doing a *Simpsons* at the Hollywood Bowl. Would you perform the monorail song with the Hollywood gay men's chorus behind you and a giant symphony orchestra?' It took twenty-five years, but what a neat arc, to go from sitting in a room and having an idea, to the Hollywood Bowl."

As usual, I'm curious about hosting. Conan moved from writing and stand-up into hosting in a big way. And my guess is that we may agree on this. I loved hosting talk shows because I have always felt that comedy is about *listening*. I grew up listening to Wayne and Shuster on the radio. They were the biggest comedians in Canada, and my brother Fishy made sure I listened to them. And it taught me to listen to the audience, and listen to answers when I ask questions. Johnny was great at that. So is Conan.

"Hosting is a totally different job. As I'm the host, and I think that's something I always try and keep in mind—I need to bring out the best in other people. The worst is when your guests aren't as funny as you are, 'cause you never know. You have to connect with someone no matter what. You know who is the easiest? Funniest? And most cruel? Marty Short. By the way, the only time I start to think that maybe I've achieved something is when I find myself at a dinner, and Marty Short is there, and he will address me by name. And I leave my body. I really do. And actually the same thing with Steve Martin. Goofing around with them for a second—I act cool, and then I go to the bathroom, and I'm just like, 'Ah! I can't believe that happened! That's fantastic!' "

I have known Steve Martin for more than forty years. He and I were on *The Smothers Brothers* together. He was just twenty-one when he started to write there. Honestly, Steve was, and is, remarkable. His stand-ups were just joyful. And Marty is one of the nicest people I know. A genius.

Again, Conan agrees. "But you should know that Marty will say the cruelest things to me. What he loves to do is come up to me, and go, 'Conan, you look fantastic,' and I go, 'Thank you, Marty.'

" 'I just want to say—whatever work you're having done, twenty percent more, and then stop.'

"He came to my house, and I have a nice house. He goes, 'This house is fantastic,' and I go, 'Thank you, Marty.'

" 'No, it's beautiful. Like, the lawn and the pool . . . I mean, when you think about this house, and then your talent—it just doesn't line up.' "

So, upon further thought, Conan and I agree on many things. Maybe even most. Especially on comedy. As Conan says, comedy is not a science. We don't understand it, and it's kind of magical. And some-times it works beautifully, and sometimes it fails utterly. You can get the greatest comedian in the world for a show. Sometimes it's not quite there. Sometimes it's just—you're opening a bottle of wine. You don't know exactly what you're going to get. And for some things, there just are no explanations. Johnny always needed guests at the last minute. He would sometimes call me or Newhart at noon to guest and tape the show at 3 p.m. I could never get over that. People would cancel at the last minute. I thought, "It's *The Tonight Show with Johnny Carson*! It's the biggest show on TV. What do you have to do that's more important than *The Tonight Show*?" I just couldn't figure it out. Ever.

Conan shakes his head. He, being a master improviser and writer, reads voraciously, and is always himself on the show, so he can arrive at the last minute and kill it. He explores other sides of his own personality.

"If we have an author on, or a political figure, or an economist, I can ask some serious questions—I've read enough, and I'm interested in things, so I can have a good conversation. But I can also be the silli-est person in the world. I'm in complete control. I get to do whatever I want. Not bad."

CHAPTER 10

BEHIND SOME OF THE
BEST COMEDY ON TELEVISION

People often ask me why I became a director after such a long career in stand-up. How did I end up going from being a comedian and theater actor to a director of some of the biggest hits in television sitcoms—*Mad About You, Designing Women, Newhart, Friends, Seinfeld, The Golden Girls,* and, to this day, *Curb Your Enthusiasm.* Well, I'd done everything I needed to do to be a good director: I'd been an actor in front of an audience, I'd been an actor without an audience, and I'd written shows, so the transition was natural. I knew about all aspects of creating a show. For example, I made sure the sets were always loose and comfortable—it's impossible to do comedy when you're tight or tense. My goal was to make it easy for everyone to do what they needed to do, and most actors I worked with will tell you that I did it. I loved guiding actors so they could create their characters the best they could. I was also able to unlock talented actors and actresses and make them shine. That said, I never unlocked Bea Arthur.

I began directing situation comedies in the mid-1980s. It was time for me to go off in a whole new direction. I'd gotten tired of the stand-up comedy life, tired of traveling and breathing cigarette smoke and staying up late and being wired at 3 a.m., all alone. I still wanted to direct—but comedies only, given that *The Seventh Seal* or *Das Boot* aren't Chevy Chase and Goldie Hawn and weren't exactly waving scripts in my direction.

Everybody told me that taking on sitcoms was a bad career move, that sitcoms were dead, that only hacks and has-beens directed them, that it would prevent me from ever returning to features. Naturally, that only challenged me to thumb my nose and prove them wrong. By the time I figured out they were probably right, I was having too much fun and making too much money to stop. And unbeknownst to everyone, the entire sitcom situation would change in a year or two. Also, I learned one important thing right away about directing sitcoms. When you're directing a sitcom, you're essentially a conductor. Not the musical kind. The electrical kind. All the real power on the set—wielded always by the head writer–producer, or "showrunner," and the sitcom's star actor or actress—flows directly through you from one end of the power structure to the other. It tingles. But not in a good way.

Here's how it works. Inevitably, at some point during the rehearsal week, the star, usually a former stand-up comic, will call me over and recite some version of this speech:

"I can't say these lines. They're all wrong. Wronger than wrong. The writer doesn't have my voice, because no one could get my voice, because I created it to do stand-up comedy and etched it into the public consciousness in front of tough drunken chain-smoking audiences and made a ton of money and got a big network deal, so why change now? I can't fire the bastard because we created the show together, but I have to keep on fighting for my own voice, and these lines are too jokey, they don't work, and I have to throw them all out and just go my own way."

And I say, "You're absolutely right."

Then I amble over to the showrunner's office, usually decorated with statuettes and Emmy nomination certificates and photos of his *Harvard Lampoon* staff mates and his Porsche and a Lionel train set, the great kind no real kid can afford, running all along the floor, and I say, "You know, he likes a lot of the stuff, but he feels a few of the lines don't really capture his voice."

And the writer gets mad, but not totally at me, and says, "Make him say the lines, goddamnit! Because I stayed up all night writing them while he was hanging out at Sky Bar, and you know he's no good when he makes it up as he goes along, and you might remind him that he used to pay my good friend Richie to write killer jokes in his 'voice' whenever he was lucky enough to get on Craig Kilborn."

And I say, "You're absolutely right." Because guess what? Sometimes he is. Then I walk back to the actor's trailer and say, "Don't worry. I hear where you're coming from, and you're absolutely right—most of this stuff is all wrong—but why not save maybe two of the best jokes out of the twenty that you're throwing away, just so [insert showrunner's name here] doesn't get discouraged?"

And he says, grudgingly, "Fuck him!" And then, "Maybe."

And because he really is a talented comedian, he does pick the best two jokes, and he's fairly happy because now everybody really knows who's the boss, and he can say all the bad lines in the meantime while asking for eighteen replacements. And guess who's responsible for writing them? The showrunners' writing staff, which consists of sixteen writers, eight who actually write and eight who just order out for food, none of whom have seen the inside of the Viper Room—or their parents, pets, apartment, or significant others—since August. And they all look like they have flown Air India coach.

This incredible high-wire act goes on all day long and never stops for five days. It only stops during the filming of a show when you have an audience in the grandstands and when something doesn't work. Then the writer and the star bond and team up against the director and yell, "Why the fuck didn't you make this work? The rhythm must be off. The blocking is wrong. The cameras are in the wrong place."

But I'm ready for them. At this point, it is extremely important that the director—me—jump into a huddle with them and say very fast, "You're absolutely right. This sucks. You know what it is? It's the three of us against this fucking audience, and we can make this work if we all stick together and think really funny really hard and make something work right here on the spot." And believe me, at this moment, if you are looking for a funny line, the gaffer or the key grip or even an agent can walk by with a line, and everyone will look his way and try it because we are all so desperate.

So on show night, everyone ends up absolutely united—against the very audience we're trying to amuse and entertain. And it's not the easiest way to work, but it works.

On the brighter side is the fact that the sitcom director, though essentially powerless, is treated like a prince. Every whim is catered to. If you're tired, a chair will appear magically under your ass from somewhere. If you hold up your hand, someone will hand you a bottle of water to drink. Everyone is catering to the director because, well, if he doesn't yell "action," no one is going to get home. And nobody wants to risk talking to the showrunner or star, who, unlike the director, can actually fire them.

It's also great to work with great comedians. You only get to do that if you're a comedian yourself, because few comedians will trust anyone other than somebody who's died in front of an audience to make judgments about what will make people laugh or not.

That's how I got my first sitcom directing job. In 1982, Danny Thomas was coming back to television in his last series. It was called *One Big Family* and was produced by Danny's son, Tony. The big fear of Tony Thomas and the people syndicating the show was that Danny, like most old comedians, would stubbornly insist on using only the material that had gotten him this far. That would make the show a big hit in the ages seventy-five to ninety-four demographic.

They thought that only another comic would be able to convince Danny to recite hip, up-to-date lines written by his grandchildren's kindergarten classmates. And they were right. Astoundingly right. When push came to shove, and it came right on schedule, Danny would talk only to me.

In Yiddish.

Nobody else could understand us. Now, we all know that Danny Thomas was Lebanese.

So, *Yiddish?*

A new script would arrive. He'd smile at the writer, give him a thumbs-up, giving the kid quite a thrill, turn to me, and say, *"A shtick drek."* (Translation: "A piece of shit.")

I'd say, *"Nish geferlacht."* ("It's not bad.")

"A shtick drek es a shtick drek."

And we'd both smile back at the writer, whom I knew now wouldn't be getting home until Shavuos (that's forever).

In the meantime, Danny entertained me every day with filthy stories—a little surprising from a guy who had a shrine to Saint Jude at the entrance to his house. Most of his cigar-waving stories were about the golden age of show business: which legendary entertainers fucked around on their wives, which bizarre sexual practices they preferred, whom they practiced them with, and so on.

Al Jolson, Danny said, was a notorious tightwad asshole who was always getting himself "knobbed" under the table, usually for free, by chorus girls. I never worked up the courage to ask what "knobbed" meant, but I got the idea. I did get to ask Danny how a Lebanese Christian, which he was, learned to speak Yiddish so well and, shall we say, so colorfully.

"How the fuck else am I going to talk to Abe?" he said, meaning Abe Lastfogel, the powerful William Morris agent who for most of his career was Danny's showbiz "rabbi."

"Well, Danny," I said, "why don't you let the world know you have this fantastic gift?"

He asked, "What for? Yiddish is a dying language!"

After *One Big Family* was canceled, the young suits actually had a good idea: teaming me up with another "old" comic, Bob Newhart, who at the time was starting his second sitcom, *Newhart,* the one set in the inn in Vermont, which he began at the advanced age of fifty-three.

I already knew that Bob understood the medium of television, trusted his writers, and didn't have the ego of the older stars who needed to have everything their own way. And yet, in his low-key demeanor, he knew exactly what was right for his character. That left me all the time in the world to schmooze with Bob and fellow comic geniuses like Tom Poston and Dick Martin and Don Rickles. I knew and respected Bob from stand-up; he was a man truly beloved by all. He was understated beyond any other comedian I know, who could sideline me, and everyone else, with a look, without saying a word. And playing a psychiatrist for years on his own show was such a brilliant role for him, because it allowed him to interact with other actors but still keep his often silent look as his funniest weapon.

Yes, that's Bob Newhart, and there isn't a person in our business who does not revere this gentle, classy man who has been a quiet but loving friend to so many in our business. And directing his show, *Newhart,* was one of the great pleasures of my life. It was the most fun show that anyone could do, and I am not the only one to say so—ask anyone in entertainment, and they will tell you that when you are working with Bob Newhart, you're gonna have the best time. It was a loose atmosphere, and there was no tension ever, with the most creative, brilliant, collaborative people. Every day Bob would ask me, "Who do you want to have lunch with? Don Rickles? Dick Martin? Dick Shawn? Lucille Ball?" Every lunch, every day, was a party at the commissary, always with funny people. It was the best time I ever had on a show. All these years later, the show that has a similar, absolutely wonderful atmosphere for working is *Curb Your Enthusiasm.*

Bob doesn't see that as so unusual. "You establish that kind of set, and it shows on camera—that everybody's having a good time." When Bob started out, I was in Chicago. Our friend Dan Sorkin, who revolutionized being a radio DJ by playing live comedy albums as much as possible, would play Bob's album. When I heard it for the first time, it was a new kind of comedy, because no one ever just talked comfortably and intelligently to the audience, without hollering at them. Bob remembers, too. "There was a sea change in comedy—no one got together and said we're gonna change comedy. We just found another way of doing comedy. Mike Nichols and Elaine May and Shelley Berman and Johnny Winters and Woody Allen and Lenny Bruce and Mort Sahl—and me. It presumed an intelligence on the audience's part. That album was so significant. I was a college guy, kind of young, and it made a difference. I remember thinking, 'Wow, this is what stand-up is all about.'"

Bob explains, "What happened was that the Warner Brothers people were coming through Chicago, and they called on Dan. And Dan said, 'I have this friend I think is funny.' Meaning me. He played a tape for the Warner people, and they said, 'We like it. We'll give you a recording contract, and we'll record you at your next nightclub.' I said, 'Well, see, we have a problem there.' 'Cause I'd never played a nightclub. And it took them almost a year to find a club that would take a chance on somebody who had never played a nightclub. There was a place called the Tidelands in Houston, Texas. And they booked me there for two weeks. I'll never forget it. I walked out, absolutely terrified. Somehow I just mustered up all the bravado I could for two weeks, pretending I knew what I was doing. Shortly after that, I played the Elmwood Casino in Canada. Died, every night. Two shows a night, for a week. The Canadians didn't go for it. They were polite, very nice. But they didn't look up. So that almost drove me back to accounting. But then I played Winnipeg, Rancho don Carlos, and that went well, so I said to myself, 'Okay, I'll stay in this business.'"

The Bob Newhart Show ended its six-season, 142-episode run on CBS on April 1, 1978. As much as comedians today owe a debt of gratitude to Bob Newhart's album *The Button-Down Mind of Bob Newhart* and his razor-sharp timing in his twelve-year-long stand-up work, so must TV comedy shows pay homage to *The Bob Newhart Show* for reinventing the sitcom. "I think we all were influenced by it," director, writer, and comedian Judd Apatow explains. "It was different from what we had seen before it." The show, which earned two comedy series Emmy nominations, was based on the unexpected kind of reactionary humor Newhart had perfected in his stand-up act in nightclubs. It created a kind of blueprint for such comedies as *Seinfeld* and *Curb Your Enthusiasm,* both of which I directed. "The secret to building a show around stand-up is maintaining the integrity of the persona you create," says Newhart. Conan O'Brien agrees. "Bob does not need to find himself on TV. He knows exactly who he is."

On *The Bob Newhart Show,* Bob starred as Dr. Robert Hartley, a kind of psychiatrist who is somewhat exploited, as in "walked all over," which was a first on television. He dealt with his loving but smart-mouth wife, friends who were sometimes simple and always needy, and colleagues/patients who were often clueless and sometimes just smart-ass. The show also found humor in the subtleties of everyday life, a subject that comedians and shows today, including *Modern Family, The Office,* and *Black-ish,* have used with huge success. Dave Davis and

Lorenzo Music (who you probably remember as the actor who played the mysterious elevator operator on *Rhoda* and had written a segment for Bob on *Love, American Style*) developed the show (it was created by James L. Brooks and Allan Burns) and wanted to emphasize reality, not silliness or farce. Bob's a regular guy dealing with the same obstacles we all face, morning until night. The bottom line is that the show is just plain funny. And that was all Bob.

It is truly hard to believe that it has been forty years since the show ended after its six seasons, and it is still as funny and as relevant as it was all those years ago. How did it start? There were many not-so-famous people involved, but all turned out to have a huge impact on television in all their work. When Bob was not available, they hired Sid Caesar. (Lorenzo Music, a super-talented writer and a good collaborator, worked with me on *The Smothers Brothers Show*.) A few years later, the duo did a script for Bob for *The Mary Tyler Moore Show*. Once again, Bob wasn't available. After they became story editors on Mary's show, MTM Enterprises asked Lorenzo and Davis to do a pilot. "We knew exactly what we wanted to do" says Dave Davis. "We wanted a show with Bob."

Bob had worked with Lorenzo on *The Smothers Brothers Show*, as I had. But he wasn't excited about doing a TV comedy. He was happy doing stand-up and had never liked all the hours that it took to do a regular, weekly TV show. In came the great and beloved Allan Burns (he had created and written, with James L. Brooks, *The Munsters, The Mary Tyler Moore Show,* and *Rhoda*), bringing with him Grant Tinker (co-founder of MTM and later chairman and CEO of NBC), who convinced Bob to give a TV show a try. It helped that Arthur Price, who was also a co-founder of MTM, was Bob's manager and knew that Bob was tired of doing stand-up for the last twelve years because he now wanted a normal life with Ginny and the kids.

Now, Bob had never been a demanding comedian or actor. He remembers, "I didn't want the show to be where Dad is a trite dolt that everyone loves, who gets himself into a pickle and then the wife and kids huddle together to get him out of it. I'm a listener and I react to what people say. I wanted the character to have that kind of appeal, too. We needed a profession that fit that. And no one wanted a show with gags or farce or any slapstick. So Lorenzo and Dave came up with a psychiatrist dealing with real problems people could identify with." It was more like having Bob, the character, be quietly sarcastic, using words with some satire, and talking to his patients with humor. And Bob knew that in dealing with MTM as a company, there would be great respect for writers. They also knew that they wanted the focus to be on the marriage of these two people, on their relationship, and that meant no kids. In a funny way, Bob's patients were like his kids, so they could have that kind of story line, since the patients were already an important part of the show.

I ask Bob how Suzanne Pleshette was cast, since she was so perfect as his counterpart. Suzanne had been on *The Tonight Show* when Lorenzo saw her and thought she would be great for the part. He called Bob's agent, Arthur, who called Suzanne, who, it turned out, was pregnant and wanted to do a show where she would stay close to home. And, says Bob, "it turned out that we had great chemistry. Suzie and I had a great relationship. Those things are hard to find, like Marcia Wallace to bring added comic relief as the receptionist. The story goes that Bill Paley, then the chairman of CBS, had seen Marcia on *The Merv Griffin Show* and thought she'd be a good addition as a receptionist. Imagine that!"

The rest of the creative plans just fell into place, remembers Bob. Turns out that Dave Davis was in group therapy, so Lorenzo thought that would be a great addition to the comedy, and that casting would allow the producers to bring in lesser-known comic actors. A terrific pick was Jack Riley—a veteran, respected comic actor who knew so much about therapy that they could write dialogue for him that made him sound like he was his own psychologist. Jack was such an unpretentious actor—he could say anything ridiculous and you just believed him. He never smiled (which was ironic because he had a lovely smile in life) and had a dry delivery of humor. And Bob's constant reactions to Jack, of a kind of disbelief, were really funny.

Other tidbits from Bob:

"I am not big on rehearsals. I know my lines."

"The background of stand-up is that when I sit down on Monday for a reading and there's a great line, I want to do it that night. I don't want to wait until Friday. I was afraid we'd over-rehearse it and it would lose that immediacy. We'd read the script and I'd say to myself, 'I know where I can put that and that,' so all I really have to learn are these three pages. You know many actors do that. Brando did it."

"People are always asking me if I have a favorite scene. I do. I love the scene where I am talking to a ventriloquist with this dummy who tells me that the dummy wants to speak to me alone."

"David, both you and Henry Winkler gave me the same great advice, once. 'Be authentic.' That is the definition of wonderful comedy."

"The late, wonderful and talented John Ritter, who was also my friend, was MTM's go-to guy for many parts. Not only was he cast in many parts in multiple comedies, but whenever somebody else failed at a part, before the show was shot, our producers would call John, and he'd come in and nail it. He was just a great talent and a great guy."

I tell Bob how much I learned from working with him when I directed him on his show, and we had such a great time. That's when we began our almost daily lunches with Don Rickles, one of Bob's dearest and oldest friends, and any other comedians, like Dick Martin and Danny Thomas, who were always free and hungry. Those daily lunches were not just a laughing session, but we never knew who would join us at the last minute—sometimes it was Dick Martin. I learned just how comfortable a set is when it is someone like Bob running it. I also learned that I could hide my lines anywhere on the set, and no one would know where they would be.

Bob knows just what I mean. It became an art form, it really did. He remembers: "One time, on *The Bob Newhart Show,* I was crossing to the little breakfast area we had. And I had my lines on the back of this cereal box. But it was turned, facing the wrong way. So, as I'm crossing the set, I reach out to the box and I turn it around. Now what reason would anyone have to turn a cereal box around? My lines were on it, and I didn't know what I was gonna say."

To this day, Bob is most proud of his show. He loved the writing, the cast, was constantly amazed that it lasted for so many years, and even more astounded that, more than forty years later, people still come up to him and relate, with great fondness, their stories of watching the show all those years ago. I must say that to this day, I think it totally unfair that the show, and the cast, including Bob Newhart, never won an award. The show was overlooked in all categories, in all award ceremonies, for all six years of its run. But here is one award or recognition you may not know about—in 1962, Bob Newhart won the Golden Globes first-ever "best TV star"—but it was *not* for *The Bob Newhart Show*. It was for an NBC variety show that ran for one season in 1961, an adaptation of Bob's comedy album *The Button-Down Mind of Bob Newhart*. And Bob did win a Grammy for Best New Artist, Album of the Year, and Spoken Word (they didn't have a comedy category then, Bob explains).

Bob is ninety-one now, and he is still doing stand-up. Around ten dates a year. "It is a narcotic," he explains. "As long as I am well, I can't imagine not touring. I have been doing stand-up for sixty years. It may be a pain in the ass, especially at my age, but when you get there and walk out on the stage, and you hear a great audience laugh, why would I want to stop? I can't imagine saying, 'You know, I am really tired of making people laugh.' I have said, 'I just can't imagine not doing it.'"

What I learned from Bob is being a mensch and four-camera shooting, and I learned editing from Ray Duvalli, the camera coordinator at *Newhart,* who'd created the art on the minor 1950s hit, *I Love Lucy*.

So once again dumb luck raises its stupid-looking head. I end up at the right place at the right time, and I'm the Cecil B. DeMille of four-camera film sitcom. Now other young directors are following me around the set, hoping to learn my secrets and steal my next job.

They didn't beat me out for *Designing Women,* where I got lucky again—I got to see the show's creators, Linda Bloodworth Thomason and Harry Thomason, who were the masterminds of Bill Clinton's first presidential campaign, while simultaneously filling CBS's 9:30 p.m. Friday time slot.

Linda and Harry were FOB (Friends of Bill) of the first order. For a while, the *Designing Women*'s costume designer, Cliff Chally, was also dressing Bill and Hillary. On the campaign trail, Bill wore the same bright-colored sports coats as Anthony Bouvier, the *Designing Women*'s

Black assistant, played by Meshach Taylor, as solid a comic actor as you can get. Linda and Harry were Clinton's media advisors, and besides scripting *The Man from Hope,* the uplifting biographical video shown during the 1992 Democratic National Convention, much later Linda probably wrote the immortal line, "I never had sex with Miss Lewinsky," which Bill blew on his first and last take.

One Friday night, I'm getting ready to direct *DW* when I get a call from Harry, who's with "the governor" in his greenroom just before his second debate with George Bush the first.

"Do you have any advice for him?" asks Harry.

"Oh, *sure,*" I say, certain he's joking.

But as long as he's asking, I tell him in a smart-alecky way that, in fact, I have something to tell Bill just minutes before the most important telecast of his political life.

I say, "I noticed in the first debate that Clinton was doing what most politicians do, looking around for which camera is shooting him and looking directly into it. He thinks this allows him to connect to the audience. Wrong. It just looks fake and stagey and calculated.

"So, okay," I add breezily, "tell 'the governor' to stop doing that. Tell him not to look into the cameras, but at the person he's talking to. Especially if he's talking to a person in the audience. If they get his profile looking at the person in the audience, they'll show both of them at the same time, and *that's* where the connection is made."

"That's a great idea!" says Harry, which in show business means absolutely nothing, and hangs up.

And I forget all about it until much later that night, when I watch the debate replay and notice that Clinton is looking everybody in the eye—and doing great. And Bush is still following the cameras around— and by comparison looks like a ventriloquist's dummy. And I sit up wide-eyed in bed, terrified at what I've just done. Which is the correct reaction, since the next day all the pundits declare that Clinton, who hadn't done so well in the first debate, has clearly won the second.

I'm too scared to brag about this to the suits at Warner Bros. Television, which produces *Designing Women,* so they don't know that I, a legal alien, have changed the course of American history. Which is paranoid, in retrospect, since they wouldn't have cared if they had known. All they know and care about is whether *Designing Women* is getting good ratings during the last half of the 1992–93 season, and they need me because Linda and Harry are off in Washington producing the inaugural gala and in preproduction for "Travelgate."

I loved directing *Designing Women*. The show itself was wonderful— the writing, the acting, the directing (if I say so myself), the relationship among the spectacularly talented women, the story lines way ahead of their times (the show started in 1986), spelling out relationships among women—it hit every button just right.

And the actors. The four starring women were different as actors, and thus ended up as different as their characters were written. And they were perfectly suited to their roles. When I directed the show, I so appreciated that they helped and nurtured each other, took pleasure in each other's successes, big and small. They were a true team, had a great group comic vibe. And it showed in the comedy. Not one raised voice. Not one stressed attitude. This all resulted in the "funny" falling simply, directly, pointedly, and perfectly. These four actresses were as good as anyone, singularly and as a group. They were smart, had skills and the faith that any one of them was as good as the others—they didn't have the masculine virile egos that male actors often had at the time. This group actually not only got along but were all different versions of phenomenal talent.

Jean Smart was an anchor for women—so tall, so straightforward, but eager to clarify any vagueness in the comedy. Adorable Annie Potts—happy, smart, naturally funny, always knowing her lines, and delivering the humor with unequaled humility and charm. Delta Burke, a truly skillful comedian, was as she portrayed—a true, charming Southern dame; she was not acting with that portrayal. The "funny" thing was that she portrayed Suzanne Sugarbaker as kind and gracious and polite, and with Southern attitude, just as she was in her life . . . a dame. And you would be hard put to find anyone who worked harder and was more eager to learn. And Dixie Carter, as her sister, Julia, elegant, smart, managing the firm, eager to keep the peace and get the clients but no pushover, was kind of a comedy anchor, with her calm demeanor and surprisingly biting lines. As their director, I found their comedy so gelled—it was not over the top, it was not in your face, but it had strength, and chutzpah, and biting observations with smart and smart-ass repartee.

As a director of sitcoms, I am not a "changer on the set" kind of guy. I am not a control freak. I am a collaborator, and I especially love women actors. I grew up with women, so I can work with them, guide them, take in and appreciate their sensitivities to the material, their lack of ego, and the work. The women of *Designing Women* never complained about the often brutal hours, recognized and respected that since I was directing and producing and writing the shows, it was a concentrated amount of work. I found that we nurtured each other, resulting in great work, great comedy, and a great time. I would not have given up one second of that process with these talents. Not one.

Designing Women actually premiered a year before *The Golden Girls,* but I directed both shows way into their runs. The first Golden Girl I met, my first day on the set, was Betty White. She was the epitome of genuine and genuinely funny. Comic actress Betty Marion White Ludden passed away in 2021 at the age of ninety-nine. I think she was America's longest-working comedian/actress. Betty White, who played the adorable Rose Nylund from St. Olaf, Minnesota, really *was* the most adorable human being on earth and the most cheerful person to work with. She was ninety-five when I last worked with her, and her memory was just as sharp as when I started with her on *Golden Girls,* decades ago. She completely lit up the set.

Comic as actor and actor as comic for over eighty years? Without question. And a great one. Known for? So let's step back a little. Okay, a lot.

Although Betty started out in radio, she was best known early in her career as Sue Ann Nivens on *The Mary Tyler Moore Show,* a part she played for four years, leaving an indelible mark on that show and on comedy. Then she was Rose Nylund on *The Golden Girls*—that was for seven years, and her role of one of four "elderly women" left comedy in a tailspin (she was sixty-three at that time). And who can forget Elka in *Hot in Cleveland*—that ran for six years. And this list does not include

The iconic Betty White on the set of *Inside Comedy,* 2014. We always bonded over how much we loved our animals.

her years of appearances on *Password, Match Game, The $25,000 Pyramid,* and *Saturday Night Live.*

Let's keep counting: five Emmys, three American Comedy Awards, three Screen Actors Guild (SAG) awards, and a Grammy. For several hundred episodes of the shows above.

I think we would all agree that the one thing that pops into our minds when we think of Betty White is happiness. She was always smiling, then laughing, making us happy, too. I assume that Betty was always an optimistic person. She agreed but paused to point out, "That can annoy people. If you're a cockeyed optimist, they get fed up pretty soon. When they were casting me for *The Mary Tyler Moore Show,* to play Sue Ann Nivens, Mary said, 'We need to get someone that's sickeningly sweet, like Betty White. A Betty White type, sickeningly sweet.' And then they cast me as the neighborhood nymphomaniac. And it all worked out."

Sue Ann had fans everywhere. Remembered Betty, "I had to prepare for the nymphomaniac part. Sue Ann was the happy homemaker. She could do anything. She could fix anything; she could mend anything. And they'd ask my Allen [Ludden, her beloved husband of twenty years, who died in 1981 and has never been replaced. Once you have had the best . . .], 'How close is this character, you know, the nymphomaniac, to Betty?'

"He'd say, 'Well, they're the same character, except Betty can't cook.'"

Betty was everyone's idol—she was always prepared, she was always happy, and she was always funny.

"That was a blessing," said Betty with a big smile. "We had such a good time. I was the luckiest old broad on two feet, with three wonderful gals to work with [Bea Arthur, Estelle Getty, Rue McClanahan], and another great three on *Hot in Cleveland*—Valerie Bertinelli, Wendie Malick, and Jane Leeves."

Here I stepped in. Betty, remember, I directed *Golden Girls*. I came onto the set. I'll never forget, you were adorable. And I had to give a note to Bea Arthur, and I said, "Bea, could you, instead of standing there, might you just sit on that line?"

And she said, "Why in God's name would I do that?"

I said to her, "No need to bring the deity into this. It's just a director giving you a note to sit down; if you don't want to, I'm okay with that."

Betty remembered it well. "Bea had her own opinions, let me put it that way. Just say no, but don't yell at him. I know, I know."

She was tough, Bea. Betty agreed.

"She was tough, and I think Bea hated me. But I don't know why. I loved her, I really did, and her talent was incomparable. Even if she didn't want to sit down at that point. She was so different from Ruesy [Rue McClanahan], who was our butterfly. And Estelle Getty. She played this old lady, and she was not an old lady. So she had to wear the wigs and all the old lady makeup. So, one summer, when we were on hiatus, Rue got a face-lift. And the makeup man nearly went crazy because he had to put all these lines on her face. It caused some consternation, let me put it that way."

I mentioned what great comics these women were. "David, it was the writers, the writers. That's where it is. You can't do it if it isn't on that page. Actors love to take credit for, 'Oh yes, I played so-and-so.' But if it isn't on the paper, you're out of business. And I never, ever fail to give them every bit of the credit."

Did she love the sitcoms better than, say, *Saturday Night Live*?

"They asked me, earlier on, about three times, to host. But I said, 'It just doesn't make any sense. I'm so California-oriented, and such a California girl. And that's so New York. I'll be like a fish out of water.'

"Well, finally my agent [Jeff Witjas], whom I adore, my great and dear friend, finally leaned on me and said, 'Yes, you're gonna do it.' I was panic-stricken. First of all, I can't read cue cards, I just don't know how to work them. But you can't memorize everything on *Saturday Night Live,* 'cause they've got, like, forty sketches. And they keep changing.

"So I said, 'I can't read cue cards, I just can't do the show.'

"Well, Lorne Michaels brought Tina Fey and Amy Poehler and the girls back to support me, and we had the most marvelous fun. But it was panic-making. But they have a cue card man back there, who was so marvelous. He said, 'When you're doing a scene with Tina, don't look at Tina, look over her head, and I'll be way in the back with a big printed cue card. And she's doing the same thing over your head, so don't be nervous about it. But your eyes won't be like over there, they're right into camera.' I thought, 'Why didn't I discover this years and years ago?' And you know what, David? I got the Emmy!"

Estelle Getty, who played Sophia Petrillo (the wisecracking, Sicilian mother of Bea Arthur's character, Dorothy), had a mental block that made her always flub the punch line. Every single humorous thing that she had to say, she'd flub—but she'd only flub in front of an audience. So I was asked to come in and help with Estelle's problem.

I decided to tape her in the afternoon with an audience, and then tape her later, after the audience was gone. We added in the laugh track, and it worked great, but she still never got her lines right when she was in front of the audience. I thought maybe it had to do with an unknown childhood fear of hers, something that kept her from moving forward. But in Estelle's case, as I learned later, it was something completely different. It was only after Estelle passed away in 2008 that I learned that her inability to remember a line was an early sign of Lewy body dementia, a progressive condition that would cause her to freeze momentarily and forget where she was. Estelle was a terrific comic actress, and *Golden Girls* was a success because of her.

And then there was Bea. Bea Arthur.

To Bea or Not to Bea.

A Golden Girl? Well . . .

Let's take a step back.

Bea Arthur—she was a whole different story compared to Betty and Estelle. In fact, I found her to be terrifying. I remember a dinner party I attended given by Hal Cooper, a well-known director of sitcoms, whom I'd apprenticed for when I was starting out. He'd also invited Bea Arthur, knowing I'd directed her in *Golden Girls*.

Now, I'm not really a party guy, but there I was sitting next to Bea, Gene Saks (her husband and a Broadway director of many Neil Simon plays), and a few other couples. They were talking about the Torah, and I was just listening, not saying anything, until someone asked, "What's the Talmud?"

Now, I don't need to be the best kid in the class, but I did study to be a rabbi in my misspent youth, so I said, "The Talmud is the book of laws about how you live your life."

And Bea just said, "Is it?"

And I said, "Yeah." She seemed bothered by that.

She was getting a little drunk, and another issue came up about the Jewish dietary laws. This time I didn't open my mouth, so Bea said, "I want to know what Jewface has to say about this." And looked directly at me.

"Jewface?"

She called me "Jewface" all night. (By the way, Bea *was* Jewish.)

It wasn't just me, though. I found out later that Bea Arthur terrified every new director on the show. The crew thought that she liked to make people's lives a little unpleasant so that hers might be a little more pleasant.

One week, she gave me a lot of trouble on the set. She had a ritual where she'd sit down with me after the show and have a gin and tonic. After having had a few G&Ts, she leaned her arm on me and said, "David, why do people take such an instant dislike to me?"

And I said, "It just saves time."

That remark spread like wildfire, and the whole crew laughed hysterically. She grabbed me and sort of hugged me.

"How did you come up with that so fast?" she asked.

"It would be a natural for someone coming out of Second City," I replied.

To be totally honest, I had never had that kind of conversation or experience when I worked on *Friends,* which played for ten years (and many more years in reruns), and got a record-breaking fee of $500 million to continue to stream—this for a show that first aired more than twenty-five years ago! At the risk of sounding like I am blindly in love here, directing this classic, a show that was always true to its creation, honest and candid yet constantly original, was always an absolute delight— every second, every encounter, every single give-and-take. This is somewhat unusual given that these actors had been playing these roles, being these characters, for years by the time I came along, and that normally, as success becomes this huge, the egos grow and interrupt the flow, sometimes bringing toxicity and stress to the process of directing. Not here. Not once. *Friends'* characters and humor were always (no matter how many times you watch each episode) authentic yet somehow continuously surprising, which is amazing over all these years. Some people say the direction is always great—I say it's Marta Kauffman's brilliance in creating and developing these kind of deliciously funny characters (with her writing partner, David Crane), story lines that are based on real moments in life, and making them memorable and funny every single time. Marta's sincere devotion to telling the truth, with consistent humor, storytelling at its best, is what puts her on the level of the most elite writers of humor that is everlasting. And Marta and Dave were wonderful to work with—professional, collaborative, egoless— and they loved the characters they created, which I think transferred to the actors, because there was not an ego, that I could see, in sight, either. (Interesting story: Marta and Dave both went to Brandeis at the same time and were in the theater program together. She was tapped to direct *Godspell,* offered David a role, but he didn't want it. Later, Marta asked him to create and direct the show with her, and they worked together for thirty years.)

Then there are the stars of *Friends*—six different actors, sharing characteristics of their talent while always being true to their individual characters. As a group, they were easy to direct because their characters were already set and developed, and their family of their "friends" were familiar to each and all of them. It would have been easy to underestimate these uniquely talented actors because they were so young, so gorgeous, and worked so well together. And they were beloved by their millions of fans.

Matthew Perry was always witty, lighthearted, and really gifted. He was able to take his innate charm and give the banter a likeable, ironic edge that set his character apart. Lisa Kudrow was a smart actress, serious about her work, who was focused on details and never needed a note (but would be receptive when she got one). "Phoebe" could have easily become a silly caricature whose humor was more daffy than entertaining—but she never did, due to both Marta's writing and Lisa's respect for her character. Jennifer Aniston was so light in her comedy, which belied her hard work to be true to the aura of her character's goodness, love of life, and patience for those around her. And her timing was exceptional. Courteney Cox took what Marta created—gorgeous, obsessive, determined yet cautious "plain girl" turned beauty, whose various careers on the way to being a chef were just so funny. Who can forget when she had the behind-the-counter job at a diner where she wore a blond "stripper" wig and huge rubber breasts and played against Jon Favreau as a tech billionaire who loved her! She made us love her, and she made me love her, as she was both brave and smart in her acting. Hardworking David Schwimmer was a perfect part of the team because his character didn't need to get the laughs all the time, and David was so secure with that. He worked hard to move the story forward, managing to combine sarcasm with truth, without ever seeming to be acting. And, of course, Matt LeBlanc, who I think was somewhat

underrated in his comedy, was an original talent who created an original character, one who took the personality of a "dumb" boy/man and
gave it a loving charm, something that is not easy to do. He was beloved
by all. So the beauty of the success of *Friends* was that gifted creators
were able to bring perfectly and truthfully created characters to life with
hugely talented actors, all making *Friends* a joy to direct.

I have to say that I had the same exhilarating and rewarding experience in directing *Mad About You,* but the story is a little different. How
many actresses do you know who can handle both comedy and drama
and win the highest awards for both? My choice for best in both is
Helen Hunt, whom I directed in *Mad About You* over the eight years of
the show's run.

Now "marry" Helen to Paul Reiser, whose top-heavy titles are al-

Directing on the set of *Mad About You,* 1996. I loved working with Paul Reiser and
Helen Hunt. I believe this was around the time that Helen tried to set me up with
her mother, but Paul didn't think it was such a good idea. It never happened.

ways connected to success, adulation, and admiration, who is an award-winning comedian, actor, musician, producer, writer, and all-around wonderful, good man, and you have an absolutely all-time great duo whose successful show was brought back for a twelve-episode limited series revival in 2019.

Even though *Mad About You* starred both Helen Hunt and Paul Reiser, it was Paul who was the creator (with Danny Jacobson) and executive producer, and who wrote the theme song (with Don Was). Paul was also the dominant force in the writers' room for the entire eight-year run, working from 5 a.m. to midnight, until he was sure that the words were right. Later in the run, Helen joined the writing team, and both Paul and Helen were in and out of the writers' room (she was a good writer herself). Paul was also busy running around schmoozing everyone on the set, which resulted in the show's blossoming, and, most of all, in what is the best lesson from and description of this comedy: Paul trusted that the audience didn't need a laugh a minute, that controversy was not something to fear, but to embrace, jump into, and make an important part of the comedy.

Paul (whose mother's name was also Helen) was and is a huge talent. He graduated from the special high school for those super-smart kids, Stuyvesant High School in New York City, and got a degree from Binghamton University in piano and composition (add that to the titles above). It was there that he first encountered theater, especially stand-up comedy. He met director Barry Levinson, who was working on a film, *Diner,* which would become a classic. Barry offered Paul the part of Modell, who was a stand-up comedian, and everyone noticed the talent on-screen. Since Paul's identity all these years has been so tied into *Mad About You,* you may have forgotten that Paul was in more than thirty films, including *Beverly Hills Cop I and II, Aliens,* and *The Marrying Man.* His TV career began with the show *My Two Dads,* and then *Mad About You* happened (164 episodes over eight years—think of that).

I have worked with Paul Reiser for many years, eight of them on *Mad About You,* and in all honesty I can tell you that those accolades above are just the beginning. His kindness and generosity, in life and in his work, are legendary. His discipline puts those of us who consider ourselves workaholics to shame. His attention to others' opinions and recommendations is always one of total respect. His devotion to his family—he has been married to his wonderful "therapist wife," Paula, for decades.

And then, of course, there is his humor—you had better be on your toes when you are around him because he is always at his best then, and his pointed observations are very sharp and unforgettable. He is not super-organized, but he knows what is funny, and to Paul, that is dealing with ordinary moments in life, through a different lens. For example, I remember the Thanksgiving show called "Giblets for Murray" (their dog), which I directed and which fans still love, and it tells you everything about the kind of comedy that was *Mad About You*—full of huge moments, from surprise to shock, and little brilliant gestures that made it all perfectly funny ("Do you have to leave the toilet paper roll empty? Really? Do you know what 'changing the toilet paper' means?"), because their comedy was all about what normal things people do, the way they relate to each other and go through their normal days, but occasionally their dysfunction bursts out in an outrageous fashion, which is so funny. Things like making a Thanksgiving pie—and leaving out the sugar. A little thing—but let me walk you through that episode, which showcases the comedy at every turn, setting this show apart from others, seeing how the comedy builds as we take an ordinary scene and turn it into chaos and crisis.

Rehearsal: Preparing for Thanksgiving dinner. Paul and Jamie are making the turkey together. They prepare it. They put it on the table. Murray the dog jumps up on it and practically swallows it whole (not difficult to direct). Jamie and Paul run to the store to get another turkey. They bring it home and put it in for a quick cook. As Jamie removes the turkey from the oven, places it on a platter, and carries it to the set Thanksgiving table, there is a knock at the door. Jamie's parents are outside. They are early. Jamie panics. She can't open the door carrying the platter with the turkey. She pivots 180 degrees, still holding the turkey on the platter, and throws it out the window (we go through five turkeys preparing this scene).

Another comedy technique used a lot on *Mad About You* is called "misdirection." An example of misdirection is when you are made to think something you are seeing is one thing, but when the camera (or the actor) moves, from another angle you realize it's something completely different. If done right, the element of surprise can be funny (in our case), or scary, depending on the genre. In *Mad About You,* a misdirection would be created by setting up a shot so the audience sees a woman from the back in Helen and Paul's apartment, and she appears to be knitting, and when the camera comes around, the viewers see that it's a big, burly man who is talking to Helen. It's a good comic relief, and it always works.

Paul was also a force as an actor, which made for a combination that was always true to what their comedy was—make the show about the way the characters interact with each other, and don't be afraid to give up the laughs to others. And Paul and Helen had different approaches to studying the characters and their lines. Helen would sometimes retreat to a corner, sometimes another room, and study her lines. This meant that she was always well prepared—totally, perfectly, with every nuance in place, every gesture just right. Paul—not so much. But that's because he always wanted options, and I gave them to him, because he was a collaborator at heart. Do I sound like a fan? Absolutely.

Now let's get those astonishing Helen Hunt award-winning credits on the record first, for acting, directing, and screenwriting. As Jamie Buchman in *Mad About You* (1992–1999), she won three Golden Globe Awards and four Emmys for that work. She won the Academy Award for Best Actress as Carol Connelly in the romantic comedy *As Good as It Gets* (1997) and got another Oscar nomination in 2012 for *The Sessions.* Helen also made her directorial film debut with *Then She Found Me* (2007). Lately, she has also been directing episodes of such television series as *House of Lies, This Is Us, Feud: Bette and Joan,* and *American Housewife.*

When I first directed Helen, she shyly told me that she had collected all my albums. That was because of her dad, Gordon Hunt, who was also great at everything—he was a director of children's theater, and then all theater, he was an opera buff, he taught acting, and, oh yes, he was the love of her life and one of the nicest (and most talented) people I have ever met. It didn't hurt that he loved my comedy and regularly watched me on *The Tonight Show.* That must be how Helen first became my fan and memorized many of my comedic pieces. Often, and while we were working, she would recite parts of my albums to me. (I couldn't get over that—can you imagine? The star of the show I am directing recited bits from my albums.) We worked so hard during the shoot, and she was so intent on hearing what I, the director, had to say. Even once we started going to spinning (the exercise, not the drugs) class together, we ended up talking about the show, asking what could be better. Always working. Just astonishing to me to this day.

For me, since I directed her for so many years and really knew her work up close, Helen is one of the best female comic actresses I ever worked with. She would come to work on the first day after she got the script and fake it, pretending she was just reading it like any actor would on that first day, but she knew it by heart—she had memorized it in one take. She was the most principled and disciplined, totally focused actor. But what stood out most about Helen Hunt, and this is not just throughout all her years on *Mad About You* but in all her work, is that there was—and is—a delicacy about her comedic work. We all recognize, and admire, the obvious, often brave, more in-your-face, brashly worded comedy. Helen's never was, not even when she raised her voice to make a funny point funnier, to give back to Paul when he threw it to her. The challenge was to get to that belly laugh. Helen's comedy was instilled with elegance, a translucent aura that—and it was usually suddenly—would make you laugh so hard as to hold your sides. She was a puzzle, that Helen Hunt, because she could be light as a feather one minute and a ballbuster the next, while never, ever, losing her loveliness and class.

And she was a truly good director. She listens to everyone, and always with respect to the other directors. The thing is that she is so much better than those around her that it behooves anyone who works with her to listen to her thoughts. Sometimes the crew found them- selves working long days because she was so serious about her work; she was a perfectionist, so she wanted to do things over and over again until it was . . . perfect. And she was right. Period.

Two personal Helen stories remain in my heart—and they involve her parents. One is funny. The other, well, you judge. One time, Helen's mother, Jane, was visiting the set, and she walked over to me (when directing, I often stand on the sidelines, watching the cast and giving slight directions when I think it's needed). As I was standing there, she asked me to get her a cup of coffee. So I did. As I was giving her the coffee, Helen said, "Mom, what are you doing?"

"This man just got me a cup of coffee."

"Mom—he is the DIRECTOR! You do NOT ask the director to get you a cup of coffee."

Now I feel bad. Yes, I am low-key, and it wasn't a big deal to get her a cup of coffee. I was just standing there thinking about the next shot.

My other "favorite but not really so favorite" Hunt story: As we said, Helen's father, Gordon Hunt, was a director of theater and animation—a truly lovely person—and Helen mentioned that he wanted to direct television, so I welcomed him on the set with us as we were working. He's then on the set with us for months. So one day I asked Helen, "How about if I let your dad direct this show?" and she said, "Wow, that would be great, but I don't think I can talk Paul [Reiser] into it."

Now, I don't make such a decision lightly, hiring someone else to direct a show I am supposed to do. I tell Helen's father, "You know how to do it. Don't worry about anything; don't fake anything. This is my crew. You know them. They know everything that they have to do, and they're going to protect you anyway. And incidentally, this is how they work with me. So they don't even need me." And then I talk Paul into it—he's reluctant to let me do it, but he does. I go off to shoot some Kmart commercials with Penny Marshall and Rosie O'Donnell, and they make a fortune for me, and I come back, and everyone is happy.

So I make my money on Kmart, Gordon directs that show—carefully, respectfully but with strong guidance, with his own touch of what I sometimes call "serious humor." With determined focus, he lets the actors feel their humor so they can still let loose with their own touches. Now that's a talent. So Gordon has his first directing gig, and he does a great job. I come back, they're all glad to see me, I'm glad to see them, and we go on. And then I get nominated for a *Mad About You* episode for a Directors Guild Award, as I happily and gratefully have been before, and to all our surprise and delight, Gordon gets nominated for his episode of *Mad About You.*

I go to the awards ceremony. Helen and Gordon go as well. I'm sitting there, as is Helen's father, and they say, "The DGA award for a comedy series goes to Gordon Hunt for *Mad About You.*" He had directed that one nominated show—and I directed fifty shows—and he won! I was thrilled for him, truly I was, but it was the most ironic thing in the world to win for the first show he directed. Later, Gordon went on to direct thirty episodes, but, honestly, to this day, that moment seeing Gordon Hunt accept the DGA award for directing his daughter's show warms my heart. Gordon died in 2016, at age eighty-seven.

Mad About You lasted eight seasons, and in the last year, it was a struggle to keep the creative spark alive. A form of cabin fever set in. Which might explain why one week Helen Hunt tried to set me up on a date with her mother.

"No no no no no. No!" said Paul, his eyes spinning at the thought of all the queasy conflicts of interests this implied, when I told him what Helen had suggested.

He went to Helen and said, "This is much too weird a situation for me. I can't take a note from my director when he's just come from fucking my co-star's mother."

So although Jane Hunt is a beautiful woman, I had to give this semi-incestuous thrill a pass, even while the show and my personal life were intertwining in increasing ways. This is going to sound weird, but besides directing the show over many years, I played several parts on the show, including the offstage voice of a man trapped in an elevator, one of my favorite phobias (yes, I hate elevators and avoid them at all costs), and an Armani-wearing rabbi.

During one of the show's best years, my "lovely then twelve-year-old daughter" Rebecca went through an interesting phase where she decided that Rebecca was a boring name and announced to everyone she knew that she would now be known as Sonya Steinberg. Naturally, this intrigued Paul, who, just for the fun of it, refused to use the S-word. So when I brought my daughter to a show I was directing, he said, "Hi, Rebecca! How ya doin'?"

First she stared at him without answering, and then said, "Who do you think you're talking to?" her voice dripping with utter contempt for the man responsible for funding her housing, schooling, and extensive wardrobe.

"You!" said Paul, absolutely delighted.

"My name is Sonya, as you know," said my "lovely daughter" icily, and this made Paul even happier, so between shots he followed her around the soundstage, calling out her ex-name and getting nothing but The Stare.

Why am I telling this story? First, I love it. Second, in the last episode of *Mad About You,* Paul and Jamie Buchman find themselves twenty years older, divorced, and the parents of an icily contemptuous young woman who's changed her name from Mabel to Sonya. Janeane Garofalo played the part beautifully. My "lovely daughter," who looks exactly like Janeane, was openly contemptuous of the casting. This last show broke all ratings records.

While I was directing *Mad About You,* I got that call to direct Rosie O'Donnell and Penny Marshall in a series of Kmart spots. Given that I have been directing comedians on sitcoms and in commercials for decades, I had learned one characteristic they all have in common—they prefer being directed by other comedians because they share a sensibility, a kind of private language that results in a shorthand of sorts and a successful collaborative result.

Among the commercials with comedians that I directed in 1986 were the spots for Pizza Hut with the then-unknown Garry Shandling and Roseanne Barr (two years before *Roseanne*). When you use new comedians, it's a celebration inside you, the director, to be able to see someone finding another way to do comedy. When directing them, it was also like speaking another language because they were both unusual, unlike any other actors. All I had to say was "Action" because there was so much of themselves in their words, in their mannerisms, in their actions. I would give them the basic idea ("don't overdo anything," which was unusual with their personalities), and they would get on camera, and you could hear the ringing laughter from those around them. They were original, pure and simple.

Garry Shandling, in the Pizza Hut commercial, improvising, adding his own personality: "Pizza is a real single man's delicacy 'cause you can pick it up on the way home, there is no commitment, and you can eat it in your underwear." What a character. What a comic. What an actor. What a writer. What a man.

Garry was the star and writer of one of the most original comedy series ever produced on television. He was a frequent guest and guest host on *The Tonight Show Starring Johnny Carson,* and he was probably one of the best stand-up comedians you will ever see. He was so easy to talk to—not because he was easygoing, which he wasn't, but because you can give him any line, any opening, and he is off and you are laughing nonstop.

"Garry, you look good, man."

"Thanks, David. I thought I was going to have to say it. I think I look fantastic. I can't see a mirror from here, but I was hoping to get a glance of myself. Too bad my mom isn't here. I could always see myself in her eyes. You know why I talk about my mom a lot? I tend to use whatever's bothering me at the time. After college, I moved here by myself, and when I moved, my mother sued me for palimony, saying, 'Twenty-two years you live with me and you move out just like that? I don't think so!'

"My mother, who was Jewish, wanted to marry me. The fact is, for many, many years I would pick women who were the complete opposite of my mother, which is white, gentile cocaine addicts. I used to joke a lot about my father, and my mother said to me, 'How come you only joke about your father and not me?' Thereby opening up, parting the sea, and allowing me to talk about her until she said, 'Gee, why are you saying those things about me?'

"So, you know, you can't have it both ways. But the fact that she was into my act and saying, 'How come I'm not in your act more,' does that give you a beginning of understanding the issue? I mean, there comes a point when you let your child not only lead his own life, but let him do his own act onstage. So, I think that's a perfect example, right—doesn't 'How come I'm not in your act more' just say it all?"

Hard to believe, but Garry actually studied electrical engineering at the University of Arizona and went to graduate school at UCLA, where he took a comedy writing class, and that began his writing career. I always figured someone had to be funny in his family for him to have been exposed to his kind of unusual humor.

"Nope," he says seriously. "Not that I know of. And the reason I say that is that my family was in Chicago, and I grew up in Arizona. So now we're at the Woody Allen influence, which is when I was thirteen or twelve or something. Woody had done a guest spot on a morning show where kids would write in and ask questions about how things were made, and the segment was on how they make baseball bats. And he took us through a tour of the Louisville Slugger baseball company. And he was holding a bat and he said, 'They're made of halavah, so when you strike out, you can eat it.'"

Now you can tell why *The Larry Sanders Show* was a landmark show for comedy, but Garry's comedic talent was not just in stand-up. I gave him his first commercial for a Pizza Hut spot. He never forgot that I gave him his start. For Pizza Hut, I also gave a start to Roseanne Barr and Adam Sandler, before he became a comedian, but he was already funny. Adam was fifteen or sixteen years old when he auditioned for me, and they didn't want someone that young for the commercial, but I thought he was as sharp and funny as can be, instantly funny, almost like a professional but with the spontaneity of a comedian. But Garry's spontaneity, his kind of insane and always unpredictable sense of comedy, came out of his own soul, his own kind of torment. His persona on television was really who he was—anxiety-ridden, guarded with his feelings, somehow on the verge of losing control. By 1986, he and my good friend, the prolific comedy writer Alan Zweibel, created *It's Garry Shandling's Show*. It ran for four years, and then for many more in reruns, winning many awards for the show and for Garry. What was so unique about the show was that Garry broke the "fourth wall" and talked directly to the audience, and incorporated the audience and elements of the studio into the story lines. And that humor was almost as insanely funny as anything on television.

In 1992, Garry created another huge commercial and critical success, *The Larry Sanders Show*. That ran for six years on HBO and was nominated for fifty-six Emmys. It was based on all those times Garry guest hosted *The Tonight Show*. How did he get to host it? That was the biggest prize for a comedian.

"I was writing for some television shows, but I got bored with it, so I went to perform at the Comedy Store, and I was awful, and I thought, 'My God! I don't know what I'm doing!' so I really worked hard for three or four years, and Jim McCauley, who was the talent booker on *The Tonight Show* back then, saw me at the Comedy Store, and I did one ten-minute set, and he said, 'We want you on next week.' I go on *The Tonight Show* and have exactly the same kind of set, which changed my career. That and the first time I guest hosted—and it was, and is, the most emotional moment in my career—not even my own shows or anything have compared to that moment. It was monumental. I think it was probably connected to growing up watching Johnny. It was just an organic place for me to be."

Garry goes on, quietly and thoughtfully, "I think my work is a search for artistic expression, and whatever my limits are, they are, and then I explore and push. I was at the Austin Film Festival last year, and I showed one episode of *It's Garry Shandling's Show,* and one episode of *The Larry Sanders Show,* and someone in the audience asked, 'Which of those is the closest to you?'

"And I didn't have a good answer. I thought the first show is most like me, but probably Larry Sanders is not what I'm like because that was a departure—to be able to play in different emotions—but I think they're all versions of things that definitely interest me and are internal."

Amazingly, Garry was offered to take over both *Late Night with David Letterman,* when Letterman moved to CBS, and *The Late Late Show,* and declined both offers to stay with his beloved *Larry Sanders Show.*

Many times over the years, Garry and I would discuss all kinds of subjects, from politics to entertainment and the idiosyncrasies of both. But we almost never discussed his personal life. Garry was never married, had no kids. He meditated, was a Buddhist who just couldn't leave it alone:

Buddha didn't get married because his wife would have been yelling, "Are you going to sit around like that all day?"
"Well, I'm meditating, honey."
"Well, why don't you go meditate while you're taking out the

trash? Breathe in, take out the trash, breathe out, put it in the can.
Why don't you work on that?"

And surprisingly enough, for someone who looked so laid-back and kind of sedate underneath that anxiety, he played basketball with huge enthusiasm and boxed several times a week (he owned a boxing studio with some friends). Why?

"I loved it. I go to a little gym. You can't see it; it's in Santa Monica, next to—and this is true—a synagogue. Really, once I was in there, and we were sparring, and I was really beating this guy, and then I realize I'd walked in the wrong door and was beating up the rabbi. And I'm just pounding him, and I was thinking what a small head protector he's got. And the crowd's going crazy. And they said, 'Wow, that was the most violent Passover service we've ever had!' Boxing is a metaphor for life—it's really like acting class, David, because you gotta be in the moment. So that's my struggle in life, is to be in the moment."

I once asked him, "What is your skill in basketball?"

His answer, "To call time-out. First, to be out of breath in my game, that's my defensive technique. I'm breathing hard enough so you think you could kill me if you drive. I played in one celebrity game, about eight years ago, where the coach of the team was Jerry West. And this is really true, and still hurts my feelings—he had me defending Whoopi Goldberg."

I could never keep up with Garry because he would move from pretty funny to insanely funny in a nanosecond.

A sample: "You know, I have written a eulogy. I'm not mad at anyone; it's just something I wanted to do for myself. Sort of passive-aggressive, in a way. Because the people who know what they've done to you are gonna be pissed when they read it. I'm looking for someone to do the foreword for the note. If you would do it, that would be fantastic. Like: 'I know Garry is a stable man, so if he's done something like this, there's a good reason. And I think you're gonna be fascinated when you hear what it says.'"

I respond, "Garry, are you writing my foreword now? Is that what's happening?"

Unfazed, he replies, "I'm sorry. What foreword would you write for my suicide note?"

I said, "The loss to the comedy world is insurmountable. But he wasn't doing that much anyway before tonight, so maybe it was the right thing." Garry died in 2016. He was sixty-six. A thousand comedians showed up at his memorial service. I miss him to this day. I know we all do.

Bill Cosby had the hit show *The Cosby Show* in the '80s, when he was hired to do his enormously successful Jell-O commercials. *The Cosby Show* was a huge phenomenon—it was on television for eight years, the epitome of a family sitcom, and it had been streaming ever since until now. At that time, it was one of the most popular family sitcoms ever, so when it came time to be working with somebody for Jell-O, which was a commercial they planned to do with kids, Kraft/General Foods picked Cosby. Bill was their spokesperson over the span of twenty-five years. The company had come up with the idea to include children, to have Bill interact with them, and they had scripted a back-and-forth for them. When they called me and I stepped in, I already knew Cosby and felt comfortable trying to come up with something other than a plan to have young kids memorize lines—which would be, if not impossible, certainly difficult, time-consuming, and would rob both Cosby, a seasoned and brilliant comedian, and the young kids of their spontaneity.

You probably know this—in commercials, boards are set up with lines for the actors to read. I just knew that this conventional plan was not going to work with kids. Kids are much more fun when they're not saying scripted words, even if they could memorize them. So I worked with both Bill and the kids just to be able to talk with them. We kept the cameras rolling, had them talk to and with each other and to Cosby spontaneously, and Cosby also guided them to be funny and bring in the Jell-O—and we had them talk for some time, so that we would be able to edit together a whole commercial. That resulted in hugely popular commercials that were also amusing and engaging. People loved them, as did Kraft.

It quickly became obvious that the kids loved Cosby, because he was naturally funny with them, and we were able to catch that on tape. As for me, Cosby kept asking for me to direct these Jell-O commercials, one after the other, perhaps because they were so successful, but also because I got him out by lunch. Yes, Cosby showed up every day with the same request.

"David, I would like to be out by noon."

I would reply, "Bill, you are getting a million dollars per commercial. What's the hurry?"

I figured I was the only guy he knew who could shoot a million-dollar commercial with a bunch of kids and get the star out by noon. The truth is that, even working with Rosie O'Donnell and Penny Marshall, doing many Kmart commercials, I was known as a director who doesn't waste time, as a director who does not need to have twenty takes of a scene, who doesn't often need to do a cover shot. I direct, I shoot, and move on. This also made me popular with all the crews. I would not be exaggerating if I said that they adored me, because, really, getting out by noon? One take? Not second-guessing myself? Cosby was a master at doing one take. Well.

It is hard to imagine Bill Cosby as anything but the brilliant talent that he was at the time, and I've known him since my career began. It is even harder for me to imagine the catastrophe that is his life now, and the horrendous tragedy for everyone involved. For me, he will always be the brilliant artist, but the image of him hurting anyone, and ending up in prison, is absolutely unfathomable, and unforgivable. Tragic.

I should note that I directed many of these commercials in the 1980s, and doing this work was an expansion of my work in directing, which was to be further expanded yet again when, a few months later, my ex-valet-parking attendant, Larry Charles, decided to give me a call. Larry was absolutely penniless, an odd-looking skinny kid with long stringy hair who wore pajamas day and night. Now he's an unbelievably rich, odd-looking skinny man with shorter long stringy hair who wears pajamas day and night. In other words, a man of towering self-esteem, integrity, and eccentricity.

In the late '70s, Larry Charles worked at the Century West Club, a gym in West LA that's so fancy, it hires people to park your car for you so you don't have to exert yourself walking from the parking lot to the front door of the gym. All the valet parkers vied to park my car, which was nice for my morale, until Larry told me much later that their real motivation was the leftover roaches (marijuana) in my ashtray. When Larry was able to beat them back, he told me he was a writer and asked me to look at some material he'd written for me. I was only reasonably polite to Larry, because as everybody knows, the hardest thing in comedy is to write in the voice of another person.

One day, I was scheduled to go on *The Tonight Show* at 5:30. It was 3:00 in the afternoon, and, since I hadn't thought of a single thing to talk about and was in an absolute panic, I gave the weird kid a break and used his material, word for word. The next day, Carson told me, "That was vintage Steinberg!" I basked in this hard-won admiration and gave Larry the check I received for that show.

So, Larry Charles had dented his last Lamborghini as a valet parker. For the next few years, I hired him to write my *Tonight Show* appearances and work on lots of other projects. He then ended up as one of the producers of *Mad About You,* wrote on *Seinfeld,* and worked on many other films. Around 1980, Larry Charles asked me to hire a friend of his, Larry David, who had produced a short-lived ABC skit show, *Fridays,* and was now living in New York City, broker than broke.

Then, as now, Larry David was a brilliant, hardworking, and—get ready for a shock—non-neurotic and reasonably self-confident individual. I used him as a character in our promos, a construction worker in the background. And then it's fifteen, sixteen years later, and Larry Charles calls me up and says, "Hey, David! Why don't you come work for Larry David, like I'm doing? We're doing a new show for NBC called *Seinfeld.*"

I directed *Seinfeld,* which I loved—then went on to direct Larry's new show, *Curb Your Enthusiasm.* Directing anyone, but especially Larry David, is like being the captain of a ship—you are one of the

At the *Vanity Fair* Oscar Party with two of my favorite people, Martin Short and Larry David, February 2016. I think that's the night that Larry disappeared for an hour and took a nap on one of the couches outside during the party, but I could be mistaken.

last to leave the set. But no matter how late I left the set of *Seinfeld,* I'd always see the lights on in Larry David's and Jerry Seinfeld's writing rooms. They would be burning the midnight oil, perfecting something that seemed tossed off in a moment. What looked improvised was in fact meticulous writing on an almost granular level. For shows that were famous for "being about nothing," they were perfected and polished until the moment we started shooting. Everything was weighed and considered, and there were infinite possibilities as to how a bit could go. What seems so casual and tossed off—a lot of blood, sweat, and tears have gone into it.

Everything in comedy, especially television comedy, is about the writing. Especially when you're creating a character. Larry David is not quite the *Curb* character that he presents himself as. He's actually a generous person and a loyal friend. But he doesn't suffer fools gladly. People do get on his nerves. In a difficult encounter, you or I might walk away, but Larry would tell the person, "You're getting on my nerves." And either the person would laugh and walk away or—well, they better walk away if they're smart.

Curb Your Enthusiasm is Larry David's baby, but directing Larry on that show is almost an extension of my own life. What we did was often based on sharing our deep secrets and making them part of his character. It helped that we had similar traits. For example, he and I always wanted to go home no matter who we were with. I liked to go to my house, he liked to go to his.

Another example: we both hate it when we go out for dinner and someone says, "Let's have a drink at this restaurant but go to dinner at that restaurant." Larry would not go, nor would I. I'd always say, "I don't do that." Why schlep to this restaurant, which can take a half hour, then get back in the car, drive somewhere else, get out of the car, go into another restaurant—where they also serve drinks! Just to have dinner? I refuse to schlep to two different places. So Larry was a one-restaurant person, and so was I.

Larry David cherishes the comedy culture in a way that few people do. At first, I mattered to him because we both had a reverence for comedy history. And the fact that I wasn't afraid to lose my popularity by isolating myself from the public gaze—that registered with Larry, and I think that's what our relationship is based on. He's a dear friend to have, and he prides himself on his friendships.

So what was Larry like when he was twelve? I ask him.

"Very, very happy-go-lucky," he explains, smiling.

I am puzzled, because this is not the Larry I know. "You were happy-go-lucky? When did that change?"

"Puberty. The moment girls came into the picture. I want them. How do you get them? I can't get them. I want them naked. I want to touch them. I never wanted something so bad, and I couldn't, didn't know how to do it. And I couldn't hide the fact but I desperately wanted them, you know."

I keep prodding. "So, you're anxious, and happy-go-lucky goes away, and the person that's sitting here now, is sitting here now."

"The mess, yes. Girls really turned me into a mess, they did."

I can't stop. "Now, did you date at all?"

"You mean in high school? No. Who was I going to ask out? Some-body in the school? Then I have to see them again the next day? Just the idea that we were out together, and then I have to see them? No. I couldn't have negotiated it the next day. It would have thrown me."

I try again. "It's not a healthy way in which you approach dating. You might start by dating someone who you think might be a friend of yours—"

Larry: "Nobody I've ever dated was my friend. And, by the way, if they were, the friendship was over as soon as I rang the doorbell."

I decide to move on. I ask Larry a question I often ask comedians. "If you weren't a comedy star, could you do anything else? What would you do?"

He doesn't hesitate for a second. "I have no skills at all. I can't do anything, really. Well, I'm a good parallel parker. I can work at a hotel taking tickets and getting their cars. I think I'd be very good at it. I see the people park the cars, I don't think they're better than I am at that."

He considers this a bit. "You know, my mother wanted me to be a mailman. She begged me to take a civil service test. 'Larry, just take the test. What do you have to lose?' I don't know why she didn't think I was capable of doing anything other than that. I was getting out of college. I would have to schlep the mail to addresses. And the dogs. And the hail. You know the slogan: the rain and hail and sleet and the snow. I think I could have done the rain and the snow, but the hail would have done me in. I'm not going to deliver in hail. I would have gone to the supervisor and said, 'I'm sorry, I can't deliver in hail. You've got the big motto up there, but I'm not doing hail."

I suggest to Larry that his family didn't have big aspirations for him at all.

"That's an understatement, yeah. So I moved into the city and I got a job as a bra salesman. I put this on *Seinfeld*. With George, because this actually happened to me. They gave me a paper bag with bras, and I swear to you it sounds insane, but the manager said, 'Take the bras home and study them.'

"I said, 'I've been trying to study bras since I was thirteen.'

"And then I took an acting class at night. I don't know why acting—it seemed easy—you didn't have to write anything, like an essay. Seemed like the easiest way to go about getting attention. Which is what I desperately needed. And with attention came girls."

This I understood. "That's the motivation for every man getting into anything."

Larry continues. "So, I took an acting class, where they put on a couple of plays. But in the class, we had to do this character, use your own words to talk about what the characters were going through. I started talking, and people laughed. And that was the start of stand-up. One night, I went to the Improv with some friends. It was a Saturday night, and we're watching the show, and I'm watching the comedians, and I'm starting to think, 'I'm as funny as that guy!' I go up to Budd Friedman [who owned the Improv, first in New York and then in LA, and has for fifty years] in the middle of the show, and say, 'I'd like to go on.' I mean, that's insane. I had never set foot on a stage besides the acting class. And he goes, 'Who are you?'

"I go, 'I'm in the audience.'

"He goes, 'Have you ever done comedy? No? Then you can't go on. There are some clubs in the Village—go and perform there.' So, I said, 'Okay.' So I proceeded to announce to everybody that I was going to be a comedian. And I wrote some material for my performance at Gerde's Folk City in Greenwich Village for my first time. It was just beyond awful. I was doing terrible impressions, and stupid bits, nothing that expressed anything of who I was."

I stop him right there. "I've never known you to do an impression of anybody."

Larry agrees. "Because I don't do them very well. At the time, I did Howard Cosell, so I did Howard—you know that was the hip act. So, I did that a couple of times, and then I went to Catch a Rising Star and starting going on late at night, where I got laughs from the comedians and the waitresses."

I am impressed. "That's a big endorsement. The waitresses are more important than the comedians because the waitresses are tough. They don't laugh at anybody. They've seen everybody. So, they're saying that you've got something when they're doing that."

Larry remembers: "The audience, they weren't laughing so much. I think they sensed how uncomfortable I was. I think they picked up on that. And then I picked up on that, and I didn't know how to ingratiate myself with them. Like, other comedians would come up and they would go, 'Hey, how's everybody tonight? How's everybody doing? You having fun? You having a good time?' And I couldn't do that. I couldn't go onstage and say that to them because I could care less how they were doing. So I never asked them, and so there was like a wall between us, you know? 'This guy doesn't care about me. Why should I laugh at him?'"

Larry then moved to Los Angeles. I was one of the first hosts of a show like *Saturday Night Live* called *Fridays,* and they hired Larry to come on.

Says Larry, "You know, if you're going to copy a show called *Saturday Night Live,* try to get another title besides *Fridays.* Be a little less obvious in the rip-off. That's all. But I got the binder, and the title *Fridays* is splattered on. And I thought this was a joke. I thought it was a funny joke show. I thought they were going to change it to a real name, that this was a temp name as a laugh. And I went up to the producers and asked, 'Are you insane? You can't call this thing *Fridays.* You're going to be compared to *Saturday Night Live.*'"

After *Fridays,* Larry stayed around in LA for a couple of years doing stand-up, and then, in 1984, he moved back to New York and got a job as a writer on *SNL* that lasted one year.

"I got one sketch on in the entire season," he remembers. "I got disgusted with not having anything on the show, even though my sketches were doing well at the read-through. So one night, five minutes before air, they cut another sketch of mine, so I went up to Dick Ebersol, the executive producer at the time, and I said, 'That's it! I quit! This fuckin' show stinks! I'm out of here! I'm done! It's over!'

"So, I quit and walked home. And I went to Kenny Kramer, my next-door neighbor, and told him I quit the show. And I started to add up all the money that I just cost myself (enough for me to live on for two years), the idiotic move I just made, and I said to Kramer, 'I'm so stupid. I can't believe I did that.' So Kramer said, 'Go in on Monday and pretend the whole thing never happened.' Like the head of NBC would forget being accosted by a writer. But I figure, that's not a bad idea. So, on Monday morning, I go into a meeting with all the writers, as if it never happened. And the writers are looking at me like, 'What are you doing here? Are you out of your mind?' And the producer said nothing to me. And it worked. I slid right back in. I think I did that on *Seinfeld,* too."

On *Seinfeld,* Larry was basically behind the scenes—writing it, producing it with Jerry. Larry: "I remember the first year of *Seinfeld* was turbulent; I mean, it was hard to get the network to really accept what we were doing. They didn't like the style of writing. But the pilot got picked up, and they ordered four shows. Jerry and I wrote the first episode. I wasn't the executive producer, because they didn't really know me or trust me. They hired someone to be the executive producer, and so we handed in the first show, to this guy, and then we got called into his office for notes. I sat quietly while he gave us his notes on the show, and when he was finished, I looked at him and I said, 'No. I'm not going to do one thing. Not one thing.' And then we went back to Jerry's apartment. And I said, 'I'm sorry, but we can't do that. I'm not going to do that. Hey, you know, good luck with this.'

"But Jerry said, 'No, don't worry, we'll work it out.'

"So Jerry went back the next day and fixed the situation, and the producer was kind of neutered right after that. So we did the first four shows. And then we did the season for thirteen. And again, we filmed the whole year with a lot of battles. And then I was in New York over the summer, and we got called in for a big meeting by NBC. Everybody got called in: Castle Rock, Jerry, and Jerry's managers. And Castle Rock said to me, 'Listen don't say anything at the meeting, just let them talk, okay?'

"So again, I go in, they go, 'Okay, we like this show, we like that show, and that show, but we don't like these. (All the ones that I liked, of course.) So, we don't want to do any more shows like this. Here's what we want you to do.' And so I had promised them I wouldn't say anything, so I didn't say anything. And when I got outside I said, 'Look, good luck with this.'

"I go to Jerry, 'Good luck, I can't do it. My hand will not obey the command from my brain to do what they want me to do. So, I'm sorry, Jerry, I'm sorry. I can't do it.'

"And Jerry says, 'We'll talk to NBC.'

"Next day, I hear, we can 'do whatever you want.'

"And I realized, Jesus, the saying 'no' thing is so powerful. I mean, it's incredible. You see what can happen when you say 'no'? And I never knew it before."

I always ask every comedian, "Who influenced you?" For Larry, it was "Woody Allen, because he was writing and doing his own material, sort of playing some exaggerated version of himself. And some of Mel Brooks—the jazz in his speech, and the way he talks, almost an improvisational, a spontaneous style of talking and writing." Mel has a musical kind of quality in the way he talks, which both Larry and I always loved. The point was that we admired them, loved the writing and delivery, but we always had our own voices all the way through.

"I discovered quickly that the audience was not my friend," Larry explains. "So it was hard to bring whatever it was that I had offstage—to bring that onstage."

I feel the opposite. My influences were Woody Allen and Lenny Bruce as stand-ups, and I tried to write material like Woody Allen, to have a little edginess like Lenny Bruce. When I was at the Bitter End one night, there were just a few people in the audience, and a *New York Times* critic came in, but I felt that if anyone was going to see me, they would see that I had formed into my own person as a comedian. And the next day, *The New York Times* ran Dan Sullivan's great review of my show with the headline "David Steinberg, a Cross Between Woody Allen and Lenny Bruce." The critic saw right through me, but it still brought in crowds and started my career.

Larry explains, "People don't understand how hard it is to actually take the essence of who you are and bring it onstage, because when you try, it certainly doesn't sound that funny to strangers. The things that your friends would laugh at because they know you don't work with the audience that doesn't know you. They're not going to laugh at it."

The truth in stand-up is that you have to learn how to introduce yourself to every single new audience as if they've never heard of you and never seen you before. That's a scale of stand-up comedy. When you move into sitcoms, the air changes. I've been directing some episodes of *Curb Your Enthusiasm* for several years, and we've been having a great time. No one involved in the creation of the show, especially not Larry, ever expected it to be what it has become.

"I had no idea," says Larry. "I never thought *Seinfeld* would be anything, either. It's just not the way I think. I swear, and this is not false modesty, it doesn't even occur to me that something could be successful when I'm doing it, especially since we improvise all the time, which is because I'm not an actor. I can't act. I don't feel nearly as comfortable acting."

What's so interesting is who the audience is for *Curb*. In the last few years, it's reached a whole other level. *Curb* has a spontaneity and an honesty that people seem to like. People have never seen a character like Larry's character. You know what people ask me about Larry the most? "What is he? Is he really that character?" I reply the same way Larry does. First of all, that character certainly couldn't have executive-produced and written the show. On the other hand, there are so many things about doing that character that Larry and I love, because as honest as he is, Larry maintains, "that's how dishonest I am."

Larry continues, "Because my life is just so completely full of shit, twenty-four hours a day. Not an honest word ever escapes my lips. Everything is a lie, until when I do this character. Then, suddenly, it works. And I can't tell you what a pleasure it is for me to do it. That I can say the truth to somebody right there on the set, in any circumstance, and I can tell them exactly what I think. I aspire to be that character. I love the character. I do."

And I love directing that character. Because I was an actor and a performer, struggling and all that, I understood that it's about support. I think the only reason I had this career, *Seinfeld,* all these shows, was because I understood that Larry David needed support. And most directors would think the opposite.

A story. A few years ago, I get a late-night call from Larry. I took it in bed, where he was probably, too. I mean his own bed. My wife, Robyn, and Larry's then wife, Laurie, sleep soundly by our respective sides.

"David, it's me. Is it all right to call someone a cunt?"

"No, Larry, it's not," I say.

"Why not?"

"It's misogynistic."

"Misogynistic? That means anti-woman. But I'm saying it to a man."

"What kind of man?"

"An effeminate man. But one who's married."

"No good. Very misogynistic."

"Okay. Goodbye."

Click.

About three months later, I'm directing an episode of *Curb Your Enthusiasm*—"The Shrimp Incident"—and in that episode Larry is on the verge of losing a big deal with HBO because he calls one of its executives, who's an effeminate man, but married, a "cunt." And he calls this man a cunt because Julia Louis-Dreyfus has just bluffed him out of a winning hand in a friendly late-night poker game. He calls this man a "cunt" in what he thinks is the spirit of colorful, late-night-poker friendship.

The scene is between Larry and his manager, Jeff, played by Jeff Garlin.

ME: "Action."

LARRY (angrily): "Isn't it all right to call someone a cunt?"

JEFF (firmly): "No. It's not."

LARRY (angrily): "Why not?"

JEFF: "It's misogynistic."

LARRY (more anger): "Misogynistic? But I'm saying it to a man!"

JEFF: "An effeminate man."

LARRY (even more anger): "But he's a man who's married!"

JEFF: "No good. Very misogynistic."

LARRY (angriest): "Fuck! Shit! I forgot where I am! David?"

ME: "You're doing great! Keep rolling!"

And believe me, I meant it. In a life spent driving through comedy potholes, it doesn't roll along much better than that. All of which makes the point—not to preempt anybody's PhD thesis—that the television sitcom is a true American-invented art form, like jazz, that is tied in permanently to our pop culture.

It is hard not to rave about some comics, and there are many of those. But, honestly, there is something so unusual about Susie Essman that

Here with Susie Essman doing my podcast. A most kind, hilariously funny, and loving person, she couldn't be more different from her character Susie Greene on *Curb*. And no, I didn't ask her to tell me to go f*** myself.

sets her apart from all of us. There are comics who are terrific stand-ups. There are those who are also talented and remarkable actors. There are many who are thoughtful, and kind, good friends to all. There are some who are always funny, and I mean *always,* whether they are in character or themselves. And then there are a few who are all of the above. And Susie Essman is one.

Susie and I have known each other for years. Seeing her do her stand-up over the last twenty years has always been memorable. It's not just the funny. It's the *Jewish,* that huge smile, the totally irreverent stories, and extreme laughs. And then, after years of doing stand-up and acting and writing and producing, came *Curb Your Enthusiasm,* which changed her life, as she will always be known as Susie Greene and for her infamous "You fat fuck!" And it changed Larry David's life, as her character on the long-running show is a staple of each episode and of the show as a whole. And she could not be happier about it.

I have directed Susie on *Curb* many times over the years, and I can vouch for this truth: Larry David loves both Susies—Susie Essman and Susie Greene. Larry relies on Susie Essman because she excels on every *Curb* episode. Susie is a favorite on the show because she delivers an honest performance every time, one that doesn't feel like a joke. What stands out about Susie the actress and Susie the character and makes her a favorite on *Curb* is that she *is* the real deal—bold and unique, unlike any other character the audience has seen, unforgettable as that extremely exciting and scary character Larry created and Susie has brought alive. It is an unusual and unique talent to be able to carry things right to the edge without going over, and that is Susie Essman's genius. If you read her book, *What Would Susie Say?: Bullsh*t Wisdom About Love, Life, and Comedy,* you may think that the outrageousness and forthright personality of Susie Greene *is* Susie Essman. Not really. And that is Essman's genius, too—taking the character Larry created when the show first started, making sure Susie Greene is always true to herself, yet always taking chances to make her better.

Once again, we go back to Carol Burnett. Susie is emphatic. "When I was in high school, I never missed her show. The thing about *The Carol Burnett Show* was that they always looked like they were having the best time [and that's how we are at *Curb*. When we're on set, we have so much fun, laughing nonstop]. Seeing Carol Burnett years ago, I thought, 'I wanna do that.' One time, a friend in college and I were watching the show, and she turned to me and said, 'You could do that!' And that was one of the first times I thought, 'I *could* do that.' I graduated that year and started taking acting classes, but was extremely disillusioned by acting classes. It was all 'Go sit in the corner and pretend you're a pear' for half an hour, and I just hated it. And still, stand-up was not something I even thought of in my life. I had no idea, never thought, 'How do I get on *Saturday Night Live?*' And I went into a deep, deep depression. I was extremely lost, and I didn't know what to do with myself. I worked at a restaurant, and the only way I could make it bearable was by imitating the customers, who were all these people from Long Island. I used to do all of them. But no one was knocking down my door. Then I got onstage at a stand-up club and did these characters and realized that I had to develop a voice to become a comic. The trick was, how do I take the person that is so funny in the kitchen with my girlfriends and put that onstage. That was really hard."

And that is the bottom line. That is why stand-up is so hard. Every comedian who has done stand-up has a point of view, that voice. Finding that voice is everything. And Susie found it. "After about three months of doing stand-up, I remember thinking, 'This is what I was born to do.'" Years later, in 2000, came *Curb Your Enthusiasm.* Larry David created the show, which was a fictionalized version of his personality and his life, and he wrote it all. Susie's memory: "It's amazing, because the first season we were like—'I got a barn, let's do a show.' We didn't have trailers, we didn't have dressing rooms. The crew didn't even have porta potties. Talk about improvising!"

Once Larry created the other characters, he hired the best of the best to co-star with him, and realized that once the words were written, improvisation was the key to *Curb.* Susie explains something we both know. "The thing that people misunderstand about *Curb* is that it's not just this free-for-all improv. Each scene is so laid out and so delineated as to what's going to happen. So when you know your character, like I know mine, and you know your relationships with the other characters, it writes itself." Most comedians are not intimidated by improvisation. They have always done improv—Second City was built on it. But a lot of this improvisational stuff was unleashed by *Curb.* What made it different is Larry's genius for writing. Susie reminds me, "Remember, David, we were at dinner at your house, and Larry was talking about becoming 'the social assassin of telling people the truth.' And he took out his notebook, and out came 'Palestinian Chicken,' and we shot it."

The show has remained a cult favorite and a hit for HBO since then (it went off the air in 2011, which was Larry's choice, returned in 2017, and returned again in 2020). It has been nominated for forty-seven Emmys. Susie's co-stars are some of the best in comedy—Larry, Jeff Garlin, Cheryl Hines, Richard Lewis, J. B. Smoove, Wanda Sykes, Shelley Berman, and the beloved Bob Einstein. And it changed Susie Essman's career in comedy and in acting. But, in truth, it was the "You fat fuck" line that changed Susie's life. "People are constantly walking up to me begging me to tell them to go fuck themselves, and getting upset when I don't. Moments like, 'Call me a fat fuck, here's my cell phone. My husband's bald, call him a bald motherfucker.' This is what my life is now. And sometimes it annoys me. But at the same time, it could be worse. I can't blame them—they think that's me! They don't realize that's not how I talk. The only time I do is when I'm dealing with customer service issues. We recently had to get a new stove and microwave. We order it, I got the best model, and it's installed, and it breaks within three days. Then I become Susie Greene.

"Larry has a lot of geniuses in him," continues Susie emphatically, with that Susie smile both Susies share. "But I think that Larry's true genius is story. When I get the outlines at the beginning of the season, and I do have a comic brain, yet I read those outlines and I think, 'I have no idea how he got there.' It's just mind-boggling to me."

And that is the tie that binds Larry David and Jerry Seinfeld. The story: When Jerry Seinfeld was eight years old, he remembers a day when he was watching television with his family, and a comedian was on, and he was telling stories, and his dad said, "See that guy on the TV? His actual job is to be funny." Something obviously took because twenty years later that little kid became one of the best at that job, ever. And, today, you can't have a conversation about TV history without celebrating Jerry Seinfeld.

Jerry Seinfeld is an example of the most-skilled comic—his stand-up is impeccable and he's on the road all the time. He'll make you laugh no matter what age you are or how smart you are. He's so at home in front of an audience because he works on his material tirelessly. Like many of us, Jerry's love of comedy started at home, whether his folks understood comedy, like Jerry's dad, or like mine, not so much. "My dad used to collect jokes in a box of cards. And he would write down the jokes so that he wouldn't forget them. He always used to say to me that if he had an opportunity, he would love to have tried to do it. He told jokes at the dinner table all the time. Joke jokes. And he was a wonderful joke teller. But, David, really your moment, when guys like you came along, you and Robert Klein were the guys that just cracked the glass and made it seem like there's a whole other way to do this."

Titles for Jerome Seinfeld, best known to hundreds of millions of people as Jerry: stand-up comedian, actor, writer, producer, director. Funny thing is, he started out as a stand-up in college productions, and after creating the most revolutionary comedy series ever, *Seinfeld,* and banking hundreds of millions of dollars, living a family-centered life with his wife and three teenagers, spending his time collecting hundreds of vintage Porsches, he has returned to stand-up, touring all over the country.

Why, you ask? It is really so simple. He loves it. Purely, totally, in a way perhaps only other comedians can understand. The joy he gets from the challenge of making people laugh sends him back on the road to practice his craft. Whether it is in a club for twenty people or in an arena for thousands—simply, it is where he is happiest. Just look at that smile.

Jerry explains, "People watch me do stand-up, after all my success, watch the documentary about my tours, and think it is so hard. Really? It isn't hard at all, unless you're not good at it, and if you are not good at it, then it is the hardest job in the world. But if you can do it, it's really kind of fun and easy."

Jerry's comedy is just impeccable. It'll make you laugh no matter what age, no matter your life experience or the knowledge you have. He is so at home in front of an audience—he's done it before, he works on it, he changes it and changes it and changes it and changes it, and it works.

And that tells you everything about this man and his love of his work. Young comics who think they're going to be like Seinfeld don't realize the years he's put into it. He's like the virtuoso cellist Pablo Casals—he doesn't stop practicing, he doesn't stop trying new things. You need to be an outsider to do comedy well, and you have to recognize what it is that you're outside of. Audiences identify with outsider comedians the most. It's surprising to discover who everyone is, as opposed to their image. There is a certain mythology around the comedy world now because it's so scrutinized. An example of something I hear all the time is that on *Seinfeld,* it was all Seinfeld and it wasn't Larry. That's not true. Jerry is an amazing writer, and he wrote *Seinfeld* with Larry. They wrote it together. Having directed *Seinfeld,* I would leave the lot at midnight, after staying with Jerry and Larry, who were still writing, and there would be no other cars on the lot except for theirs, every night. I just can't get that image of how hard they worked out of my mind.

I remind Jerry that I started out Talmudic, always asking the audience questions. "Why this? Why that?"

Jerry figured that out pretty quickly, asking questions of his audience. "Start off as a comedian by doing someone else," he recounts. "Do anyone's jokes—I used to do you! When I was just thinking about comedy, you were already doing it, and you were such an idol of mine, you and Bob Klein and Bill Cosby and Carlin. You were like the constellation to me, you four guys—you had quality balls. You really did!"

Jerry graduated from college with a degree in communications and theater, but that doesn't explain how he found his passion for comedy, for stand-up. It began with appearing at open-mic nights, which led to being discovered and getting small roles in TV sitcoms. As his father had said, a job where you just have to be funny. Like others (like myself), Jerry first made an appearance on *The Tonight Show Starring Johnny Carson* (on May 6, 1981) and so impressed Johnny that he became a frequent guest on *The Tonight Show* and then on *Late Night with David Letterman*. It was all about stand-up.

After a few years of stand-up, Jerry got a part on the TV series *Benson*. "Three episodes," he points out. "And then I got fired, and the part was so small, and I was so irrelevant to the show that they didn't even bother to tell me. So I showed up for work, and I sit down in my chair at the table read where everyone gets their script the first day of the week, and everyone reads through the script, and I sit down and say, 'Hey, where's my script?' And this guy calls me over—I am out. They didn't even bother to let me know. You know, politely say, 'Get out of here kid, you're out.' But that actually was one of the great experiences that I had, because it made me so angry that they had the power to just take this away from me. And I started focusing on writing and working hard and saying I'm going to be a comedian because they can't take that away. I really valued my stand-up career for the first time in a different way after that. I really resented that. So then it was just stand-up, stand-up, stand-up, and all of a sudden I was doing *The Tonight Show* with Carson, and later, *Letterman.*"

Since I had been doing *The Tonight Show* for years, I knew how Jerry felt. It was the pinnacle. And it was terrifying. Like my first *Tonight Show Starring Johnny Carson,* for Jerry, it was a seminal moment. The biggest thing. But more complex than you might think.

"I remember every moment. May 6, 1981. That was the only time I ever felt electrified. There's nothing better for a comedian than being hemmed in, having been closed off, shut out, not welcome; that's nutrition. That's what you want as a comedian. Acceptance is a dangerous thing for comedians. But that night—was magic. Because the truth is, that kind of stand-up is the most intimate performance that there is. That relationship, when it's locked in, is so intense, and rich, that all of the negative things about comedy that people say—how difficult it is, how humiliating it can be—I embrace all that. Because I think the ledger still tips in our favor. You get so much. And you're also so much more in control of your life and your destiny and your art than anybody else is.

"And then, when it came around to NBC being interested in me to do something, I had my own career, which I was comfortable in, and that's why I could say, 'This is the way it's going to be, or to hell with it.'"

What happened next changed television history.

"Around 1989, I met up with Larry David, who I always thought was one of the brightest comedians I had known from those days. I told him, 'NBC is doing a show, and they asked me what it could be.' We went to the Korean deli across the street from Catch a Rising Star and made fun of the products around the cash register, and Larry said, 'This should be the show. Just this, two guys making fun of stuff. A show about nothing.' And that's really how it started. And when we went into NBC, and they said, 'What is that? That's not a show.' We went, 'No, that's the show, that's what we're doing.'"

Jerry reminisces, "It was so unlikely! I mean, what happened to me was ridiculous. That was not the plan. The plan was to do the TV show, hang on for a couple, two, three years. Like an obscure little cult thing.

And I'll pump up my ticket sales at the comedy clubs. That's why I called it *Seinfeld.* I thought, 'Well, at least I'll sell some tickets.'"

There is a bit more behind this. You may have heard Jerry explain that their influence for the show was *The Abbott and Costello Show.*

"It was," says Jerry, "because that television show that they did, I think it was in 1952–53, was about comedy. There was no explanation about comedy or of anyone's life. Nothing made sense; there were always a lot of inexplicably evil people on the show, and we stole that. We took that right away. We always had people on the show like the garage attendant who tells you, 'You can't get your car out, you just can't.' It's simple. And that was the law of the show, that comedy is boss."

I have always thought there was another reference in Jerry's character, which was Jack Benny, because Benny always gave away everything—everyone around him would do things that were just nuts, and he would just stare at them, as if he was the audience's point of view a lot of the time.

Jerry agrees. "I love to play straight, playing straight to me is funny—Bud Abbott is really funnier to me than Lou Costello because a really good straight man who keeps bringing the logic back is funny. In stand-up, there's all this rigorous logic, so we brought that to the show. Like when Kramer says, 'Well, I'm gonna teach people to make pizzas in their own ovens.' Well, you can't have people sticking their fingers in five-hundred-degree ovens! That's the funny part."

Lucky maybe, but also smart. Jerry and Larry (who had been a writer on *Saturday Night Live* for one year) knew Julia Louis-Dreyfus from *SNL,* and knew Michael Richards and Jason Alexander from their work as actors/comedians. And the rest is history. Originally named *The Seinfeld Chronicles,* the show became *Seinfeld,* ran from 1989 to 1998, and although I don't count awards much, this is just overwhelming: the show and its cast won ten Emmys (nominated for sixty-eight, a record), three Golden Globes (nominated for fifteen), six Screen Actors Guild (SAG) Awards (nominated for seventeen), and more.

It was huge, beyond anyone's comprehension.

In truth, Jerry and I agree. "If people live lives of quiet desperation, stand-up is a life of loud desperation. Noisy desperation, that's what it is. When I finished my TV series, I was a big star, and successful, and I had a lot of open doors. And I saw this as a dangerous thing. And so I left LA and I tried to break back into the middle. After being on top, I said I gotta break back into the middle. Going on the road and working it made me feel comfortable. To be honest, I never felt great being at that pinnacle. There was a point when the show was really at a very high level—it was *the* thing for a period of time. And I just thought, 'This is not good. This is not where I belong.' You know what I mean? I felt like, this is not comedy. I always thought comedy and star are mutually exclusive. There's no comedy star. Either you're a star or you're a comic."

I was lucky enough to direct a few. Of course, I had little to do with the success of *Seinfeld,* but since Jerry and Larry and I are all stand-up comics, they listened politely to my suggestions, used a few of them, and I won an Emmy for directing the episode titled "Tapes," in which Jerry suspects that somebody is sitting in the audience and stealing his act, a subject near and dear to all three of us.

"I actually had a similar experience recently," says Jerry. "Believe it or not, I was asked to perform at the White House. They were honoring Paul McCartney. I don't even know how I got there. And all I kept thinking the whole time is, 'Why am I here?' And getting up onstage in the East Room of the White House and performing for the president and Paul McCartney felt like my first *Tonight Show.* I haven't felt like that. Even at the White House, where you would think it would be hard—not really. It went well, and it was a huge thrill."

Jerry remembers it word for word.

"Thank you very much, Mr. President, First Lady, Sir Paul McCartney, other people. Sir Paul, you have written some of the most beautiful music ever heard by humans in this world. And yet, some of the lyrics and some of the songs, as they go by, you can make one unsure, even concerned sometimes, about what exactly is happening in this song. Songs such as 'I Saw Her Standing There,' and I quote, 'She was just seventeen, you know what I mean.' I'm not sure I do know what you mean, Sir Paul."

As Jerry tours the country now with his stand-up, other issues emerge. "I do little places, and I do my regular shows in theaters around the country. And I try and do new stuff there. I still struggle with it." And then there is age. "Some comedians, as they age, really struggle, because so much of comedy requires physical force—not stand-up as much, for you and me—but others? Look at Don Rickles, who, at eighty-four, was not in great shape. There were no elliptical machines at the Sahara in the sixties! But he defied those 'age-old' adages—he had the same energy he always did—so that is some crazy DNA in him! It's miraculous for someone that age. I got to see him at Town Hall with Chris Rock, who had never seen him in person. And this is a few years ago, in 2017, just before Don died, and everyone told us that 'he may not be in his prime, but you've gotta see him!' So we go to see him, Chris and I. And after the show, they set up a chair backstage, in this horrible, not even a real backstage area. They just put a chair on the ground and everyone stands there, and we wait for Don to come out. We wait like forty minutes. I don't know what he's doing back there."

I have to interrupt Jerry, because I know what Don was doing. "Showering," I explain. "He comes out with the towel, right? It's the old tradition—you had to do it at nightclubs. And, in the lounges when he worked in the sixties, his show would start at midnight, and he'd do five shows, from twelve a.m. until six a.m. That's a lot of showers!"

Jerry shakes his head. "When I finish my show, I can talk to you ten seconds after I'm done, I'm right there. I'm not doing anything. For Don, forty minutes later, he comes out, he sits down in the chair, Chris and I stand there, and he just insults us all for another twenty minutes. And we are laughing hysterically 'cause he is so funny!"

Jerry can't stop. "This is another favorite story of mine about Don. Before I was really known, I went to see Don in Vegas. They gave him a note that I was in the audience, and onstage (and so far, decades later, this is the farthest from my name that anyone's ever gotten in terms of mispronouncing it), Don says, 'We have George Stanbury in the audience.' And then he insulted me. You know, David, if there's a pure white light of comic energy, Don had it. He was remarkable for the antenna he had for what he could say to you. And he improvised all the time. There was no real structure to it, just so purely funny. That's why I think he was such a special comedian."

Back to stand-up. It always somehow comes back to stand-up. Jerry and I agree—which is probably why after decades writing, producing, and starring in the most successful comedy series of all time, Jerry is back to doing stand-up in clubs across the country.

CHAPTER 11

ACTORS AS COMEDIANS, COMEDIANS AS ACTORS

Many years ago, the comedian Red Buttons had lots of friends who were also comics. They included Don Rickles, Jack Carter, George Burns, Bob Newhart, Jan Murray, and many others. They would all meet regularly for lunch. The story is told that when Red got his first role as a serious actor, in *Sayonara* (co-starring with Marlon Brando), he took off and did not speak to his friends the comics for a year. And he won the Oscar for Best Supporting Actor for *Sayonara*. Red took himself seriously, so seriously that it took him over a year to rejoin his group of comics. Then, in 1961, he got a role in the war drama *The Longest Day*, and when he took off to make this movie, his group of comics sent him a telegram saying, "Goodbye, Again."

Actors as comics, comics as actors. It is really, really difficult to be a comedian. It takes particular skills and passions, and when you have those skills, when you are able to transfer that comic talent to dramatic acting, also a difficult talent and skill, and do it so well that you become celebrated and awarded for that talent, that is magic. And rare.

The talents below are some of the greatest examples of this extraordinary ability. I know them, I admire them, I respect them, and I always love working with them.

.   .   .

My friend Julia Louis-Dreyfus, whom I have been lucky enough to direct many times over the years, stands alone as an actress who is also brilliantly funny, a brave artist both in her comedy and in her public political and social positions. And she is a gem.

As Elaine, she was feisty, smartly ahead of her male cohorts in recognizing stupidity and arrogance, and so funny. Also a little scary, as you never knew what was going to come out of her mouth. And her movement of slapping men against their chests, with both of her open hands, is iconic and always funny. Julia was Elaine for nine years.

As Old Christine, she was a single mom who ran a gym, still loved her ex, and made everyone laugh. Julia was Old Christine for five years.

As Selina, also known as Vice President and then President Selina Meyer, in *Veep,* she was outrageous, insulting, self-centered, ruthless, and absolutely mesmerizing. Julia was Selina for seven years.

As Julia Louis-Dreyfus, she is singularly one of the hardest-working actresses I know, smart beyond any inkling you might have from the roles she plays, strong yet humble in her manner and relationships, and talented in everything she touches. She is also one of the most awarded actresses in comedy ever—winning eleven Emmys, one Golden Globe award (she was nominated nine times), and nine SAG awards (twenty-one nominations). Her personal life is also award-winning—she has been married for over thirty years to comedian and writer Brad Hall, is the mother of two sons, has just been through a fight against breast cancer, and has been involved in political and social campaigns aimed to safeguard our lives forever. She has been Julia Louis-Dreyfus for over fifty years.

And, oh yes, the award that meant most to her, because of its lineage, was the Mark Twain Prize for American Humor, which she received at the Kennedy Center in 2018. She was introduced by Jerry Seinfeld. Here is what Jerry said:

"When we first started making my TV series in '89, we made the first episode, it was basically me, George, and Kramer. George was kind of a Larry David character. Larry had a funny neighbor named Kramer, so we threw him in. We used as little imagination as possible. All Larry and I really wanted to do was have two guys talk in an idiotic way about completely stupid things. Which is not nothing. We did not want it to be about nothing. We wanted it to be about being stupid. So we make the first episode. I don't think anybody liked it that much. [The network] eventually said, 'Okay, you can make a few more, but you need a real female character. All you've got are three stupid guys.' . . . [That] is called a network note. . . . We thought, 'That's not a bad idea. . . . Let's add a smart woman. That's funny.' . . . Julia Louis-Dreyfus used it to launch one of the most brilliant and spectacular show business careers of all time. . . . So then we fleshed out the idea a little more. We decided, let's make it a girl that Jerry used to date, they decided to continue the relationship as friends, a completely absurd idea, could never happen in real life. . . . As lame as all this is, I was still required as an actor to play this situation . . . Way beyond any acting ability that I possess. How did I do it? . . . I just really, really liked Julia. I could not get enough of her. Nine years, I was not acting. I couldn't. I thought she was funny, charming, beautiful, intelligent, every single second I ever spent with her onstage and off, bingo, no acting required, just read in the lines in the script . . . piece of cake."

Here is what she said that night, through a few tears:

"When Mark Twain first emailed me about the Mark Twain Prize, I have to admit I totally misunderstood. I assumed that I was being asked to honor somebody else . . . and I thought, 'Oh my god! What a hassle. . . . I have to go all the way to Washington, DC'—which, no offense, is a nightmare—'and make up flattering things to say about how funny someone else is? No effing way.' And then I reread the email and I realized, 'Oh, it's me! They're giving it to me! I get the prize.' And my attitude about the whole thing changed, it really did."

When and how did it start, this passion for and genius at comedy? Who did she see as a kid that appealed to her and made her take notice?

"There were a lot of people," Julia begins to remember. "I mean, Soupy Sales, for example. When I was little, I used to watch Soupy Sales with my mom. We would laugh together. But I have to tell you a little thing that you may think is interesting. When I was growing

This photo says it all. Funny, charming, beautiful— arguably one of the funniest women on television today, and so full of life.

up, me and my neighbors would do shows. We had a neighborhood theater company, called ourselves the University Players 'cause we lived on University Avenue. We also had a dance troupe called Julia and the Umbrella People, and that's the truth. I think the name sounded groovy, and you can imagine, David, how good those shows were. So here is my punch line—my next-door neighbor was a girl named Margaret Edson. Yeah, that's right! We did shows together, including *Sorry, Wrong Number*—you know, that terrifying waiting for the phone to ring show. We charged our parents $1.50 to come to the basement and watch us do this show. And Margaret Edson went on to write the Pulitzer Prize–winning play *Wit*."

Then, like so many of us, Julia, too, had her beginnings in comedy in Second City in Chicago. Did she love it? Not so much. "It was not great," remembers Julia. "I was in the touring company, so I spent a lot of time in Dundee, Illinois, at a place called Chateau Louise. And a lot of people in the group were really, really high. And it was sort of a bummer to be traveling with them. When I auditioned for Second City and, inexplicably, got in, it wasn't super-fun. I was still a junior at Northwestern, and I joined the comedy show on campus called Mee-Ow. Everything came from that [including meeting husband-to-be

Brad Hall, a terrific writer], and from that, we all got hired to do *Saturday Night Live*."

Who was in that *SNL* troupe? No lightweights. "Eddie Murphy, Tim Kazurinsky, Mary Gross, Joe Piscopo, Robin Duke, Billy Crystal, Chris Guest, Marty Short—I stayed there for three years. I'm not complaining, because it was like grad school, in a way—you know, where you get beat up a lot. Remember, I went to *SNL* when I was twenty-one, very green, and I was its audience. When I was in high school, I watched Bill Murray and Chevy and all these guys do their thing, and I was going, 'Uhhh, goo goo gaga.' I just couldn't believe it. And then to get cast, it was like Cinderella going to the ball, except it wasn't quite the ball that I had anticipated. I didn't have a big bag of characters from which to pull material. I thought, 'Oh, we'll all work together, and we'll make this good show.' But everyone was older and had more experience and knew the politics of the place. And I would honestly say that it was also not female-friendly at the time I was there. I did learn a lot, the hard way, and I met Larry David during that time, 'cause he was there, writing, in my third year. And he didn't get a single sketch on during the year, ever. Really, it's not a joke. He got one on, it made it to dress, and then it got cut between dress and air. So we were both really miserable together, and I learned that if you're not having a good time, it ain't worth it."

Julia was not alone. *SNL* was a complicated place and continued to be so for years. But I always thought that you can bond through those times, even if you're not having a good time, with another person that is not having a good time. That's a good bond. Julia agrees.

"I like the misery bond," she explains. Me, too. That is another show business bond that I feel works—you don't bond because you love the same people, you bond because you hate the same people. It's the same thing. Julia has another take on this:

"You know what that reminds me of? I have a little small pile of cartoons that I cut out. One had the heading 'Why kids don't have their own talk shows.' And it's two kids, maybe age six, and they're seated—desk, guest, host. And the host says to the guest, 'Don't you hate Eric?' It's fun to hate other people together."

And then, not so much later, came *Seinfeld*.

"Larry called to tell me he and Jerry were working on a series for NBC about two guys, and they needed a girl. Larry sent me these four scripts (they made this pilot, *Seinfeld,* and I wasn't in that). And then NBC said, 'Okay, we'll pick up all four.' Real stamp of approval! 'And, you need to add a female character.' So Larry sent me these scripts, and in two out of the four episodes I had something significant to do. The other two, not so much. But I thought that the writing was a real cut above, 'cause it was. It didn't resemble anything that was on television at the time. The jokes weren't setup, joke, setup, joke, setup, joke—which, by the way, has its place, believe me, but it was very different."

What also made a big difference, she says, is that "I had the good fortune of already being approved by NBC because of *SNL,* and because of another series I had done, *Day by Day.* So I went and I met Lar, and I met Jer. I didn't really know Jerry, sort of recognized him as a stand-up, but I didn't really know the world of stand-up 'cause I didn't do that. We just sort of sat around and talked. And we ate cereal and just read a scene together. It was just him and me and Tom Cherones, who was a director at the time, and that was that. They made the deal over the weekend, and we shot the next week. It was really quick. And, truthfully, I could sense that I loved it. But I figured it was going to be canceled 'cause I thought the network was too stupid to keep it on since it was so off—so really unique. The rhythms were different, everything was different, and I thought, 'There's no way this is going to stay in place.' And yet, it did. NBC tried to get it off a few times. We have Rick Ludwin at NBC to thank for the show staying. He fought everyone and just kept it. It was obviously hard work. Some days were harder than others but ultimately we liked the show maybe even more than the audience liked the show." It was a great, happy experience.

Having directed many award-winning sitcoms over the years, I know what a difference it makes if those involved love the show. That's kind of crucial. If you love what you're doing, that's great. Whatever that feeling is translates in some ways. As Julia remembers, "We would just howl at this stuff. We would die laughing. It was joyful. But I never thought it would have the lasting effect it has. I didn't know it would have this kind of . . . iconic-beyond-belief effect. I mean, how can we possibly know? You can't. Jerry and Larry will tell you—we were just doing our work." And it showed in every *Seinfeld* that I directed. Hard work. Brilliant plotlines that were seemingly, but not really, about nothing. And a cast made up of truly brilliant actors who were always true to the characters they played.

Same is true for *Veep*. I tell Julia that I just had lunch with Larry David and told him we were getting together. He said, "You're seeing Julia, so please tell her that *Veep* is the best work she's ever done. I love the show." And Larry David doesn't love a lot of shows. "I love the show, too," says Julia, quietly and with pride. "It is a remarkable show, and I lucked out to get this gig." I tell Julia that, as a director, I am amazed at how fast *Veep* moves, how brilliant the overlapping dialogue is, how she keeps a rhythm going so that anyone's going to be heard, walking, running, moving. *Veep* really is offbeat in every way. And Julia is so funny! I mean, every time she says "fuck" it gets a laugh just because it is a great word. One of the greats.

Julia interrupts, "It's *the* great word, yeah. And then there's great political stuff in it. When I first heard about this idea, from a comedy point of view, I thought, 'Really?' Then this idea came to me—'unhappy vice president.' I thought, 'Oh my god, of course. It's perfect. It's a gold mine of material.' It was right in front of our faces. And no one had ever done it. It's when another person has the job you want. Nobody aspires to be number two. Particularly in this country."

Now *Veep* is over. It is available to stream forever, but Julia has moved on. What is next? I am not sure, but what I am sure of is that Julia will make a mark on all of us. It will involve a woman of strength and bravery and humor and a personality true to herself. It will have political and social impact, and Julia will be that woman, through and through, for many years to come.

Serious, like Julia; always respecting comedians, like Julia; reveres joking and silliness, also like Julia. But as I am sitting across from Steve Martin, whom I have known for more than forty years, we are trying to catch up, and suddenly there is a fly stalking us. I realize Steve and Julia are not at all alike, as Steve just watches it. Julia would have smacked it.

"He is after me!" I say.

"It's all part of my plan," explains Steve. "See, we can no longer say, 'You wouldn't hurt a fly.' It's audio-animatronic."

"What does that mean?" I ask, knowing the answer will not be predictable.

"It means it's mechanical."

"It's mechanical? What?"

"Audio-animatronic," he says again quietly. With authority.

I should be used to this kind of "commentary." But even though Steve and I go back many, many years, he remembers things differently.

"I once saw you naked in a swimming pool," he recalls.

"You did not," I reply with some arrogance.

"I did. At Tommy Smothers's after-hours party, one time in the sixties, when everyone was just, 'Oh, da chance to get naked with girls in the pool? Yes!'"

"Back off. There's no way—I don't get naked any time if I can avoid it. But there were parties at Tommy Smothers's house."

With Steve Martin, holding a photo of us from forty years ago when we were on *The Smothers Brothers Comedy Hour.*

"There were, yeah," says Steve.

"You are lying," I reply, knowing full well he wasn't. "So what do you remember of those old Smothers Brothers days?" I ask.

"Well, I was so excited, first of all. I was twenty-one when I started. The youngest kid there. It was so thrilling to work eighteen hours a day and to have my material on television, even if it was only the word 'the,' which sometimes it was. And to be at the center of something that was happening and hot—it was the equivalent of *Saturday Night Live* in its day. They were revolutionary. And meeting all those people: one minute, a comedian working the Ice House, and the next day, standing in a room with Pete Seeger, working out my bit—his bit. I was really terrified and excited at the same time."

And that's Steve Martin. He is always honest and aware that we were all in something big, while it was happening. It was sort of what they used to call the "counterculture." This time his memory is clear, and right. "You felt like you were the center of the universe, you know? You were young and thinking, and you had a political position before you knew that there were other positions, too. We learned how to think for the other side. Like, oh, there are other opinions. Complete fun, and hard work, too. I was there all the time."

The Smothers Brothers Comedy Hour was so well written. It was the first comedy show written so carefully and breaking ground all the time. "That was Carl Gottlieb," Steve remembers, "one of the very good writers on the show, who had worked with the Committee, which was a very important improv group out of San Francisco." Gottlieb actually went on to co-write the movie *Jaws,* and co-wrote, with Michael Elias, Steve's huge hit *The Jerk.* And Bob Einstein, Steve's writing partner (and brother to Albert Brooks) on *The Smothers Brothers Comedy Hour,* went on to a very successful career in writing and performing as "Super Dave."

Again, Steve Martin remembers clearly: "Bob and I worked in a windowless room. And I lived below him in the same house in Laurel Canyon. We were very, very close. We had a great time, just laughed all the time. He was one of the funniest people I ever met." Bob Einstein was absolutely and purely funny. I had directed him over the years in *Curb Your Enthusiasm,* and he was the biggest pain in the ass. He didn't want to do anything that the director, me, said. But it didn't matter. He was so funny.

Even though *The Smothers Brothers Comedy Hour* was a big hit, it still contained somewhat precarious acts, especially the monologues. Steve remembers it as I do:

"In the beginning, I used to look at you doing your monologues and think, 'Why him?' But you did these great, fantastic iconoclastic monologues, and you got in a lot of trouble."

But even before this writing gig on *The Smothers Brothers Comedy Hour,* Steve had done stand-up comedy. "I was doing stand-up comedy from as soon as I got out of high school, age eighteen," he remembers. "I worked at Knott's Berry Farm, at the Bird Cage Theatre, where we did sort of a melodrama, and there was a little five-minute slot at the end of the melodrama called 'The Olio Acts,' and you went out and got to do four minutes of whatever, and I did a comedy magic act. Then I took that and expanded on it and went down to the clubs in Orange County, with my banjo and some jokes and the comedy act."

"Do you remember any of the earliest material that you did?"

Steve answers, "Almost all of it was lifted. From joke books, and Carl Ballantine, the great comedy magician, was a great source. I did that from maybe age seventeen to eighteen, and then when I hit age nineteen, I had an epiphany while I was at college, and that was: You have to write it all yourself, otherwise you would never be an original. And if you weren't an original, you would never have any success. So I had to take out everything that had some precedence to it. I was very lucky. Television was just coming in when I was about six, so the first thing that came on was *Laurel and Hardy* and *Abbott and Costello,* and I got to see Jerry Lewis, all coming through the television."

Steve continues, "When I was studying in college, poetry, philosophy, and the arts, it was just like having your mind expanded. I realized, 'That's what I want to be. I want to be one of those guys.' And I loved comedy, so it was perfect. There were people being very original in comedy, Bob Newhart and Bill Cosby. As I got older, I got to watch Steve Allen, Don Knotts, Tom Poston, and Jack Benny, and I was inspired by, and fell in love with, comedy from these great masters."

As I had also started in stand-up, I wondered if it was hard for Steve (it wasn't for me) to make a transition to writing on *The Smothers Brothers Comedy Hour* when he aspired to do stand-up, to be a comedian. But, like me, Steve thought comedy was being in professional show business. We both loved it, and learned so much. Although Steve was a little different—he also played the banjo. "That's what I was doing in my act at the time—playing the banjo." Folk music was very popular when we were younger. And the Beatles were sort of outspoken and fighting back, in a way, besides writing and playing really good music.

"When I worked at a fantastic club called the Great Southeast Music Hall in Atlanta, Martin Mull was playing there," he says. "It was a big space, seated maybe four hundred people, and it didn't have seats, just plywood tiers covered with a carpet, pillows. Martin Mull was the ultimate professional. He played guitar and sang funny songs. He was great, and we just hit it off. Then, after the show, we ran outside and did the same show there just for the money. Put a hat down and played again. It was really fun times. But that did not make it any easier."

Exactly. It's the hardest thing to do, because you can only get better by suffering onstage in front of a lot of people who are not laughing at you. Steve is still touring today—now with a band, still with the banjo, and the jokes. He talks, he jokes, he plays. And he is still the best version of surreal humor there is—he can take any abstract notion, make it seem like it is silly, but give it the serious humor that is uniquely his. I don't know any other comedian who has influenced nearly everyone in comedy (check out how many times other comedians mention him in this book), who is an uncanny genius and can be utterly serious while being totally goofy at the same time.

"I delight in it. I really do," he says. "Because now I have music and other musicians onstage, and we have a rapport, and so I'm not really alone like I was. When you are alone onstage, you can be in the middle of a moment, but your mind is actually in the next moment, you're thinking ahead, of what's next. You're always at the mercy of a million things that are going on. Today, as I tour, I know that the comedy portion might be two minutes, and then a song, three minutes, and then there's another comedy portion because it's easier to change out material, so you're always a little bit fresh. And now I think, 'Oh, boy! I've got this wonderful line,' and for about a minute and a half that I just love, it's brand-new, and it makes me laugh when I say it. And you don't know why, and you don't know where, and you don't know when they're gonna laugh at it, and it's remarkable."

At one point, Steve stopped doing stand-up.

"I was at my wits' end. I was no longer creative with what I was doing, and I was just repeating what I had done. I remember I had an old recording of Lenny Bruce, sort of toward the end when he was under siege, but he was still talking about his act. He said, 'When I was onstage, I ad-libbed maybe three minutes tops' in an hour show, and that's a lot. Sometimes, the joy of it is actually just doing your best, most perfect show. And then sometimes there is actual spontaneity onstage, and it's just wonderful, and the audience can smell it, you know? They like it."

How true. When you do stand-up, you give the illusion of spontaneity. No matter, Steve's act was so lively. I remember the time I ran into Marty Short, a mutual friend of ours, and I had just seen Steve. I said to Marty, "I just saw Steve's act," and I don't know why I chose this as a metaphor—I meant it in the nicest way—I said, "It was positively Hassidic."

And Marty said to me, "I have no idea what that means. Hassidic? Why would you bring a Jewish reference into Steve Martin's act?"

But what I meant is that it was *joyful*, as joyful a stand-up act as I had ever seen. It was the opposite of bitter and hard, which was going on so much at that time. As serious as he was, Steve just had a lightness to him.

"Not an accident," says Steve.

Big lesson here. How you play anger as a comedian is everything, because comedians, when they get angry, should never scare the audience. Actors, when they get angry, always scare us, but comedians don't. That's why Steve Martin is most comedians' reference for why they got into comedy, how important he was to them, and how they see Steve's influence on their work.

Steve doesn't see that impact. "I really can't take a lot of credit. Sometimes it's just who's around at the time when you're growing up, and I was around at the time when a lot of these people were growing up." It's much more than that. All these hugely successful comedians respect Steve from the movies, from the touring, and everything else, but it seems to go back to that early *SNL* moment when all these people who were younger connected with him.

Been there. It's a great feeling. And then, what you have to watch out for is not doing the same thing over and over again, and that's probably why you eventually stop. And that's what finally happened to Steve.

For me, the moment was directing. For Steve, it was acting in the movies.

Steve Martin: "There was an ignited moment in the movies at one point, and I said, I'm here, and it's working. That was actually *The Jerk* in 1979, which was a big hit ($100 million, which was huge then), and then there was a period of struggle because I had thought, 'Well, this is gonna be an easy transition from stand-up to movies. Hey, I've been in front of an audience. It's the same thing.' But it wasn't, and it wasn't really until after *All of Me, Father of the Bride, Roxanne, L.A. Story,* and *Parenthood* that heartfelt performances started to appear in my come-dies, and where I started to be a commodity that was wanted. An actor." A successful actor, he had other hits, including *Dead Men Don't Wear Plaid, The Man with Two Brains,* and *Planes, Trains and Automobiles* (with my dear friend John Candy).

And then the writer/stand-up comedian/actor hosts the Oscars. Three times!

"First time, I hosted alone," Steve says. "I was quite nervous, but it was like artificial nerves because I knew I could do it. I knew the material was good, and I knew I'd been onstage live in front of people a million times, and I'd hosted situations and I'd done it, but I was still nervous. And I thought it went pretty well.

"The second time I hosted was the night the Iraq war started, but I had experience, strangely enough, when I worked at the Bird Cage Theatre at Knott's Berry Farm, in 1963, and Kennedy was assassinated. So there was this feeling of horror everywhere, and I thought, 'Well, we probably won't be doing a show, that's for sure.'

"And the producers came back and said, 'We're gonna do the show.'

"I thought, 'This is gonna be awful.' And so we went on to do the show, and it was one of our best houses. I guess there's some truth to saying that people are looking for an escape, because everyone was depressed. So I kept remembering that night of the Iraq war and tried to think of a philosophy, which was to 'acknowledge it right off the bat.' There was all this talk about cutting down on the glamour and the glitz, and the stage set was just the glitziest thing, so when I walked out, I said, 'Well, so much for cutting down on the glitz,' and I got a big laugh, and then I just proceeded to do the show, the best show I possibly could. I was still a little nervous, but the show went fine.

"And then, the third time, when I'm hosting with Alec Baldwin, I thought it was a really good changeup, and it just felt good. So I was waiting for this wave of nerves to come over me, and it just never did. I was so relaxed. I had a good time all the way. Carson was always my role model for the Oscars. Always, Carson. Nobody like him. What had I learned? You do the best, tightest, seven, eight minutes, and then you get out of the way. You don't come back and do another twelve minutes, or a skit, or anything. The audience wants to get to the envelopes, and that was my premise. Every fifteen minutes you're playing to more losers. By the end of the show, there are a handful of winners and a whole audience just starving. They want food. And liquor. They've lost, and they're bitter, and I don't want my lines falling into that."

And there is always the writing. His passion. His brilliance. Steve has written for *The New Yorker* over the years (his wife, Anne Stringfield, is a writer there). And today? Back to books, of course. Didn't you just know Steve Martin would return to writing? What is possibly left for Steve Martin to do to humiliate every other versatile comedian in the country? He started out as a writer, remember? So he was always a writer first. He wrote his first full-length play, *Picasso at the Lapin Agile* in 1993, for the Geffen Theater in Los Angeles (Tom Hanks read Picasso), and it toured the country.

The latest—Steve wrote a show that made it to Broadway, with songs that he co-wrote with Edie Brickell, and he has a new album with Edie. Remember, Steve started out playing that banjo (he won a Grammy for Best Country Instrumental in 2002, and then one in 2009 for *The Crow: New Songs for the Five-String Banjo*). He has been successfully touring the country in a show he does with Marty Short, called *Steve Martin and Martin Short: An Evening You Will Forget for the*

Rest of Your Life. He is a major collector of contemporary art; he had his first child, a daughter, in 2012; and he is still playing that banjo. And, most of all, his comedy is still based on serious goofiness and is being channeled through his plays, books, stand-up, and films. He continues to be a visual comedian. Remember how, when he started out, he wore that crazy arrow running through his head, and also when he sang "King Tut" wearing an Egyptian headpiece? Well, my dear friend Steve Martin still gets pure joy out of sitting on a stage, quietly, alone, and seriously playing his banjo.

No banjo, no piano, no accessories, nothing for this huge talent, Chris Rock, except his honest comic genius. But where did he come from? Stand-up—no surprise. But as Chris worked at building up his stand-up, he also got small parts in shows—like *Showtime at the Apollo,* which was a big deal back then. Eddie Murphy had a deal at HBO, with a

On the set of *Inside Comedy* with Chris Rock, 2011. It's very rare to find comedians today who aspire to do hour-plus-long sets. Here Chris and I are talking about that. He's impressive in so many ways.

show called the *Uptown Comedy Express,* which was more or less the first *Def Comedy Jam.* Chris appeared on that, too, together with Robert Townsend, Arsenio Hall, Marsha Warfield, and Barry Sobel. He had also begun appearing in films, like *New Jack City* and *I'm Gonna Git You Sucka,* which was a big hit—but he had one line. He continued to have a career as a stand-up; he had a strong presence, meaning that he would stand there, wait quietly, then check out the entire audience, taking his time, before he would open his mouth to say something totally outrageous.

And then came *Saturday Night Live.* Chris, Adam Sandler, David Spade, and Rob Schneider all started at pretty much the same time. Remembers Chris, "We all got hired together. It was a great time for me, like going to X-Men school or something, because we all kind of felt like we were better than the comics around us. When I was at *SNL,* Conan O'Brien was a writer on the show, and so was Al Franken. It was unbelievable." The process was grueling, and to Chris (and many other writers), it was somewhat inexplicable.

Chris remembers, "I'd write two pieces a week—a regular sketch, and then one for a 'Weekend Update,' and then they'd have a read-through. Monday we'd meet the host, and Tuesday we'd write. And we had until Wednesday at ten a.m. to hand in all the sketches. So we'd end up spending all day there Tuesday and writing all night. Then at one p.m. or two p.m. on Wednesday, there'd be a read-through. Of the forty to fifty sketches submitted, they'd pick about nine or ten. It was a strange system. Why would you have all these people writing shit that's not ever going to get on the show? It made no fucking sense. So later on, when I did my own show on HBO, and we had the pitch meeting, I would make sure that no one would write something I didn't at least think was kind of funny. If we needed twelve things, I would make us write fourteen. Not fucking sixty! And if a writer didn't have a good idea, I'd make him write with somebody else. And every three or four weeks I'd switch people's offices so there wouldn't be any cliques. I had a great time at *SNL,* but it was really like school."

Even before *SNL,* Chris thought he was hot stuff. But . . . he wasn't? Chris: "I was still young. I was learning stuff. I wasn't that good. Even though I got *New Jack City* and all these things, I'd never taken an acting class in my life. I would meet people on the show, and they would say, like it was hot shit, 'Hey, I was in Second City.' I had never even written a sketch. So my whole time at *SNL* was just a learning experience. And the guys in front of me were better than I was. I can't sit here for a second and go, 'I should have been on instead of Dana Carvey or Mike Myers or Phil Hartman or any of those guys.' They were just amazing, and I was on the bench. Hey, Kobe Bryant was on the bench his first two years, too."

Chris grew up in Brooklyn—Crown Heights, to be exact, then in Bedford-Stuyvesant. He was bused to schools in white neighborhoods, where he was bullied and beaten. Soon after, he dropped out of high school and went to work, which helps us to understand the history of his life that he uses in his comedy. So we have to ask, was anyone funny in his house? Not exactly.

"My grandfather was pretty funny, and he was the guy who probably influenced my performance style. He was a preacher, a preacher who loved women. He hit on every woman he saw. When I got older, I realized that was my apprenticeship. I basically watched him prepare a set every week, as I sat in church and listened. When I think about it now, he was amazing—he never really wrote the sermon; he'd just write down the bullet points and run with what was kind of a skit. I write my jokes the same way, so he definitely had a big influence on me. And my dad celebrated the comedians of the time—like Redd Foxx. We had the Cosby albums. We listened to *Noah: Right!* and all that stuff. I think there was a Moms Mabley album in the house somewhere.

"I was weird. There were the kids who took apart radios and stuff. I took apart jokes. I was really interested in the inner workings of a joke. Like, how did you say that word to get that reaction? And I was only six or seven! I was fascinated hearing comedians do their bits. I watched Alan King when he was on *The Ed Sullivan Show,* and he had the aura that said, 'Hey, I'm very authoritative and a big stand-up guy.' Oh man, that's what a comedian is supposed to be like. And then I found Eddie Murphy, and the reason I was a big Eddie Murphy fan was because he was the first actual *young* comedian. Eddie Murphy was never a grown-up. This guy, out of the box, was like, 'I'm twenty-two, I'm getting pussy, what's up?' We all wanted to be Eddie Murphy.

"So one day I am in line at Radio City Music Hall for Eddie Murphy tickets. It was February 11, 1985. This was back in the olden days when there was no Internet. People actually had to go to the theater and wait in line to get tickets at the box office, and this line was three or four blocks long. While I am in this long line, which I figured I'd be in all day, I am reading the paper and see a bunch of ads for comedy clubs. And I just had this little epiphany! I walked out of the line, went from Radio City to the Comic Strip. But they said it wasn't audition night, so I walked to Catch a Rising Star, about thirty or forty blocks, and they said, 'YES! It's an audition night tonight—pick a number!' So I just hung out all day. There were probably thirty of us wannabe comedians outside, and there were seven slots available, and I got number seven. I went up that night to do my three minutes, and I got a couple of laughs, and as I was walking out, Mike Eagan, who ran the club, said, 'You passed.' I thought all comedians had to wait—I didn't know there was passing and not passing. I'd never been in a comedy club before, so I didn't know the system. From that moment on, I was probably at a comedy club every single night for about nine years."

That is a classic story: stand-up comedians going to clubs, night after night, learning timing, learning to gauge their audience, what works and what doesn't. It takes over their—our—lives. When I was at Second City all those years ago, I at least had the camaraderie of my fellow comedians, and the luck to have mentors like Paul Sills and the rest. For Chris and the comedians working alone, it was difficult, sometimes lonely, always obsessive, and demanded total absorption, often at the expense of anything else in life. But Chris is dignified and elegant even when his comedy—the connection with the audience—is major-league, first-class comedy. This is difficult—particularly because it is so personal—as he talks about his family, about dating, about divorce and how it relates to him. He never uses props. He just connects—he doesn't just entertain; he connects on a very basic level. And on his schedule, in those beginning days, it was obsessive, and exhausting.

"I was in New York so I could go on three times a night," Chris remembers. "All at comedy clubs—Strip, Catch a Rising Star, the Comedy Cellar. I essentially went a decade without dating, without taking a woman out on a Saturday night. Because it was literally like, okay, if you want to go see a movie with me it's going to be during the day on a Wednesday."

Chris was beginning to be known. "When you get a one-line part in *I'm Gonna Git You Sucka,* it's enough to get you in a club and to get you laid. Though I'm not saying you're getting the highest quality of being laid. You need more than one line for that."

One could say that's the motivation for almost everything in life. You know, comedians own it, but I have a feeling that for people like Einstein, it's the same thing.

After *SNL,* and before Chris did his own HBO show, which was a huge step, he seemed to have everything together. He found his voice as stand-up and kept his uniqueness. But he was not satisfied. "I'd been in a couple of movies. I'd been on *SNL*. But I hadn't been particularly good in anything. Okay, serviceable, a nice-enough guy. At *SNL,* they literally hadn't had a Black guy in eight years, since Eddie Murphy, which meant that I was always compared to Eddie Murphy, and, you know, I'm still not as good as Eddie Murphy. But was I as good as David Spade and Rob Schneider? Yeah. I was as good as the guys I shared an office with. But I wasn't being judged against them. I was being judged as this whole other thing. *In Living Color* was on at the same time, which meant everything about my position was magnified, and you can't grow under that kind of scrutiny.

"So my career was kind of over after *SNL*. I'd pop up on a *Fresh Prince,* but I really couldn't get any work. This was when I knew it was over for me, because I was doing small parts. So, it's that dynamic: you used to walk right in the door, and now you're waiting at reception. But you know what was the best about that time? The people. The comedians I met. Danny Aykroyd was so nice. He let me use his trailer every day after he left. He let me eat with him. Steve Martin, Phil Hartman were so nice to me, but I was done. I gave up trying to get famous and decided I just wanted to be a good comedian. I refused to even go on acting auditions—I just worked at the clubs every night, like in the showcase clubs, where, you know, you do fifteen, twenty minutes. By the way, showcases have ruined comedy."

He is right. Showcases have changed comedy, because everybody's getting ready for a television set, whereas before, there were showcase clubs at which people actually developed a show. I don't know if it happened after *Seinfeld* or *Cosby,* but stand-up comedians who used to be happy being stand-up comedians, all of a sudden many wanted to do eight minutes to get a television show. As Chris says, "That whole attitude ruined stand-up, but it's like baseball and pitchers. Nobody can go seven innings anymore. I go on tour and people are shocked: *'You did two hours!'* I'm like: *'Everybody used to do two hours!'* So I'd just work every single night."

The truth is that when you give up trying to be famous, which is a liberating thing, you're going to get good at what you do. You don't have to be career-driven. You just get to work, to define and refine your act, your art, to connect with your audience, and learn, learn, learn. Chris got better and better, got his voice, started doing long shows, and people started showing up on the club level. "There were fights because people couldn't get in!" Chris remembers with some incredulity. That's when he knew he had something.

"Years later, I was at Goodnights Comedy Club in Raleigh-Durham—the finest comedy club in the country, by the way, and any comic will tell you that—and I was in the middle of the show, and suddenly, I say to myself, 'Oh shit, I'm getting good at this!' They were laughing so hard that I was starting to look around, like, 'Who the fuck are they laughing at?' And that's the moment the laughs come, and you know that something's happening. And then the bits get longer, but you still never believe that you are going to get on *The Tonight Show* or *Letterman* or anything, so it didn't matter if I had a nine-minute bit and not two minutes preparing for a TV show. I was so not going to be on any of those shows, so it didn't matter to me.

"And then I did *Bring the Pain,* my second special for HBO, and my whole world changed. I got famous. I did a lot of Black people stuff, the 'Black people are nig*ers,' and the crack and the women stuff, the cheating stuff. You know, the political stuff gets the most attention, it's topical, and they sell twelve hundred tickets at most. Some of my favorite guys are political comedians, but they don't play the stadiums. The relationship stuff sells the tickets. If you want to play Staples

Center, you've got to talk about people fuckin'. You've got to get into the complexities of men and women. Even when I'm touring around the world, the topical stuff comes and goes, but that relationship stuff works everywhere."

I was doing stand-up in the sixties and early seventies, and when Nixon started to act up, I started to talk only about Nixon, and I had the opposite reaction—I became more famous for my Nixon material. So depending on the political subject and the fever of the times, it can get great traction and attention. I did then, but I couldn't do it after that, because it was only a moment when Nixon was who everyone was talking about. Steve Martin actually got really big and just didn't do political stuff. Just silly fun brilliant stuff.

Now Chris Rock is famous for stand-up comedy, and he opened up a show in Madison Square Garden a few years ago, 19,812 seats. So I ask Chris, where does he go to work that material out since he is so recognizable? I've never understood how hard it is for a comedian to say, "Well, I'm just going to try out my stuff on this audience who's paid money to see me." Although Jerry Seinfeld seems to be doing that regularly now that he is back on the stand-up road, which he loves.

Chris still goes to small clubs. As he explains, "On this last tour I worked things out in a little college town near Rutgers. Every tour is like a fight to me, and I do what fighters do. Fighters go upstate and set up a camp, so that's what I do—and in eight weeks, I can fight anybody. You give me eight weeks, and I will have a fucking great act. So that time I set up a campaign, right outside of West Palm Beach, Florida. Probably most of my tour I do for a month, where there are a lot of old people, most of them Jewish. And if I can make old Jews laugh at this shit . . . When I get it in front of the young people, it's like swinging two bats in the on-deck circle. It's like, if I can do this shit underwater, when I get aboveground, it's going to be amazing."

The Black comedians had their own world, but the audiences were made up of everyone. Chris agrees. "And there was really no 'Black comedians'—there were comedians, and the ones who came from Black lives had Black history, their own comedy sets, and their own opinions about others. Pryor had such a vulnerability about him. He wasn't cocky at all. You actually got the sense that he could break down and cry. He had every tool imaginable, so he could tell great jokes. And he did great characters, great voices, and he could tell a great story."

Chris also had the greatest time in which to be funny. "If you put Eddie Murphy in those years, you'd probably end up with the same guy," he says. I saw Cosby at the Apollo Theater in 1969, and it was the best stand-up act I've ever seen. "I saw Cosby in 2007," says Chris. "And it was the best stand-up act ever. Like, he's still that funny. You just have to come around at the right time. And you have to be right for that moment."

Chris Rock has won four Emmys, three Grammys, and hosted the Oscars. Pretty impressive on its own. He is still dominant, important, at the top of his game, playing by his own rules. Smart and funny, he continues to tap into things that may seem mundane in your life, but he sees it through another lens that makes you go, "Yes! That's me! I get it." And when the comedian is saying what you are thinking, that's the successful connection for any comedian—and especially for Chris Rock. Chris has always said, "Stop competing. Your success is your own." Yes it is, Chris. It surely is.

As it is for the comedy of Will Ferrell, who was born in Newport Beach and raised in Irvine, California, a master-plan community, one of the first cities to be planned with a public school, a supermarket every couple of miles, and perfectly wide streets. It was a great place to drive yourself crazy and then become funny as a result. Sophisticated dignity that gets the audience into the palms of their hands marries Chris's comedy with Will Ferrell's. You would not have guessed that given Will's background. Will's mom was a professor at a junior college who taught ESL, English as a Second Language, which was basically just teaching English to non-English-speaking people. His dad was a musician who played with the Righteous Brothers, on and off starting in 1975, which meant he was on the road a lot.

"Part of growing up was going to see Dad play in Vegas," remembers Will. "I saw the excitement of showbiz, but also the flip side. My dad would play at a nightclub for a year, and then it would end. So as a

The always brilliant, funny Will
Ferrell, telling his "get off the
shed" story on *Inside Comedy*.

kid, I had it set in my head that I was going to have a 'real job' carrying
a briefcase and wearing a hat. Of course, I didn't do that. The hat got
lost along the way.

"My dad was funny. He'd do a little bit of shtick on the stage with
Bill Medley every now and then. I was obviously a big fan of the early
Saturday Night Live years and *The Tonight Show* because, prior to cable,
that was the only time you could see comedians do their thing.

"I was pretty earnest, a conscientious class clown. I'd mess around
for a little bit, but if the teacher said, 'That's enough,' I'd say, 'You're
right. That was enough.' In elementary school, I learned how to do
physical comedy. I'd pretend to hit my head on the door to get a laugh,
things like that. It was a way to make friends and to be funny, and then
in high school it was a little more overt. I was conscious of it. I had
more of an Andy Kaufman approach. I'd come to school in my pajamas
for no reason, and people would say, 'What? What's going on?' And I
would say, 'Oh, you didn't know? You're supposed to wear pajamas. It's
Pajama Tuesday.'

"I was popular and had a lot of friends. I played sports. I was the
kicker on the football team, which is the funniest position on the team,
if you think about it. You just have to sit there and wait, hoping that the

quarterback screws up so you can go in. And you have a lot of down-time during practice just to do bits.

"Being funny came from just enjoying it, as opposed to a lack of getting attention. I loved sports, and I thought entertainment was too hard, so I went to college to study sports journalism. I thought, 'That's more of a real job,' and it's something I really loved—there's a little entertainment there, too. But I got done with college, and I realized, 'Oh, that's just as hard.' Everything's hard. I still had the nagging thing of wanting to try comedy, so I did try stand-up when I finished college. I took a stand-up comedy workshop, which consisted of a microphone and a little Peavey amp in a junior high classroom. It was a six-week class that ended in a performance. I'd previously gone to a bunch of open mics but was just too scared to go up. So, I thought, 'This will force my hand.'

"Here's my opening line:

"'Hi. I'm Will Ferrell, and a lot of people don't know this, but I was the original vocalist for the theme to *Star Trek,* and if you'll indulge me, I'd love to sing it for you.' I sang the whole song, and it would usually get applause. Then I'd say, 'The reason why I can sing that way is because I have no testicles.'

"For my act, I cobbled together about twenty minutes, at the most. What I found was that, usually, you only get five minutes starting out, but my setup was often an hour and a half before I got to the punch line. In improv sketch comedy, I found safety in numbers, that there's nothing more exhilarating than stand-up comedy when it's working well. I think everyone who performs should have to try it because it really tests your mettle. And when it goes wrong, you want to die.

"The difference between sketch comedy and doing stand-up is that when the stand-up audience doesn't like you, they're not saying, 'We don't like the set.' They're saying, 'We can't stand you. You, personally. We hate everything about you. Why did you even come out here and waste our time?' I think it's almost the bravest art form there is. I'd actually gone to see a sketch show my senior year at USC and got pulled up onstage to participate. I left that night going, 'Wow, I want to do that.'

"And then, of course, there are the comedians who influenced me in unimaginable ways. Steve Martin was really influential because in the seventies, when everyone was political, he stepped outside of it and was just absurdist. I loved his sense of freedom and commitment, and that faux persona of 'I'm incredibly handsome and talented.' I'd listen to his comedy album over and over again because that combination of silly but super-smart all at the same time was something that obviously registered with me.

"And then I get on *Saturday Night Live* and things started to happen, and talk about a surreal moment: Bill Medley from the Righteous Brothers is introducing me, having me stand up in the middle of the crowd. That was just so bizarre. During the O.J. trial, we did a mock show called 'O.J. Today,' and I was the first new cast member to be on the show that season. At dress rehearsal I thought, 'Oh. This is easy. This is great.'

"Then Lorne came up to me and said, 'No pressure, but the whole show is riding on your shoulders.' When they started to count down, it all hit me, and I flubbed the first line. Afterward, everyone said, 'It was a really human moment. It showed that the show is live and that you were nervous.' But in the midst of it, I realized, 'This is the hardest job I'll ever have, and also the most fun job I'll ever have.' The one character that I think got me the *SNL* job was a suburban dad who was yelling at his kids to get off the shed. I did that in my audition, and then I started hearing that I was being called the 'Get off the shed guy.'

"There were many characters I loved. My George W. Bush impression, rather than people finding it negative and controversial, actually had the opposite reactions. I had a lot of people say, 'Hey, I'm Republican and I love that show.' I made Bush feel very human in a way. He did very few press conferences as president, and I think the audience was just yearning for him to engage with them."

Another *Saturday Night Live* success story: "My life at *SNL* lasted seven seasons. Seven absolutely extraordinary seasons. Then I wasn't sure what I was going to do, but Adam Sandler had left, and Mike Myers and Dana Carvey had done *Wayne's World,* so it seemed like it'd be fun to try movies after the show. I'd only shot *Old School,* and I left the show with that not having come out yet. Then I began to create a world of characters I loved. I developed *Elf* because I thought, 'I've never seen that before, but it could be the end of my career at the same time.' The one character that is near and dear to my heart is Ron Burgundy from *Anchorman*. It took us close to three years to get *Anchorman* made. Adam McKay, who I met at *Saturday Night Live,* and I had written it on spec. We literally got ten rejections in one day. It was such a struggle to get that movie made. We couldn't believe we actually got to shoot it, and that it was actually in the theaters and did pretty well. I feel lucky that when I look back at these movies we've made, I like them all.

"Then Adam McKay and I created Funny or Die. We were the first ones to really tap into what the Internet had to offer for comedy with the Funny or Die sketch 'The Landlord.' It was Adam who had the idea for his daughter, who was two at the time and a great mimic, to play a nasty landlord. We took an hour to shoot it, and then, next thing you know, it's got almost eighty million hits. We used to have to ask everyone to put videos on Funny or Die. Now people want to do it!"

Will points out that although all the actors on *SNL* he mentioned were men, it wasn't completely made up of men. *SNL* had some extraordinary women—as did all of comedy. Many traced their beginnings to Second City—both the Chicago and Toronto versions: Barbara Harris, Melinda Dillon, Joan Rivers, Judyann Elder, Melissa Hart, Judy Morgan, Gilda Radner, Shelley Long, Bonnie Hunt, Amy Sedaris, Tina Fey, Catherine O'Hara, Nia Vardalos, Abby Sher, and more. The list continues with Kate McKinnon, Amy Poehler, Cecily Strong, Julia Louis-Dreyfus, Rachel Dratch, Jan Hooks, Kristen Wiig, Jane Curtin, Maya Rudolph, Ana Gasteyer, Molly Shannon, Nora Dunn, and Laraine Newman. And in a class all her own, the master comic and actor who went on to make a huge mark in film, television, and theater, Whoopi Goldberg.

Does it count that Whoopi Goldberg and I have *almost* worked together a lot? I wish we had, and I hope we do, but our paths have crossed many times over the years, especially together with Robin Williams and Billy Crystal, given that they raised over $50 million with Whoopi through Comic Relief. As far as her work is concerned, I have watched Whoopi survive and thrive despite all the glass ceilings that were put on top of her in her beginnings. Along the way, Whoopi has acted in many huge blockbuster films (more than 150), winning an Emmy, a Grammy, an Oscar, and a Tony (she's an EGOT), and going from theatrical comedy to drama to moderating *The View* since 2007.

I especially remember Whoopi in 1984, because I was working in New York at that time, and that was when Mike Nichols discovered her, when he saw her perform the monologues she had written. Mike created her show for Broadway, which ran for a year. I saw *that* Whoopi Goldberg. I was stunned then, especially as a young comedian and actor myself, watching her once-in-a-lifetime performance, and am truly still stunned when I remember how groundbreaking, emotional, and brave it was. And so funny. (It was that show that Steven Spielberg saw when he cast her in *The Color Purple,* which won her an Oscar nomination for Best Actress in 1985, showcasing her extraordinary talent as a serious actor.)

Nichols was so proud of Whoopi's one-woman show. And the public was totally entranced. I was blown away. Who can forget Whoopi as Fontaine, the dope fiend who bravely waded out into the audience, shaking up the crowd with his honest dialogues about pot and AIDS, and, in one of the most unexpected and earth-shattering pieces, performing a monologue on Anne Frank's room as the family hid from the Nazis, with Whoopi's point being not just the Nazi horror, but Anne's insistence that man is actually *good,* that we all have "heart." Combining these moments—sometimes more than moments—of great pain and, at the least, smiles, mostly from Whoopi's talent for making the audience identify with who and what she was portraying, showcased her deep intelligence and heart-wrenching, poignant pathos. I will never forget Whoopi turning into a handicapped character who was so real, so painful.

I have noted the unusual genius of the comedians who are also masterful, important dramatic actors, like Steve Martin, Robin Williams, and more. For Whoopi, the accolades for her serious acting did make her a star, but, for me, it is her brave comedy that marks her almost one-of-a-kind brilliance. Throughout her career, her comedy was as honest, as based in truth, as it could be, which made it gut-wrenching while still somehow funny.

Whoopi is an unbelievable mimic, and her ability to honestly portray humor masked in pain is absolutely unequaled. Her characters, often called avant-garde, were, to me, original, brave, and heartbreaking, while still head-shakingly funny, as Lily Tomlin and Richard Pryor would surely agree, because they understood and were unequaled in their own similar groundbreaking, biting satire that was also funny.

And make no mistake about it, in my experience, being heartbreakingly funny is hardest, as the writing, the creating, the bringing to life of these characters Whoopi created takes all that genius and makes it unforgettably and simply brilliant. Whoopi has tackled—many years before it became more common and obvious—discrimination, sexuality, and politics as arguably no woman, and certainly no Black woman, had.

Whoopi is the consummate artist. Period. And I wish we had worked together, as I also wish about Elaine May, a brilliant comedian and writer; Belle Barth, one of the blue female comedians, as blue as the males, with a sense of humor like a sailor, and who paved the way for Joan Rivers decades later; Phyllis Diller, unafraid in her comedy, so funny, and also not afraid to be unattractive and proud of it, with a signature huge laugh; Totie Fields, known for her broad comedy with words, who actually started out as a singer on *Ed Sullivan;* and Imogene Coca, the other half of Sid Caesar on *Your Show of Shows* (she won an Emmy for her work there), who had started out in vaudeville and was known for her comedic expressions.

Many years later, when I saw Amy Schumer at an NRDC benefit, I went up to her and told her, "You remind me of Judy Holliday." I didn't think she would know who Judy Holliday was, but she did. Judy was the opposite in terms of aggressiveness, but something in Amy's tone of voice reminded me of her. Amy started out in stand-up, won a place on TV's *Last Comic Standing* competition, and then became a hugely successful comedic film actress, winning an Emmy and a WGA Award as well as receiving Grammy, Golden Globe, and Tony nominations.

Obviously, the queen of comedy on television was the beloved and revered Lucille Ball, who was the first to break the comedy barrier between men and women. Lucy actually began her show business career as a singer, and then, in 1951, with her husband, Desi Arnaz, created her iconic *I Love Lucy* show, which kept going seemingly forever. Lucy was not just funny, she was a beautiful person who came from tragedy—she lost her dad when she was three (he was only twenty-seven), her mother and stepdad abandoned her to relatives, she was very shy in school, where she was outshined as a teenager by classmate Bette Davis, and she overcame rheumatoid arthritis—and persevered. She was smart, smart, smart (she and Desi retained full ownership of *I Love Lucy* but took a salary cut in exchange for being allowed to shoot the show in Hollywood rather than New York), in front of the camera as a comedian, as an actress (not many people know she acted in seventy-two films), and of course, in *I Love Lucy.*

Lucy and Desi Arnaz created the show under the Desilu banner—they wrote it and were perfectionists in every part of the producing. Nothing was ad-libbed. Every word, every facial expression, every laugh was planned and rehearsed, again and again. Lucy's work as a smart and breathtaking comedian truly paved the way for not just funny actresses like Mary Tyler Moore, Penny Marshall, and Cybill Shepherd, but also for Robin Williams. And this will probably surprise you: her work as a producer changed television, as Desilu produced huge television comedy hits like *Our Miss Brooks, Make Room for Daddy, The Dick Van Dyke Show*—and two non-comedies, *Star Trek* and *Mission: Impossible.* The studio was sold, in 1968, for about $17 million (over $100 million today) and was a milestone: a woman comedian/actor/producer/writer had owned and sold a studio.

I Love Lucy ran for six seasons with original shows, was the number one show on television with the highest audience numbers to this day (67 audience share), and had an afterlife that has been forever. It was the first comedy starring a woman, dealing with story lines like marital issues, women in the workplace, and pregnancy. And Lucy herself went on to star in two more shows—*The Lucy Show,* which ran for six years (1962–68), and *Here's Lucy* (1968–74), which is truly an astounding record. Of course Lucy won Emmys (four), was inducted into the TV Hall of Fame, got the Kennedy Center Honor in 1986, and received the Governors Award from the Academy of Television Arts & Sciences (home of the Emmys) in 1989, the same year she died.

So most of this you sort of know. Comedic icon. Woman ahead of her time. You might identify her comedy as "slapstick"—but that kind of sells it short. Her comedy, which was choreographed down to the smallest gesture, came from Lucy being one of the most disciplined comedians I ever knew. Her comedy seemed free-form, and in a way it was, because it was spontaneous, unafraid, and just truly funny, except that she knew every single thing she was doing, and all those gestures— hands and legs and especially those captivating eyes, the hair tossing, and the uproarious laughs—were rehearsed and written to the tiniest detail. But here are some other firsts and a heart-wrenching piece of history you may not know. Yes, Lucy was the first woman to head a studio, Desilu, which she bought from Desi and where she became a very actively engaged studio head. Desilu, moreover, and *I Love Lucy,* pioneered a number of methods still in use in TV production today, such as filming before a live studio audience with a number of cameras.

But to really know Lucy, and to understand the depth of her character and morality, we have to go back to 1936. When Lucy registered to vote that year, she listed her party affiliation as Communist and signed a certificate stating that she was registered as being affiliated with the Communist Party. The same year, she was appointed to the State Central Committee of the Communist Party of California and hosted a get-together at her home in Hollywood for new members of the party. Now, remember, this was not that unusual at the beginning of that era, as Communism was equated with socialism, and many entertainers believed in that. And, by the way, Lucy's grandfather called himself a socialist. (Ironically, years later, in the 1952 presidential election, Lucy voted for Dwight Eisenhower for president.) But in 1953, Lucy met with an investigator working with the House Un-American Activities Committee and insisted she was not a Communist.

Now, the climax of this story goes to Desi. Lucy told the story like this:

"We were filming episode 68 of *I Love Lucy*, 'The Girls Go into Business,' and Desi, who always—always—did the warm-up of the audience, instead told the audience about my grandfather, and then said, 'The only thing red about Lucy is her hair, and even that is not legitimate.'"

Another characteristic of Lucy is something else you may not know and is one of the things that I love about Lucille Ball—and that was her support of other entertainers, especially women. Lucy hired her co-star in *I Love Lucy*, Vivian Vance, for years after. She was close to (and also hired in her shows) Judy Garland, Ginger Rogers, and Ann-Margret. And, most of all, in 1966, Lucy became a friend and mentor to Carol Burnett. She was a guest on Carol's highly successful CBS-TV special *Carol + 2*, and, in turn, Carol reciprocated by appearing on *The Lucy Show*. It was rumored at the time that Lucy offered Carol a chance to star in her own sitcom, but Carol chose to create her own variety show. The two remained close friends until Lucy's death in 1989. Carol remembers, "Lucy sent me flowers every year on my birthday. When I woke up on my fifty-sixth birthday, in 1989, I discovered from the morning news that Lucy had died. Now imagine this—later that afternoon, flowers arrived at my house with a note: 'Happy Birthday, Kid. Love, Lucy.'"

I always thought that Lucille Ball and Marty Short would have made a great duo. Talent, sure. But they both exemplify the kind of comedy that has a natural, totally spontaneous quality, that is—and isn't. Both are consummate talents to the highest degree. Both created characters that people not just laugh at, and with, but adore. And that is a special gift. But I also dreamed of another amazing couple—like Lucy and Carol, how about Lucy and Bette? Don't you wish you could have seen them together?

Sometimes as a writer, as a producer, as a director, as a comedian—and as a person—you are at a loss for words. Actually, more times than you think. Because when you have been around as long as I have, when you started out in improvisation and then did stand-up and acted and

Bette Midler and I go way back to the early '70s. We were on Carson's *Tonight Show* many times together. I remember one time in 1973. She sang "Boogie Woogie Bugle Boy," told stories about her life, and blew everyone away. A wonderful storyteller in every way, an adorable person.

directed . . . you get used to talent, and while you continue to admire and respect it whenever you encounter it, there are times when you are blown away by the power of the person. So you know where I am going with this: Bette Midler, of course. Hello, Bette!

Singer (not enough of a description of the woman who belts out the classics she created that are so unforgettable that the same audience of tens of thousands turn out to hear them at every sold-out concert to this day, and she's sold over thirty million records!), songwriter (she wrote those classics), actress, comedian, film producer, and philanthropist.

Where did it come from? How did "Bette Midler, a lively girl from Hawaii" (Bette's own description) turn into a star whose power and career are based on courageous, enormous, and unique talent, a legacy of simply beautiful music and earth-shattering performances onstage and in films? What I do know is that the girl (named after Bette Davis) who started out having few friends in elementary school suddenly changed. "When I got to high school," she says, "I was the belle of the ball. I suddenly realized I was funny. I got into the drama club, where I did little plays. In fact, our junior class presented the first play that the high school had ever put on, and I was one of the people who was a catalyst for it. It was *Our Hearts Were Young and Gay.* Who knew? And I was one of the leads.

"And I have to say, to hear these kids laughing over the footlights was absolutely fantastic. And I thought, 'I want to be an actor. I need to be an actor,' thinking I would be an actor like Ethel Barrymore. Of course, I didn't know Ethel Barrymore. I had no idea what she did, but she was very dignified, and I liked that, so I patterned myself after her, doing speech festivals because I spoke English well (I was a state champion—many people in Hawaii spoke what was called Pidgin English). I would play both parts like in a drama reading. And I got a big trophy—it's still my favorite trophy. Except for the trophy that I won for perfect attendance in Las Vegas." Hard not to laugh when Bette is your lunch date, when one guest after another stops by with accolades, and Bette is gracious to everyone. I can see she is delighted, and proud.

Bette's dad was in the army, stationed in Hawaii. She spent a year at the University of Hawaii, where she was in the drama department, but that was difficult for her. "I'm a little bit of an autodidact," she explains, "which means knowing things by just teaching myself. So after a year, I quit and went to work at a radio station. I lasted two weeks. I counted up all my money, came to New York, and immediately got a job as a chorus girl in *Fiddler on the Roof.* Then a girlfriend from the show introduced me to the idea of singing in nightclubs. She dragged me down to a club, brought my three songs, and gave them to the piano player. And I got the gig. I did that for years and started making a name for myself. First I had three songs, then I had five, then I had twenty minutes. Once you had twenty minutes, that was an act, and you were allowed to get a job in a nightclub, opening for someone who was important."

You never know at which moment your career will change. I know that well, as does every comedian and singer and actor who ever performed. Bette opened for George Carlin at a club on the night that he decided he wasn't going to do his regular act anymore, that he was going to be edgy and avant-garde. That was, to say the least, surprising. Bette says, "It was horrifying. Nobody knew what was coming, and I was the opening act. He started riffing, and he was fantastic, but the crowd started to boo him. The next day, they asked me to be the headliner because they'd fired him."

And then, in 1970, came the baths (the Continental Baths, a local gay bathhouse in New York). "I had an acting teacher who knew the man who owned the baths, who said, 'I want to have a nightclub in my basement.' My acting teacher said, 'I know just the girl. She has an act of twenty minutes. Call her.' And it honed my comedy skills, and the guys were the most receptive audience to my comedy. After I was doing it for a while, the guy in charge hired a new piano player, Barry Manilow. It was love at first sight! He was a genius, he was funny, and he got the jokes. He could play in any style and especially loved rock and roll. We started putting bands together, played to sold-out crowds, and more and more people started coming to the baths. We became something of a sensation." Hit albums, sold-out tours, a TV sitcom (*Bette*), sold-out theater performances—whatever Bette did, she blew her audiences away.

During the last forty years, Bette has released fourteen albums as a solo artist. Hits? Too many to count. These will ring your bell—"The Rose," "Wind Beneath My Wings," "Do You Want to Dance," "Boogie Woogie Bugle Boy." Her film career includes multiple Golden Globe Awards and Oscar nominations for films like *The Rose, Ruthless People, Outrageous Fortune, The First Wives Club, The Stepford Wives,* and many others. Awards: I recount them here because they are for work across all types of entertainment—three Grammys, four Golden Globes, three Emmys, a Tony (that was in 2017, for a revival of *Hello, Dolly!,* which was sold out from the minute tickets went on sale), multiple Oscar nominations, and, yes, those over thirty million records sold worldwide.

And then there was *The Tonight Show Starring Johnny Carson,* which, as you know, was a huge part of my life. And Bette's. "I did *The Tonight Show* in New York," remembers Bette, with nostalgia in her eyes. "On the way to my audition, I was in the town car with Budd Friedman, who was my manager. I was wearing one of my thrift shop rags, and when I got out of the car, the damn thing ripped all across my butt. I literally had to hold my dress together with a paper clip. I got onstage, and I was so angry that I was in another zone and really sold the song. I wouldn't have gotten the gig if my dress hadn't ripped." The song? "Empty Bed Blues."

I remember that night so well, not just because Bette was riveting, but because Johnny and I discussed her performance more than once when we were together. "Empty Bed Blues" knocked everyone's socks off. Johnny and I thought Bette was doing a version of Janis Joplin. But really she was just being Bette.

It was the film *The Rose* that changed Bette's life though, because the singer who sold out clubs and concert halls became an instantly acclaimed actress with an Academy Award nomination.

Other films followed. Surprisingly, Bette remembers one script with much fondness. "I got a script for a play called *I'll Eat You Last*. It was a one-woman show about Sue Mengers, an outrageous and successful agent in Hollywood, whose most famous client was Barbra Streisand. I thought the script was really funny. I'd never done a show that I wasn't in charge of. I knew Sue Mengers a bit—a girlfriend once brought me to her house, and I fell in love with her. She was hilarious. She was pro-fane. She was nutty as a fruitcake, and nothing bothered her. Somehow, the whole world came to Sue, and I really loved that about her because I'm quite shy. Everyone who knew Sue had a story about her, but she never had a memorial, so *I'll Eat You Last* was really like her memorial." The play was a huge hit, with Bette receiving accolades for a truly unforgettable performance, and she toured with it nationwide.

But one of my most memorable times with Bette was a notorious night at the Hollywood Bowl, the first gay benefit held in Los Angeles, where Bette and I performed. You can read the entire story from my point of view, and from Lily Tomlin's, who also performed that night. But there is one thing to know that is distinctly Bette—she had been performing to and for gays her whole life, since those first nights with Barry Manilow at the baths in New York all those years ago. That night, as I watched her sing, I was moved by her compassion, which was in every note she sang, and by her bravery, to be able to be funny, to mock herself and the audience, and yet show them that compassion is everything. And that's Bette—the ultimate entertainer, a performer with a huge fan base that follows her from concert to concert, from appearance to showcase.

This is not the case with Mike Myers, a comic actor who excels in film and television. Mike and I share a bond that is unbreakable. It's not just ours, though. It is being a Canadian. When I received the Order of Canada last year (Mike had also received this honor), I was moved to tears at the ceremony. I did mention Mike as a fellow Canadian comedian. Had I mentioned all of them, I would still be talking. Since we don't have a time limit, here are Canadian comedians and comic actors who have dotted the entertainment world with huge impact: John Candy, Catherine O'Hara, Eugene Levy, Andrea Martin, Dan Aykroyd, Norm Macdonald, Seth Rogen, Samantha Bee, Tommy Chong, Lorne Michaels, Martin Short, Mike Myers, Jim Carrey, Ryan Reynolds (maybe not a comedian but a great comic actor), Michael J. Fox, Tom Green, Howie Mandel, Leslie Nielsen, Will Arnett, Caroline Rhea.

Enough of a who's who?

Mike Myers will like this. He is so proud to be Canadian. And like many of the others, he was on *SNL* (six years), had great film roles (*Wayne's World, Austin Powers*) that received terrific reviews, was in *Inglourious Basterds* in 2009 and the Oscar-winning *Bohemian Rhapsody* in 2018. And also, like many of us, Mike started at Second City, in the Canadian touring company. He left to work in England, then returned to Toronto and starred in their main theater. But it was the sketches that he and Dana Carvey adapted from their *SNL* days that became the film *Wayne's World* (they sang the song "Bohemian Rhapsody," which became iconic).

When Mike and I get together, it's just plain fun. And when we do, we often begin recounting, again and again, our stories about Canada. "I grew up in a very strange house, where my dad (who was British) would do singsongy catchphrases like 'Michael, you're not good enough.' Which is a little sad. Actually, I made that up. He was very supportive, I just wanted to add a little drama.

"I started performing when I was eight years old, in a British commercial for British Columbia Hydro, which is what they call the electric company. And then I did one for Datsun 610. So, as a kid, I was already performing. I thought I might want to be an architect, and my dad said, 'Why would you want to do that? Why wouldn't you want to be an actor?' I'm the only performer I know whose dad was just like, 'No, just be an actor.' And then when I became an actor, I was so proud to see so many other Canadian entertainers. I was so proud to see you, David, on *The Tonight Show Starring Johnny Carson.* I did love Wayne and Shuster. I was very proud that Lorne Michaels and Dan Aykroyd were from Canada. And I didn't realize Gilda Radner was from Detroit, because she worked in Canada a lot, so I thought she was Canadian, too.

"My father died in 1991, and I went into a funk, no two ways about it. And when I created *Wayne's World,* in 1992, where I was strapped to the front of a rocket, and all of a sudden life is moving a million miles an hour, I realized that the only person that I ever wanted to see any of it had just died." And this tells you something about the character of the man whose comedy is frenetic, surprising, hilarious, absurd, farcical, uproarious—all traits he actually includes in the comedy that is so memorable, the comedy he so loves.

"Then I got hired on *SNL.* I handwrote the material for it on a yellow legal pad. On the fourth show that I was on, I was very nervous, so I put my yellow pad on the read-through pile. Another writer came in and read it and said, 'This sucks.' And threw it on the table and left. I was devastated. But I picked it up and I put it back on the pile. And I walked home because I couldn't afford a cab (we got paid three hundred dollars a show, a thousand dollars if we got on the show, and we did twenty-two shows). The next day, we saw that the sketch had gotten into the pack, but it was the last sketch. The last few sketches, people are like, 'Aw, really?' So Dana Carvey (my supportive co-writer) gave me a look like, 'Let's do it, dude,' which was very generous of him. Dana had explained that *Saturday Night Live* was a little bit like the court of the Borgias, so never drink anything that anyone offers you. So the sketch got on, the last sketch of the night. I did the skit, I sold the shit out of it, and I brought the house down. And the crew, who have always been unbelievably supportive of me, sang the 'Wayne's World' theme on the way out. And on Monday, the members of the crew said that everyone on the subway was talking about it."

In life, Mike speaks at a hundred miles per hour. He is unstoppable. "In 1997 came my dearest *Austin Powers,* which kind of came from my family. It's my fuzzy memory of being forced to watch British culture, and coming to love it. I didn't research anything for *Austin Powers.* I wrote it in two weeks. I knew he was gonna have bad teeth, because the English won the war and lost their teeth (you can be an unbelievably great celebrity, even as recent as David Bowie, and be happily and easily described as snaggletoothed). The character is sort of a James Bond parody. Gene Siskel had given me, in his review, a tremendous compliment. He said, 'Mike Myers has managed to come up with a brand-new form of entertainment, which is the tribute movie. A tribute movie whose franchise has made over $750 million.'"

Mike always likes to hide behind his characters. If the writing is good enough, which it always was, it works, as you can see with *Austin Powers* and *Wayne's World.* Mike was still creating characters in the revamped *The Gong Show* (the executive producer was Will Arnett, another extremely talented Canadian in the comedy world). When it first appeared in the 1970s, it was considered a kind of campy, nothing show, a kind of amateur talent contest where they cut off the losers mid-performance—and it was a huge success. In this reincarnation, Mike plays the jaunty, devil-may-care British host Tommy Maitland, and I defy you to recognize Mike in this person. But you always recognize Mike in his characters, because they always—and I mean always—manage to combine hilarity with humanity.

Most of us comedians did not inherit our comedic talent. Ben Stiller did. No question about it. And it was actually his specific talent in the kind of comedy that gave him huge success and fame—exaggerated, slapstick, farcical, absurd situations seemingly out of control but in

actuality totally controlled and created. His parents, comedy veterans
Jerry Stiller and Anne Meara, also excelled in comedy; they were known
for their back-and-forth routines popular on many variety shows. So
even though Ben's talents also include serious acting, writing, producing, and directing—as you well know, he is most celebrated for his
absolutely hysterical huge blockbusters (bringing in more than $2 bil-
lion) like *Reality Bites, The Secret Life of Walter Mitty, Zoolander, There's
Something About Mary, Meet the Parents, Dodgeball, The Royal Tenen-
baums,* and more—we give his parents huge credit for surrounding him
with their comedic sensibilities and talents.

I always love talking to Ben, because the conversations are
unpredictable—swinging from funny to serious is just par for the
course for him. His memories of growing up in a home where his parents appeared on *The Ed Sullivan Show* (thirty times) are of a fun-filled
childhood. "You don't know anything else as a kid except what you're
living with. I was more interested in the comedy world than in going
to school because it seemed like more fun. But, of course, I wasn't seeing the hard work and the pressure, so when I decided I wanted to be
like them, they were supportive. They were a little concerned and over-
protective because they had to deal with rejection themselves. But my
sister and I weren't around for the times that they were struggling, so, as
kids, we didn't think of that. All I thought of, when I was ten years old,
was that I wanted to direct. I always loved *Jaws* and *The Godfather,* and
watching comedians like Albert Brooks and Steve Martin, but I didn't
know I wanted to be an actor. I loved watching and making movies
with my friends."

The inevitable auditions came along. "After auditioning for three
years," remembers Ben, "the first acting job I got was in a revival of
an off-Broadway play called *The House of Blue Leaves* by John Guare. I
was horrible at auditioning and used to choke a lot on the callbacks. I
choked on a fourth callback for *My Cousin Vinny.* You know that auditions don't really give a full sense of what an actor can do, and I always
kept that in mind later on. When Judd Apatow and I were producing
and directing *The Cable Guy,* Owen Wilson came in to audition and
did so-so, but we'd seen a short film that he did, *Bottle Rocket,* which
later became a feature. I remember thinking it wasn't a great audition,

but I give Judd credit because he knew Owen would be good. And one of the first jobs I got after *House of Blue Leaves* was *Empire of the Sun,* and I was so grateful that I didn't have to audition because Steven Spielberg was so confident in me."

The truth is, like me, Ben loves directing, especially directing actors he admires. For example, he says, "It was incredible directing Jim Carrey in *The Cable Guy*. He's a force of nature. He would do twenty-five variations of the same line to try all the possibilities. Writing it was such a rewarding collaboration because Jim had so many ideas that we funneled into what Judd and I already had, which made it both satirical and real. We were all so young and didn't know what we weren't supposed to do, so we were able to take chances."

Judd Apatow went on to direct many successful films, but not many people know that he started as a stand-up. Ben does. "Judd was a stand-up who'd write for other people like Roseanne and Garry Shandling. We met in 1990 for an *Elvis Costello Unplugged* taping at MTV. We knew all the same people, hit it off immediately, and talked about comedy. I asked him if he wanted to help out on a sketch show I was doing for HBO, so we started hanging out at the comedy clubs and working together right away. It took us two and a half years to start creating a pilot and go through all the different versions of it until the show, *The Ben Stiller Show,* finally got picked up. We did thirteen episodes, and they aired twelve before canceling it. But we were just so excited to be doing it that, even when we got canceled, we weren't bummed, because the journey to get on the air had been so long."

The Ben Stiller Show was one of the most underrated comedy shows ever. It was so very good. And then it took almost ten years for Ben to direct the huge hit *Zoolander* (an animated version was on Netflix in 2016), the kind of insane satire of the fashion industry (a sequel was released starring Ben, Owen Wilson, and Will Ferrell) and a huge box office hit. Was it fun to make?

"It was great. Drake Sather, the late stand-up comedian and comedic writer, came up with shorts for the VH1 Fashion Awards about people in the fashion world, and asked me to do the male model character. We did the shorts, and then we went through thirty drafts of the script over three years. The studio didn't really get what we were doing at the time, so *Zoolander* didn't get a big buildup. We came out a week and a half after September eleventh. It was tough. We couldn't think of any reason not to release it, and we thought it could be nice to have a comedy as an option after that kind of tragedy."

I'm so curious, since Ben's films are so uniquely his, what movies influenced him. You may not be surprised, given Ben's sensibility, and his comedy made up of surprises, sassy and audacious moments, bold-faced writing, and those hysterically blunt mannerisms.

"I was obsessed with *Caddyshack*. When it came out, I was working as an assistant scuba instructor in Nantucket, and everyone would stand around impersonating Bill Murray's character. I have a strong connection to Albert Brooks movies as well. He was brilliant at creating a persona of himself, which he started in his stand-up and then recorded in his comedy albums. My sister, Amy, and I would listen to them over and over. Albert took his own experience and used it to make really funny movies that didn't always have happy endings, which hadn't been done before."

I thought *Tropic Thunder* was so bold in every way. The whole satire of the movie business was spot on. That was all Albert, says Ben. "That comes out of all the Albert Brooks and *SCTV* humor, making fun of how seriously actors take themselves and the ridiculousness of it. Unfortunately, a lot of people don't see that side of the industry because they're not in show business, and there's always a challenge of appealing to a broader audience while capturing what I found so funny. That movie is about indulgence and excess, and we needed a big budget to execute that, so it kind of folded in on itself. It was a good lesson because despite all the money we spent on special effects, if we couldn't make the audience laugh, it didn't matter. Actually, it was Albert Brooks who inspired me to be a director. I started out on *Saturday Night Live* as an apprentice writer there because what I really wanted to do was make short films. I wanted to do what Albert Brooks had done there."

I, too, am an Albert Brooks fan. He's a huge talent in writing, directing, and comedy. As a person, he's talented beyond description—odd, subdued, full of integrity, a genius writer, and a humble guy. Maybe a little more than odd—Albert can disappear into his room while guests are partying, and then rejoin the crowd with humor and warmth. You kind of have to march to that drummer in your head with his kind of talent and success. Albert's work was a big influence on Ben's because his sketches were like little films. But others, too, have pointed to Albert as a big influence. He is that actor/comedian who received an Oscar nomination for his role in *Broadcast News* and got accolades for his role in the movie *Drive*. His voice is known to animation buffs for the classics *Finding Nemo, Finding Dory,* and *The Simpsons*. But his most glorious accolades have always pointed to him as pure genius—and that is as director, writer, and star of *Modern Romance, Lost in America,* and *Defending Your Life*. He also appeared in *Taxi Driver,* the Scorsese classic, where he improvised his dialogue. I had the pure joy of directing him in *Weeds*.

Yes, Albert does it all. He was a writer on *SNL,* and during the first year of the show, he directed six short films starring Paul Simon, George Carlin, Rob Reiner (Albert went to Beverly Hills High School with Rob), Candice Bergen, Richie Pryor, and Elliott Gould. He was on *The Ed Sullivan Show* as "The World's Worst Ventriloquist" (1971, one of Ed's last shows), and was called "The Funniest Person on the Planet" by David Letterman whenever he appeared on his show. He also appeared on *The Tonight Show Starring Johnny Carson* (Johnny called him "an unusual performer who didn't want to be plugged"— and Albert cracked him up every time he was on the show), and he is mentioned by most comedians as influencing their work (see especially Steve Martin). And Albert still consistently voices animation hits like *The Secret Life of Pets* and *Finding Dory.*

Albert Brooks's brother was the late, amazingly talented Bob Einstein, my dear friend, he of the "Super Dave Osborne" character and his one-of-a-kind portrayal of Larry David's friend Marty Funkhouser on *Curb Your Enthusiasm*. I repeat—Bob's brother is Albert Brooks. And his dad was Harry Parke. Explained Bob, "My dad went by the name Parkyakarkus. He played a Greek restaurateur. He had been on radio for years, with Eddie Cantor, Al Jolson, and then he had his own show. We loved him. He was a well-known comedian. And when he died, I was fourteen, and it was just the worst. He was appearing at the Friars Roast Dinner for Lucille Ball and Desi Arnaz. He had just performed, he killed the audience, went to sit on the dais, and died of a sudden heart attack. I heard about it on the radio in the morning. It was horrific. He was an insanely brilliant man. And what I got from him was—he never threw humor away. He would say something, it was funny, there was not a lot of experimentation, and he would say, 'Just talk and be funny.'" And yes, since Bob was Albert's brother, this does mean that Albert Brooks's real name was Albert Einstein, and surely I don't need to explain why Albert changed his name.

I first met Bob on *The Smothers Brothers Comedy Hour*. He remembers it as a pivotal moment in his life. Not because he met me, but thanks to Tommy Smothers.

"In all seriousness, and I haven't said this enough in my life, I thank Tom Smothers for any success I've had. He had the balls to give me and so many people a chance when we were young punks. And he put his career on the line in our hands, which was pretty stupid. He gave Steve Martin his chance, too. Steve was very nervous as a young kid. He was working at Knott's Berry Farm, and his act was silly. At the time when everyone was doing Vietnam humor, serious stuff, he was doing stuff with a candle in his arm. But Steve was such a super-bright guy, who turned out to have an amazing career. We wrote scenes together mostly in the office, even though we were roommates living together. We tried to push the envelope as much as we could. And a lot of that stuff worked great."

And then there was the night . . . Let us explain.

Bob recounts what happened. "Remember Officer Judy on *The Smothers Brothers Comedy Hour*? Judy Collins was on, and whenever we would have a guest on who was that special, we'd try to do something silly with them. I just thought it would be so ridiculous if I was a policeman that was singing one of her songs. And then at the end of the song, Dicky would say, "Tommy, what was that?" and Tommy would say, "Coming over here, I was arrested for speeding, and the cop asked if he could do a schtick on the show." So that's how it started. The next week, I arrested Liberace. But it seemed that everything we did, we got lambasted by the censors. And so we started putting bad words into the script. Like 'fuck,' and 'shit,' and the censors would go crazy and take that out but let everything else go by. So that's how we got away with so many things—until we were thrown off the air."

Of course, I remember it well, too. I was on that show. Bob remembers that, too.

"You, David, were doing the sermon about God," he says. "So in the sermon, the next thing we knew, we were all handcuffed and up against the wall and sprayed with mace. David, it was such a great piece."

Bob then started writing for Redd Foxx, with me, since I was producing and writing at the time. We did some great shows for Redd. Fred Silverman, who was the greatest programmer of all time, told me that he was going to ABC, and would go after Redd Foxx from *Sanford and Son*. He said, "If you produce the Joey Heatherton show, I'll give you a three-year deal at ABC," and I said no. I mean, I loved Joey, she's gorgeous, but I figured we're gonna have trouble getting guests, we have no money, it's a summer show, and no one knows what this show is.

When Joey hears this, she says to me, "David, I've already got a commitment from Frank Sinatra, Fred Astaire, Dean Martin, and Bing Crosby."

I said, "Are you kidding me? Those are gonna be our first four guests?"

"Yes."

"That's a guarantee?"

"Yes."

Our first guest was Gary Burghoff, and we had to give him a song. That list—it didn't exist. We went to ABC, and Fred gave us the deal.

Fred says, "I want you guys to do Redd Foxx."

So Bob and I go to a meeting with Redd Foxx, who is truly, and by far, one of the funniest men in the history of the world. He comes into the office, and he's staring us down, and he goes, like Charlie Chan, into a revolving bookcase. And disappears into the office. I'm telling you the truth—the fireplace turns into a bookcase, it's gone. He comes back out, with white stuff all over his nose, and he says, "How you doin'? How you doin'?"

I said, "Redd, you got white shit all over your lip."

He said, "Always happens when I have sugar donuts for breakfast."

So we agree to do the show. First show, we have an audience of four hundred people from the Farmer's Market.

"Ladies and gentlemen, Redd Foxx!" Magnificent set, music, big band is playing, audience is going crazy, no Redd.

"Ladies and gentlemen, Redd!"

No Redd.

I stop the tape. I go to his dressing room. I knock on the door.

I hear, "What?"

I open the door, and the girl who is doing his hair is sitting on him. I see his head under her dress.

I say, "Redd."

And from under the dress, he said, "What?"

I said, "We're on camera."

He said, "Can't a man relax?"

Then I said to him, "Redd, we only did one little sketch for the audience. Could you go talk to them?"

"Yeah!" And whenever he said "yeah" to me, I knew I was screwed. He goes down and he takes the mic in front of these four hundred people.

He says, "How many of you washed your assholes this evening?"

I'm hearing purses click, and I see people grabbing their hearts.

Redd says, "You know, they got all kind of flavored douches on the market—strawberry, persimmon, pineapple. I told my wife about it, but with my luck, she came back with tuna."

I said, "Gimme the mic."

"Is that enough?"

I said, "Yes, that's plenty of entertainment."

I loved him. He started in the '50s. Before everybody, Redd was doing it. He helped so many people. He gave so many people a chance. And his comedy was as edgy as you could get on television and radio at that time, and completely cringe-worthy filthy and sidesplittingly funny. You would be embarrassed to be laughing at Redd's humor, everything from showing up at everybody's Passover Seders where he was supposed to recline, and he would take the pillow of the guest next to him and fall asleep, to talking about the different flavors of douches at a dinner party.

Years after Bob Einstein and I worked with Redd, Bob created Super Dave. Or more accurately, *The Super Dave Osborne Show,* a Canadian-American variety show where Bob played Super Dave, who ran a theater, performed outrageous and often scary daredevil stunts; things always got screwed up, and Dave would be injured every show. The stunts were outrageous—he flew on a yo-yo, was catapulted across a giant football field, and at the end of each outrageous stunt, he would appear injured. It was ridiculous and hilarious. It debuted in 1987 and ran for five years. The character was Bob's creation, and he also played him on various comedy and variety shows, and on his own show on Showtime. It was shot in a theater with an audience, and Bob stayed in character, even when his notable guests—like Ray Charles, Celine Dion, k.d. lang, Jerry Lee Lewis, Kenny Rogers, Sonny Bono, Steve Allen, and the Smothers Brothers—cavorted in various costumes.

Bob remembers, with fondness and amazement, that it worked:

"You never know what'll work. Who the hell knows? Everyone I talked to in show business, with the exception of you and a couple of other people, are liars. On the news, they'll say, 'That's my favorite, I love it.' Off the news, it's 'Screw 'em . . .' So I wanted to do a character that was really full of bullshit and full of himself, but also got hurt. And when he got hurt, the real him came out. So that's what it was, and it was what I absolutely love—physical comedy. I had to top my own stunts all the time. It was so hard! My favorite stunt—and everyone seems to love this—is still when I'm on top of the bus, and I'm going on a five-hundred-mile singalong tour to stop profanity on the highway. 'Cause you can't swear when you're seat-belted to a piano going down the highway."

I am laughing as I reread these words. He died way too soon, and I miss those 8 a.m. calls waking me up, asking how I did on set the day before. I really loved Bob.

· · ·

You've heard it before—after graduating college, an aspiring comic goes from club to club trying out stand-up routines, dreaming of being onstage or on TV. Not Wanda Sykes. Not too many Black, gay, female, hugely successful comedians worked at the NSA. The National Security Agency. Five years. So the fact that she ended up co-starring and guest starring on *The Chris Rock Show* (for which she won an Emmy), *The New Adventures of Old Christine, Curb Your Enthusiasm,* and *Black-ish* needs some explanation. And it is a great story.

Wanda explains: "I grew up in the Maryland, DC area. My father is a retired colonel in the army, and he was stationed at Fort Meade and the Pentagon. When you live in that area, you end up working for the government in some way. So when I graduated from college and moved back home, those were the opportunities that were there for me. I filled out my forms and tried to pass a drug test to get a job at the

With Wanda Sykes, a brilliant comedian and comedic actress, on the set of *Inside Comedy.* A true joy to be around.

NSA, and it worked out. It was bizarre. I was a contracting specialist, so I bought things—and I hate shopping. The engineers designing the spy equipment would send the blueprints to me, and I'd send those out to contractors to get prices. I'd always try to figure out what they were making. Somehow, among all these career army employees, I was always funny. I made my co-workers laugh."

And so she found comedy at a talent showcase in Washington, DC. She then began appearing on television and was discovered by a true comedy hero to comedians just starting out, Caroline Hirsch of Caroline's Comedy Club in New York City. There, Wanda opened for Chris Rock, joined his writing group, and also appeared on his show. The writing team won an Emmy, and Wanda went on to appear on *Curb Your Enthusiasm* and to come to terms with being a gay woman.

Carol Leifer, the well-known, well-liked, and very talented comedy writer, has said that she dated all these guys, and all of a sudden she'd had enough of that and fell in love with a woman, and has been married to her forever. And she came up through the comedy circles, too. I wonder if Wanda's story is similar?

"Very familiar," says Wanda with that honest laugh. "My version kind of mirrors Carol's story. In relationships with guys, I'd get to a certain point where I'd feel like, 'If the guy disappears right now I think I'll be okay.' It wasn't until I got divorced that I thought, 'I forgot, I'm gay!' Then everything made sense to me. Stand-up is male dominated. I fit in so well and developed great relationships with the other comics because they saw me as one of the guys. There was mutual respect, so it wasn't, 'I'm gonna laugh at Wanda's jokes 'cause she's got a nice set of tits.' It was genuine."

Where did the "funny" come from?

"My parents are funny, but in a way that doesn't work with strangers. My mom and dad do great impressions of people at their church, and it's hysterical if you know these people. We laughed a lot in our home, and that was the age when they had all these great variety shows, so we were exposed to comedy every night. Moms Mabley, the Smothers Brothers, all these great comics were on TV. Moms Mabley was really underrated for how funny she was. She had a huge influence on me. My mother said I'd walk around with a nightcap on my head, like she did. All this comedy stayed with me, but I didn't know how to do it as a career because I was in such a structured environment. I didn't even venture to take theater classes because I knew my parents wouldn't pay for them, and they'd want me to study a trade instead. It wasn't until I was able to take care of myself that I let myself do what I really wanted to do, which was comedy.

"So I entered a talent show that a radio station was sponsoring. The second I got big laughs, I knew, 'This is my thing! This is what I do!' I didn't win, but Andy Evans, a local comedian who was emcee-ing, was blown away because he hadn't heard of me at all. I'd dropped in out of nowhere. So he showed me around to the comedy clubs, and that's where I met Dave Chappelle. He was sixteen at the time, and we became good friends, although I think he was using me, because when his mother couldn't make it to the club, he told people I was his aunt, since he needed an adult with him in order to stay. He was so good right away!"

Wanda then wrote with Chris Rock on *The Chris Rock Show* (for which she won an Emmy), which is when Wanda and I started to run into each other at comedy tapings, at every award show, and on the set of *Curb* over the years, and we always gravitated to spend time with each other. Years later, Wanda came on my *Inside Comedy* series, where we couldn't stop talking, and I was honestly admiring of her strength, her ballsy humor, her bravery, and her truly engaging personality. Wanda's humor was not about funny words—it was about her attitude, and her security even when throwing out outrageous, honest humor, with strength and courage.

Wanda: "I'm a Black, gay woman. I think the only way to make the GOP hate me more is if I sent them a video of me rolling around on a pile of welfare checks."

As for Wanda bonding with Chris Rock on his show, it was a mutual admiration society.

"I always tell Chris that I owe him," Wanda says fondly. "I learned so much, because, basically, everyone stumbled in front of the camera. Jeff Stilson, Louis C.K. . . . just a lot of power. That was my first writing gig, but I really became known as the crazy lady from *The Chris Rock*

Show because I was the fake guest. The Bill Clinton–Monica Lewinsky scandal was going on, and I played one of the president's secretaries and said, 'The president is racist.' And Chris asked me why, and I was like, 'Because I've been sitting at that desk for three years, and he's just walked right by me and hasn't touched me once.' I named all the other Black women in the White House and said he wouldn't even spill coffee on us, and meanwhile he's throwing himself at these white girls. It was just ridiculous. I knew how far I could go, but I wanted to go a little further."

Later, in 2009, it came full circle, as Wanda hosted the White House Correspondents' Dinner, the first African American woman and the first openly LGBT person to get the role.

And then Larry David came into Wanda's life. That comes with its own stories. From 2001 to 2011, Wanda played a recurring role as . . . herself. She was Cheryl David's funny good friend who stayed friends with both Larry and Cheryl after their divorce. It was a coveted place to be—full of the most talented improvisational actors, the greatest writers who were constantly working hard on the writing, surrounded by talent in every corner. But, I ask Wanda, was it fun?

"I love working with Larry," she explains. "But *Curb* was probably one of the most stressful gigs I've ever done. In 2001, I got a call from my agent telling me that the *Curb* producers were shooting an episode, and they wanted me to do it but didn't have a story. Well, of course I wanted to do it. But I also wanted to know what the scene was about. For years, whenever all these great actors and comedians would shoot this amazing show, I never got anything to read until I arrived on set. Some days I'd get lucky and one of the makeup people would fill me in a little. If the great Jeff Garlin was around, he'd ask if I knew what I was doing that day, and I'd be like, 'No, Jeff, when does anyone around here know what y'all are doing today?' We were all thrown out into the fire, and it's Larry David, so everyone wanted to impress him and make him laugh. That was my thing, to make him break up and lose it, laughing. I loved that. I really loved that." So does Larry.

·   ·   ·

Larry also appreciates the actors around him. That was always particularly obvious when Larry appeared on *Saturday Night Live*—especially in 2015, when he played Bernie Sanders to huge accolades and surprised many people who always see Larry as playing a version of himself, not a well-known figure. It brings to mind when Tina Fey played Sarah Palin on *SNL,* another well-known figure rather than the brilliant comedic roles that bring Tina award after award.

How could she have been on so many hits, which ran for so many years, getting so many laughs, garnishing award after award, expanding her horizons with huge producing duties and more awards—and still remain so humble? She's Elizabeth Stamatina Fey, also known as Tina Fey, that's how.

Let's get those credits out of the way up front, because you cannot understand her range of super talents, her achievements, and the kind of comedy she so excels at without them. Television: *SNL* writer, then head writer, and performer, for nine years. Creator and star of *30 Rock,* seven years. Creator of *Unbreakable Kimmy Schmidt,* which was on for four years. And many, many films. Her memoir, *Bossypants,* was a *New York Times* best seller. Awards: nine Emmys, five Screen Actors Guild Awards, seven Writers Guild Awards, and the same Mark Twain Prize for American Humor that was won by Julia Louis-Dreyfus.

Tina started at Second City in Chicago, years after me. Tina often speaks about the impact *SCTV* had, which is always gratifying to hear, being that I was involved in it from the beginning. In fact, the *SCTV* group was in a show in Toronto called *The David Steinberg Show.* I put them together. We did a year of shows, and then we didn't get picked up. They preferred Canadian *Stars on Ice.* Perfect for Canada. And then *SNL* head writer Adam McKay recruited Tina as a writer. She became head writer and anchored "Weekend Update" with Jimmy Fallon. She continued to perform, then left to create other hits. And then, years after she left *SNL,* there was the Sarah Palin moment, 2008. All hell—great hell—broke loose. And she continues her prolific career to this day.

.   .   .

While we are pointing out talented women comedians who are true to their brand of humor and their brave positions on everything, Sarah Silverman immediately comes to mind—another multi-hyphenate as stand-up, actress, producer, writer, who has been talking about social taboos and controversial political issues forever. Sarah's forté is that she is sincere and honest while discussing religion, sexism, and racism as satire. Her act tackles issues that are in the cultural limelight, but she is never in your face about an issue—she can insult and be sarcastic while engaging you with that genuine beautiful smile disguised as a smirk. She embodies the art of pushing the envelope in the most intelligent of ways. And she is surprising and shocking on her way to funny, which is part of her joke. Her misdirection, a favorite comedic technique of some of the best comedians, made her consistently funny.

What I couldn't get over about Sarah when I saw her for the first time is how bold she was onstage. I could never tell where she was headed. That's the best part of doing stand-up, and I loved that about her. She was aware of what she was doing with the audience, just this side of nervous, and then released it with a laugh. She was just brave enough to make the audience a little uncomfortable. How did that start?

"My dad was funny, a real character, with a very strong Boston accent that is impossible to understand, even for me. When I was three, he taught me a whole bunch of swears, which he thought was hilarious. All these adults were shocked that a toddler was swearing, but it gave me so much attention and approval from grown-ups for saying things that were shocking, so it isn't so surprising that, from a very young age, I became addicted to this shock, and it would inform my later comedy."

We know what pushing the envelope in comedy can mean. For me, after many years of success in doing so, we also know that I got the Smothers Brothers thrown off the air. For Sarah, it was an evolution of trying different material and testing different boundaries. An example of such a joke was one she wrote in high school. "I was doing this kind of joke when I moved to New York. My friend asked me if her breath smelled like tacos, and I said I don't know, 'Do you put shit in your taco?'"

This was a different level of comedic courage from her idol, Steve

On the set of *Inside Comedy,* 2012.
Sarah Silverman telling me how she
played me in a remake of *The Odd
Couple.* Smart, irreverent, adorable
person. A great comedian.

Martin. "I worshipped Steve Martin growing up," Sarah remembers. "I
loved him so much. On my ceiling of my childhood bedroom, and it is
still there, it says, 'I heart Steve Martin.' I think I first saw him hosting
Saturday Night Live. Then his comedy specials, his books, his albums,
and then his movies like *The Jerk* had started coming out. I loved how
absurd he was, that even though he looked like such a dignified man,
he was so silly. I read everything about him. One article said that he
lived in Los Angeles and loved this artist David Hockney, who was at
the LA County Museum. And you know, I'm from New Hampshire. I
had never been anywhere besides Boston. And we went to the Boston
museum, and I got a David Hockney calendar, and I took all the pictures out, and I hung them on my wall. I'm just this fourteen-year-old
Jewish girl in New Hampshire with paintings of gay men in swimming
pools all over my wall because I loved Steve Martin."

Jimmy Kimmel and Martin Short, aside from being extremely talented, can make any party a lot more fun.

Sarah was a writer on *Saturday Night Live* for a few months, produced and starred in *The Sarah Silverman Program* for three years, guest stars on television programs constantly, and is also known for being on *Jimmy Kimmel Live!* for many years while they were romantically involved. You are probably familiar with the time, in 2008, when Sarah appeared on *Jimmy Kimmel* to show Jimmy, who was her boyfriend at the time, a special video, a song called "I'm Fucking Matt Damon," in which she and Matt Damon sing a duet about having an affair behind Kimmel's back. The video became a phenomenon on YouTube. When Sarah won a Primetime Emmy Award for Outstanding Original Music and Lyrics for that song, Jimmy released his own video with Damon's best friend, Ben Affleck, where many stars sing Kimmel's song "I'm Fucking Ben Affleck." This back-and-forth between them caused so much public attention, especially when Sarah won the Emmy, that it still comes up whenever comedians and talk show guests and hosts get together. Sarah recently had another version of her own show on Hulu called *I Love You, America with Sarah Silverman*.

Her outspoken comedy, in many appearances, continued years later, when Sarah spoke at a TED conference in San Diego, which offended those involved. Sarah explains, "The overall theme of TED, what they say to keep in mind when writing your piece, was 'What the World Needs Now.' And I talked about 'population,' how there are so many children already born, and that I would like to adopt a mentally challenged baby. But when you make a decision like that you have to embrace all the ugly thoughts that come to your mind. And one thing I realized was that the best-case scenario is that I die of old age at a hundred, and I'll still be worried about who's gonna care for my elderly retarded child. So I came up with a solution that works for me, which is, I am going to adopt a mentally challenged baby with a terminal illness. Now, you're probably thinking, what kind of person looks to adopt a mentally retarded baby with a terminal illness? An amazing person."

Now, if you think that got attention, it certainly did. Lots of it, much unwanted. But Sarah doesn't remember any show of discomfort or anger by the audience. "I'm used to having a level of discomfort," she explains. "But the crowd was great, and it wasn't until the next day, when I was driving to visit my mom, that I saw on Twitter that Chris Anderson, head of TED, had tweeted to his million and a half followers that I was awful. And I just felt so betrayed. They invited me to go there, I had my manager double-check that they knew who I was and what I did. So now I felt bad. I tried to not say anything, so I waited a couple of days, and then I found myself writing on Twitter, 'Kudos Chris Anderson for making TED an unsafe haven for all. You're a barnacle of mediocrity on Bill Gates' asshole.'"

I tell Sarah I think that is pure poetry. Sarah is not so sure. "Because I just feel like he's somebody, and I should be compassionate and not write about that—but I am a little bit proud of it, and maybe I shouldn't be. In all honesty, I feel like I put together a very well-constructed sentence." And Sarah has a personal message to TED: "If there is any lesson Chris Anderson could glean from this, in addition to, your wonderful project of TED should be a safe haven for people, and not some place where if you blow it you're in trouble, it's that you really can't fuck with comics, you know?"

.   .   .

Lasting in the business for almost fifty years, going from stand-up to television series (remember *Anything but Love* with Jamie Lee Curtis?) after television series—that brings kudos, continuous work, and continuous laughter. My dear friend Richard Lewis, who, thank goodness, I continue to run into on the set of *Curb Your Enthusiasm,* where he has been appearing since 2000, started doing stand-up forty years ago.

"I went to the Improv to check out open-mic night," says Richard. "I asked David Brenner about it. He said, 'Listen, this is the only game in town. Just go to other dives, when you think you have a good ten, twelve minutes, then come into open-mic night.' So I listened to Brenner, and I went everywhere for half a year, and I called him up and I said, 'I'm ready.' I was playing at a place that's no longer there, where you had to be pretty bad not to be the king of the hill. If a mental institution bused a day trip, that was the lineup, then me. It was so easy to follow these guys—they were mental patients. And, David, I say mental patients with tremendous respect.

"So Brenner comes in, and he says, 'You're ready.' And I went to the Improv, and it sounds like a boast, but I blew the fucking room away. Budd Friedman [the founder and owner and supporter of many great comics] came onstage, put his arm around me, and said, 'You're the new all-star of '71. You wanna stay around for the real show?'

"I said, 'Of course!' I was immediately arrogant. I went on at two in the morning. The audience had three guys who were on peyote or mescaline, four drunks, two Klansmen. No one could have killed. And I bombed. And I learned the lesson. Then, and now, all these many years later, I'm a regular at the Improv. But that night, I was so blinded by my own success that I stayed. And I learned—and a lot of comics will probably tell you this—if you have a bad show, and you bomb, wear it like a cloak, like an Ingmar Bergman coat, you know, in *The Seventh Seal.* Until you get back onstage and have a good show."

Richard is so right. That hasn't changed to this day. You have a bad show, you carry it with you, forever. So the lesson was—and is—you'd better get used to bombing, because sometimes you can't control it in any way. "When things happen to you as an artist, keep working, keep moving. I still remind people that, when you start out, you want to be a ballet dancer or a writer, you just better really want to be that, and learn your craft, 'cause there are no fucking guarantees. It's a ruthless business, so all there is to do is work on your craft and hope you get a break."

Richard did get a break, doing *Anything but Love* with Jamie Lee Curtis. "I had a good four-year run with Jamie Lee Curtis, who was phenomenal. I got the sitcom, and all of a sudden, by the end of the day, forty, fifty million people see my face, know my name. And within two months I'm selling out three-thousand-seaters, adding a show, Carnegie Hall, you know and I am basically the same guy. You need that break. I was ready years before, but I was lucky that it happened."

I ask Richard, as you know by now, the question I always ask: Was your family part of your comedy education, supportive and encouraging? "I'm almost weary discussing how little I got from the family," replies Richard, apparently used to this question. "No one in the family helped. They were in their own world. My father never saw me. Not once. My mother didn't get me. I used to beat myself up and bring her on my shows. You would think that on a television show she would turn around and praise me. Nope. I was doing a gig in New York and I brought her on the *Tom Snyder Show,* which Tom was hosting after the New York news at five p.m.—that's 2.3 million people! My mom interrupts the news to say, 'Here's his greatest joke.' She does my joke as a joke!

"I wanted to scream, it was so unbearable. She had problems; I guess she did the best she could. But another time, a week before Carnegie Hall, I did a show in my hometown of Englewood, New Jersey. It's a twenty-five-hundred-seater, sold out. And I was already in the TV series, so people knew me. And my mother came two hours early. She goes, 'Hi, I'm his mother. How are you? I'm his mother,'" introducing herself to twenty-five hundred people and then sitting down in the front. It was all for attention. She needed attention as much as me. But she did it in a way that, unfortunately, hurt me. How? I would be onstage, and when you're a comedian, we use hyperbole all the time. I'd say, 'My father had seven heads.' And my mother would yell, 'He never had seven heads.' It was a fucking nightmare. I actually won them over, but how, I don't really know. Finally, I realized that it was a burden I did not want to have. So I called my mother and said, 'You cannot come to Carnegie Hall.' I would have felt it. She sort of understood and didn't come. And you know what, David, it turned out to be one of the great nights of my life in terms of the show."

One of Richard's invaluable traits is speaking out about drinking before a show, remaining sober onstage. He doesn't preach about it, but he is open.

"I was dying from it," Richard explains quietly. "I looked in the mirror, and I went, 'Do you really want to die like this? You got so many blessings in your life. You really want to have a heart attack and go now?' And I said, 'No.' I called two friends, who took me to Cedars-Sinai Hospital, and this time, when they rolled me in the gurney, the doctor looked down and said, 'What are you doing to yourself?'

"I looked up and said, 'I am killing myself. But it's over.' That was August 4, 1994. I haven't had a drink since. It's still one day at a time. I'm just glad it happened, because it has enabled me to help other people, and there's nothing better. And that's what I do now."

I wonder if the comedy, the work, got more authentic in some ways after Richard got sober. What happened to the stand-up? I sensed an important answer, because so much of Richard's comedy is based on neurotic reactions to circumstances, psychotherapy, depression. So what did happen to the stand-up?

"It mushroomed, David. I did a throwaway once. I said, 'I have so much clarity now that I despise myself even more.' And I really meant that. If I have anything that's authentic, it is that I love destroying myself onstage. I love admitting my failures. So when I got sober, it was part of my sobriety to look in the mirror and go, 'All right, screwball, you take some responsibility.' And it made my comedy better than ever."

Years later, Richard is still doing stand-up.

"I have never lost my passion for stand-up. Whenever there's been acting, there have been a couple of series, and, lately, of course, *Curb* with Larry David. That's the best—I have kind of been playing myself on *Curb* since 2000. It is the greatest gift. So great!"

. . .

Great! This is a perfect story about who a comedian is. Let me tell you a story about Bob Saget. Many, many years ago, when he was an unknown comedian, he worshipped the old-timers of comedy. As did I. Even as a kid. When Bob was fourteen, in Los Angeles, he had seen Larry Fine, one of the Three Stooges, speak at his high school. Later, he found out that Larry was living in the Motion Picture and Television Country House and Hospital in Woodland Hills. Bob went to visit Larry there.

"I brought him black-and-white movies of himself when he was younger. I brought my eight-millimeter projector and I showed him his films, with subtitles, and Chaplin films, Laurel and Hardy, Buster Keaton, the Ritz Brothers, or the Marx Brothers. So he was looking at himself when he was young, with the projector running, and the light and no sound, and it was kind of like purgatory for him because he didn't get to hear the comedy. And then he would just go, 'Moe beat the shit out of me. Broke my ribs. Threw me on the table, pulled my hair out. Can you imagine what that was like for me?'

"Years later, I went to see Larry, who was then in a wheelchair, and suddenly he wheels himself backward to go to the front desk, to get his new teeth. He rips open an envelope, takes out the bubble wrap, takes the teeth out, and just puts them in his mouth. It was a perfect Three Stooges moment."

As with almost all other comedians, Bob did stand-up. His was a little different in that he really spoke to the audience. I mean literally spoke *to* the audience. Not walking into the audience with a mic. "I do not do *The Price Is Right* or the *Let's Make a Deal* approach. But I do engage an audience. When I go to a city, when I'm on tour—I'll go to a place, and it's a town meeting for me. I really do like to immerse myself. I look at it as a date. With a town. Or with that venue. With the people. They yell stuff out at me 'cause they know me from different things." Not a surprise—the man had been on television for so many years playing pretty much the same character, so it makes sense that his audience felt that they really knew him.

It is kind of fitting that I come toward the end of my book by telling the story of Bob Saget and his kindness to and love for a member of the Three Stooges, because I started this book extolling my reverence for and experiences with Groucho Marx and George Burns and their world, for stand-up comedy, comedians in clubs and on television, and those who excel at being both actors and comedians.

And Bob Saget was part of all those worlds. Only difference was, he was tall. Six feet four inches tall. One of the tallest comedians I knew, probably around the same height of the brilliant comedian and my good friend Brad Garrett. Taller than Kyrie Irving and David Letterman and Craig Ferguson and Larry and Jerry. Not to mention that he towered over me.

But, at the risk of being trite, Bob was tall not just in height but in kindness, as you see by his care for Larry Fine (and Bob was a kid then); in his work—sixteen films and more than thirty-five television shows, including big hits like *Full House* for eight seasons, *Fuller House* for five seasons, *America's Funniest Home Videos* for eight seasons, and years on *How I Met Your Mother* as the voice of Ted Mosby. On *Entourage,* he played a parody of himself, a part I found hilarious—a foul-mouthed, womanizing druggie. What I loved was that Bob didn't mind being oafish, goofy—taking chances with his comedy.

And the shows keep going. In rerun heaven, they seem to go on forever. Said Bob with some wonder, "They showed *Full House* on Netflix, and it beat the ABC lineup on a Friday night! Thirteen episodes for families to binge on, and they did!" You can catch Bob on all those television shows on YouTube, and since I didn't direct any of them, I have no stories about what he was like to direct, although others will tell you that he could have been a terrific director himself.

Another Second City graduate? Steve Carell. He is the sweetest man, actor, comedian, and writer. Funny in all versions of comedy. And, it turns out, a gifted serious actor as well. You probably knew him first as the correspondent on *The Daily Show with Jon Stewart,* for six years. His films were huge box office and critical hits—*Anchorman, The*

40-Year-Old Virgin, Get Smart, Crazy, Stupid, Love, Foxcatcher (that got him an Academy Award nomination), and more.

Steve grew up in Massachusetts. I never would have guessed that, as he doesn't have a bit of an accent. He explains, "That pretty much says it all. That sums me up. They call us Mass-Holes. I can't even do a Massachusetts accent. My wife grew up there. She can do a great Massachusetts accent. And I'm sort of 'Pahk the cah in Hahvad,' which is terrible. I'm actually really good at accents. I always do comedic accents. You know, like in *Despicable Me,* there's no accent there; that's just sort of, I flew over sort of Eastern Europe, and that's the accent. There's nothing, nothing actually legitimate about that. It's just loud. I was bad in the movie because it was a choice. That person as a character is a bad actor."

I, of course, always want to know who was with Steve in Second City.

"Stephen Colbert, Amy Sedaris, Ron West, Jill Talley, and various others. I was there for six years. I started with the touring company and then went to one of the satellite resident companies until I finally made it to the main stage. Then it was Stephen Colbert who got me the job at *The Daily Show with Jon Stewart.* I'd been living in Los Angeles doing very bad pilots for terrible TV shows, and Stephen called me out of the blue, right at the transition between Craig Kilborn and Jon Stewart, and said they were looking for correspondents. He asked if I'd be willing to do a field piece, and I moved to New York after that."

A word about Jon Stewart's show. Co-created by two women, Lizz Winstead and Madeleine Smithberg, it was kind of a replacement for *Politically Incorrect.* To say it was ahead of its time would be so trite. It brought satire television to new heights, made news stories more than real, gave wider perspectives to politics, politicians, and media, and did all of this by making fun of itself and of serious coverage in the media. It was brilliant. Won over twenty Emmy Awards. Steve's correspondent was deliberately political, as Stewart wanted, with an editorial voice.

"In my mind," says Steve, "my character, the correspondent, was a guy who'd done national news reporting but had somehow fallen from grace and was now relegated to this terrible cable news show, so he was bitter about it. He thought that he was smarter than he was, and took himself very seriously. The first field piece I ever did was on a guy who owned a venom research facility, which was really just a mobile home in the middle of Nebraska, but he was also an Elvis impersonator. I almost didn't do the piece because it was predicated on being mean. Stephen said that you have to make it work for yourself somehow, so I decided to make my character the butt of the joke instead. I once went to a convention of people who'd created a whole Klingon language based on *Star Trek* episodes. They were the sweetest people in the world. I didn't want to make fun of them, so I sang a Klingon song with them, took it very seriously, and got them in on the joke."

Steve went on to host *SNL*. "I've hosted two times. When you're standing backstage as they announce your name, you get a chill because the show has so much history. The fact that it's live is different, because you know that whatever happens, happens. Lorne Michaels told me, 'Your adrenaline will go so hard that when it's over, you'll collapse.'" And it was so true.

And then came Michael Gary Scott, Steve's fictional character on *The Office,* the American version of the British hit, where his part was played by Ricky Gervais. "Ricky was our executive producer," explains Steve, "but he wasn't really there on a day-to-day basis. He really entrusted us with it, because he didn't want it to be the British show. The odds were against us because we were up against some really stiff memories of an iconic show, and I didn't want to impersonate Ricky because he's so unique. So I needed to go in a different direction. At first, viewers weren't on board with it, but after a while, audiences began to find it and got the tone. It took some time."

Then came movies. Many became huge hits; most were memorably fun and wonderful, but one, not so much.

"It was called *Melinda, Melinda,*" remembers Steve. "It was a tiny little part alongside Will Ferrell in a Woody Allen movie. I played Will's best friend, and it was a surreal experience. I was petrified, because I knew going in that Woody wasn't a person who I could try to buddy up to. He just wanted us to do our jobs. Once, I did a take of what I thought was a funny line and chuckled to myself after. When we cut, he told me not to ever laugh at myself in a movie. The audience will think it's funny, but your character doesn't think it's funny."

I explain to Steve that Larry David would not agree. Larry likes to laugh at himself. He thinks people laugh at themselves in real life, so why wouldn't they on-screen? Steve agrees. "Yes! Will and I had one long scene, and Woody said that they were going to cover it with different cameras, so not to worry about it being the only chance to get it right. We rehearsed it once, and a guy with a handheld camera shot it, and that was the only take. Woody had no intention of covering it, but he wisely took all the pressure off of us by making us think we had ample opportunity to get it right."

Then Steve and Will did that huge hit, *Anchorman.* I wondered if they improvised.

"We all improvised. It was so funny I laughed until I cried. Will is such a good improviser, and it's such an absurd movie. He was walking around with a full beard, drinking out of a milk container. You don't know why it's so funny, but it just is. I didn't have a lot of lines on the page, and the director, Adam McKay, told me to just say anything I wanted at the end of each scene. So I would look around the room and think about what my kids would say. When we were in a scene talking about love, I said, 'I love lamp. I love table.' And Will said, 'Brick, you're just looking at things in the room and saying you love them.' That was in the movie. It was just ridiculous fun."

After all these years, I wonder if Steve still thinks of the comedians and actors who influenced him when he was starting out. "I've always been a Steve Martin fan. I'd listen to his albums over and over, and I'd try to figure out what was making me laugh and how he was timing everything. He was an anti-comedian to me, since he was very silly and joyful, but there was such an intelligence behind the silliness. I was trying to dissect comedy, which is an odd thing to do, because there's nothing more boring than somebody's process. Pulling the curtain back takes all the mystery away."

We exchange anecdotes about the well-known actors we have watched over the years. What about Jerry Lewis? He was tall, but he would do things to make himself seem smaller because he thought the height wasn't appropriate for a comedian.

Steve replies, with seriousness and a little disdain in his voice. "Someone who's tall and good-looking isn't funny. When a comedian becomes really ripped, they lose about seventy-five percent of their funniness. You sort of hate them, like, 'How dare you become handsome and healthy?' I'm never going to be in good shape, because I want to be employable."

Employable? Not a problem. Especially now, as Steve, in addition to his performing, is one of the executive producers of our series, *Inside Comedy*. Employable? Always.

Some comedians just make you laugh when looking at them. For me, that's Jim Carrey. Yes, he is one of our Canadian Americans, an actor, comedian, producer, musician, impressionist, screenwriter, and his latest success and obsession—cartoons drawn with pen and ink, especially of politicians who are in trouble. He's contributed to *Playboy* and *New York* magazine.

Makes sense, right? Jim is a brave, outlandish, grab-them-by-the-balls kind of comedian and actor. Strangely enough, although we both travel in comedians' worlds and are both Canadians, we only met recently. And not surprisingly, our conversations are always repartees.

Jim is kind of surprised. "Didn't we meet once on a moose hunt? Didn't I almost shoot you?"

I remind Jim, "I am from Winnipeg. We don't play with moose."

"I'm from Toronto," he reminds me. "We can actually cross the street without blowing away in Toronto."

I remind him, "In Winnipeg, you can't. It's flat as can be, and every American I know says, 'Oh, the skiing must be so great.' Actually, I always say, 'It's so flat, you can watch your dog run away for four days.'"

Jim goes with that one. "It is fantastic skiing—cross-country."

When we start at the beginning, it is a familiar story. Yes—stand-up. Jim, who has such a wonderful sweetness beneath that bravado of near insanity, recounts with great fondness, "My dad was the guy that galvanized the room; he was like a cartoon talking. He was mesmerizing. I wanted to be like my dad. When I started doing my stand-up, my father was a huge supporter of mine. He was funny, funny, funny. I have a theory about comics—that they all come from emotionally sick mothers, who needed some kind of bolstering." I am amazed when Jim shares that with me, because that was exactly my situation with my mom. Jim continues, "My mom was depressed a lot—she was a child of alcoholics. I felt that she needed love from her kids, needed us to fill that gap for her. I kind of lived in that, and I had a burning desire to make her feel good. So when I was that little kid, I looked at my dad, and I went, 'Oh, that's how you get over sadness, that's how you wanna be: funny.' I would entertain her—I'd come in in my underwear and do my praying mantis impression. You know, crawling up on the bed. You must have a good praying mantis to make it in comedy."

Moving from that to an audience became the goal.

"My father had read about these places called comedy clubs. This was the mid-seventies. He took me down to Yuk Yuks, in downtown Toronto. I was fifteen years old. And I got up and did an act that my father and I put together—imitating Tim Conway as an old man. My focus was actually the imitating. That was really the trick that I did that everybody loved. I was going to be the man of a thousand faces—I got to about a hundred and fifty. And I really was about faces. I used to do James Dean, and I would turn my face and my whole being inside out and really kind of acted these parts. Years later, I ended up in Vegas doing these impressions when I opened for Rodney Dangerfield. I thought I would die in Vegas. I just was not happy with the idea that this was going to be my resting place. I wanted a wider kind of appeal to whatever I was doing. And I just believed that there was something deeper going on. So I went to Hollywood."

And the rest, as they say, is history. After appearances at comedy clubs, Jim's grander career kicked in. We have all seen his very funny *Ace Ventura: Pet Detective* film, probably multiple times, ditto *Liar Liar,* the exceptional *The Truman Show,* and *Dumb and Dumber* (which made $257 million twenty-six years ago; Jim wrote it with the Farrelly Brothers, as well as the sequel and the animated TV series that followed), and his TV series *In Living Color.*

Jim explains, "Keenen [Ivory Wayans] actually hired me because I was so disrespectful to him when I went into my audition. I told him I loved him and then pretended to assassinate him in front of everybody. And for some reason that's what got me the job. But I was definitely committed to Keenen and the joy—beyond belief—from the first time

I met him. I had never created characters before that show. It was a whole new process to me. And those guys, that incredible cast, were on their feet, never doing the same take twice. It was really just like Second City training."

It was a truly innovative show. *SNL* had been around, but this took comedy to a whole other level that you'd never seen before. And the show was culturally interesting, because it was all African American, except for Jim and actress Kelly Coffield.

Jim: "It was fantastic because they had a complete belief in me and gave me the greatest opportunity of my life to be seen in a way that would be beneficial to me. It really encouraged me. It was a wonderful opportunity, and I feel graced by it, for sure."

Then came *Ace Ventura,* which was another huge step up. No one saw Jim moving into the movies. "It was hilarious," Jim explains, "because David Alan Grier would make fun of me. I was in the *Living Color* offices, and once we finished our writing for the show, me and Steve Oedekerk would stay late and write and rewrite *Ace Ventura: Pet Detective.* Of course, I didn't even believe in *Ace Ventura: Pet Detective* when I took it. I figured, 'I'll rewrite it if I don't like it. As long as I have a trap door and I can get out—it's cool.' Of course, Steve and I were always in the office until four in the morning, howling with laughter, getting completely pregnant with this thing. And by the end of the draft, there was no way I was not gonna do it. David Alan Grier still continued to make fun of me in front of the audience. He would say with some sarcasm, 'Ladies and gentlemen, Jim Carrey, during hiatus, is gonna be doing a movie called *Ace Ventura: Pet Detective,* and we're expecting real big things from that.'

"And everybody would howl with laughter at me. And I would just kind of sit there, red-faced. And then the movie came out. And the next thing you know, the very next time we went up in front of the audience, David was like, 'Hey, everybody, let's hear it for Jim Carrey in *Ace Ventura: Pet Detective.* It's really nice to see! Congratulations, Jim!' And he gave that David dejected face that he does so well. So yeah, its success was a shock to everybody. The amazing thing is that I got such great response from other comics that I love. That meant everything to me. Seinfeld called me immediately following the movie and said he'd never laughed so hard in his life. Imagine! Steve Martin called me and said he'd been kind of shy lately, hanging out in his house a lot, and his friends told him to come out and watch *Ace Ventura,* so he decided to go out, begrudgingly, and he said it made him believe in the world again."

So what does Jim do to follow his film stardom? He exhibits in art galleries, contributes to many magazines, and works seemingly constantly, as if he has been possessed by this need to express himself through his art. "Making art is not a choice," he has said.

Making genius comedy isn't, either.

Speaking of a kind of genius (you knew I was going to do that, right?), did you know that Ellen DeGeneres has an older brother? He is funny, too. Vance DeGeneres has been an actor, musician, film producer, and screenwriter, and was also a correspondent on *The Daily Show* for a couple of years. But his most beloved and rewarding job I hope has been as my executive producer of our television show, *Inside Comedy.* It was actually Vance who brought the idea of this show to me, as he was already a successful producer. Lucky me.

Here I am with Ellen DeGeneres on her set. But the tables are turned, as I'm interviewing her for my show *Inside Comedy,* 2011.

I bring him up here not because he is a great producer (which he is), but because his younger sister, Ellen, says he is the one who most affected her sense of comedy when she was growing up. "He was very funny early on," remembers Ellen. "And I was very influenced by him. But I don't know that I was funny growing up. Animals were an early passion of mine, so most people I grew up with (except my brother) are very surprised that I made a living doing stand-up. In high school, I used humor to fit in, but only people I was close with knew that I was funny. I was not funny in big crowds. I wasn't shy—I just didn't care to make a big scene. I wanted to be funny around a few people. Then I learned that you had to be funny around a lot of people to make money, so I expanded."

Time for the credits of this brave and universally adored talent, because it is heartwarming and will make you smile just to be reminded of the expansive career she has worked hard to enjoy, one not without its ups and downs, and one that she has navigated with class and courage. She has been hosting her syndicated television show for over seventeen years, but she has been a presence on television for almost thirty. She has hosted the Oscars, the Grammys, and the Emmys. She has thirty Emmys of her own, twenty People's Choice Awards (more than any other person), and in 2016 received the Presidential Medal of Freedom from President Obama. They both cried.

Ellen has been an LGBT activist since 1997, and after a setback in her career when she so courageously announced that she is gay (which she handled with enormous grace, dignity, and integrity), she has been a huge star, has tens of millions of devoted fans, has developed her own lifestyle brand (ED Ellen DeGeneres), and has led campaigns for global AIDS awareness and animal rights. If you have watched her show, which, of course, we all have, or follow any media at all, you know she has been married to the actress Portia de Rossi, now known as Portia Lee James DeGeneres. And that she is an amazing combination of cool reserve and ultimate warmth in her comedy. She is truly a comedian to respect and admire.

Of course, I wonder who inspired her, in addition to Vance.

"I thought Steve Martin was hilarious because he's so intellectual, yet his comedy is ridiculously easy and simple. Woody Allen also influenced me, and I read his books and watched his movies. I followed Carol Burnett and Lucille Ball, and I was also a fan of Bob Newhart, because I loved his very dry humor."

But Ellen's comedy started out very quietly. I love the way she found herself in humor.

"I'd never been to a comedy club. Someone needed to raise money for some cause, and they asked me to do stand-up. I'd never done that before. This was when I ate meat, and I walked onstage with a Burger King Whopper, fries, and a shake and said, 'I'm so sorry, but I've never done this before, and I haven't eaten all day long. If I don't eat something, I'll get too weak and nervous.' And I started unwrapping the burger and took a huge bite, and then said the next part of the sentence, and I did that through the entire meal, and then just walked off when I ran out of time. Later, I performed at a coffee shop. I didn't really play piano, but I wrote a song and said that I wrote it when I was in the hospital while I was screaming. It was just one chord. I did stupid things like that, and then I started actually writing material."

Back to brother Vance. By the time Ellen started being really serious about her comedy, and letting herself feel the success that comes with people laughing at your performance, it was "Vance who had already been on *SNL,* and he was the one with all the talent, so it was nice for me to get some attention onstage. After that, I performed at places I had to drive to, and sometimes ended up out of pocket. I didn't even have gas money. When the bar was raised, and I was performing with other comedians, it got really hard, and there were nights when I wanted to quit, but I couldn't because I had no other skills. I saw a banner in the French Quarter in New Orleans for a comedy club, so I talked to the owner, a Mafia guy with no clue as to what comedy was. I asked if I could get a job there emceeing, and he hired me because he didn't have a plan.

"So I was the MC for all these comedians coming from all over the country," Ellen explains seriously. "I was scared to death, and he kept trying to force me to curse for the X-rated shows, but I wasn't going to change, and they didn't know what to do with me because I wasn't doing the typical gendered material. I was doing stuff that I found weird and funny, a lot of prop comedy. I would go up onstage and just hold up fabric and just look at people. Then I'd put that down, and I'd hold up, like, velvet, and then I'd put that down, and I'd hold up something else. And I'd just say, 'I'm trying out new material.' I did a lot of prop comedy like that. I'd open up a can of corn and say, 'I know that was a corny opening.' I did really bad stuff like that."

Then a friend of Ellen's invited her to live in San Francisco. She did, and, she recalls, "I started doing stand-up, but I didn't get paid for most of it. In San Francisco there were so many good comedians, we all just wanted to get stage time. There was this huge comedy contest, and people from NBC were there. Everyone thought I was going to win, and I was planning on moving to LA the day after my victory. Sinbad beat me in the finals. But I got a holding deal with David Spade at Lorimar. Then I was on three episodes of a show written by Neal Marlens and Carol Black, the creators of *The Wonder Years,* and I barely had any lines. I asked them if they'd write a show for me if their show got canceled, and they said yes because they loved me. One day, Neal called to tell me that their show had been canceled, and they actually did want to create a show for me. I felt I had to tell him that I'm gay or else he'd be so mad he had created the show when he found out. He said he already knew, and he asked me if I wanted to be gay on the show. I said no, because I was closeted and knew that no one would watch a show about a gay woman."

Times they are changin'. "We had forty million viewers and two more shows left after the one where I went public about being gay [Ellen actually came out on *The Oprah Winfrey Show,* and then Oprah played Ellen's psychiatrist on the coming-out episode of *Ellen*]—one where my boss finds out I am gay and fires me, and the other where my father finds out and has a huge problem with it. Those were two of the best shows, because that's what happens when you come out to everyone in your life when you're an adult. I was really proud of those shows. They obviously changed my life, but they also changed the direction of the show. The last two seasons were fantastic, but there were boycotts. I found out that the show had been canceled from an assistant who'd read about it in the papers."

Sixteen years later, *The Ellen DeGeneres Show* continues to get big ratings, has a fervently loyal following, and wins all those Emmys. Ellen smiles. "It makes me very happy to see the kind of audience that wants to make an effort to come see me. Not just turn on their TV. But actually makes an effort to be here. It may feel like a different world, until you read the news and see that there are still children being bullied, even to the point of taking their own lives, and you see the overturn of Prop 8. But it makes me very happy to see the diversity of people who make an effort to be in my audience. I went from losing everything to being completely myself, to have the kind of viewership that we have and the kind of fans."

Ellen continues quietly, "And when I look out in this audience and see the diversity, all ages—grandmothers and young kids, all colors . . . there's everything. If we let animals in, we would have raccoons. Raccoons love me."

Raccoons don't come up much in conversations with Jon Stewart, but cows and dozens of pigs and piglets and rabbits and sheep and goats do . . . because they live with Jon, his wife, Tracey, and his family on a twelve-acre farm in New Jersey, which is also a refuge for abused animals.

Jon has been doing stand-up and writing comedy, producing, directing, and acting for over twenty years, and, in the last ten, actually acting as a political commentator in the forefront of outspoken, watchful criticism of politics and of hypocrisy in government and in our society. His commentary has always been encased in brilliant humor, first on *The Jon Stewart Show* (on MTV) and then on *The Daily Show* (the biggest hit on Comedy Central to this day). And as I write this, he has a new current affairs show about to come out on Apple TV+. In between, he appeared on others' talk shows, hosted the Oscars twice, and co-authored the best seller *America (the Book): A Citizen's Guide to Democracy Inaction.*

Childhood? Complicated. Estranged from his father, he grew up with four brothers, and he wasn't funny. So he says. Played soccer. Graduated college. Worked at various jobs you would never guess: puppeteer, HR, caterer, five-and-dime store, and as a bartender for three years at the legendary nightclub City Gardens in Trenton, New Jersey, in the late '70s—though he never performed there. Like all of us, he found stand-up. Specifically, at the Bitter End. I, of course, assumed that Jon had been working at various comedy clubs by then. I am stunned to hear that the Bitter End "was my first night," says Jon. "They had a process back then of auditioning, where they would bring people in. At that time, the Bitter End was more music than comedy. I think Monday night at one a.m. was their audition time. And I passed."

He's right. Not good. When I was starting out at the Bitter End in the late '60s, I was opening for the late Jerry Jeff Walker, who was a very close friend that I adored, and Tom Paxton—folk music was still very popular. Kris Kristofferson was down the street at the Café Wha?. (He wouldn't let any of his friends come and hear him because he didn't like the way he sang.) Jon remembers it, too. "We used to talk about that place and go, 'That's the Village Gate, man. You know who used to play there? Dylan, man. Richard Pryor,' and 'You know who plays there now? Us. And you know what, we kind of suck.' So, it's more that we felt bad for the Village Gate.

"A lot of our determination in those days was to get better. So when we started out, we had the previous class that had just graduated from New York—Richard Lewis, Jerry Seinfeld, Robin Williams, Richard Belzer, the guys that had worked the Catch and the Improv. I went on at the Cellar every night—and you got a plate of food, you know? Falafel and hummus, which at the time you didn't realize was because chickpeas are incredibly inexpensive. So you figure, 'Holy shit, I got a bowl of hummus here!' I was okay because I worked at a Mexican restaurant right up the block, so I was set for lunch and dinner. I also drove to do the Jersey one-nighters—if you needed to make seventy-five bucks, you could go out there, because, at that time, they had turned almost every type of drinking establishment into one night of comedy."

Fast-forward to 1993, when Jon began to be widely recognized, thanks to *The Jon Stewart Show,* an instant hit, and his voice became truly important. It was being heard, admired, and was entertaining. (The show's production company, Worldwide Pants, was founded and owned by David Letterman.) Six years later, Jon began hosting *The Daily Show,* and it was revolutionizing for television. Its correspondents were stellar and went on to huge careers on their own. They included the likes of Stephen Colbert, Steve Carell, John Oliver—talents who combined political and social intelligence and brilliant humor. They covered everything—the media, politicians, prejudice and discrimination in society, always with a combination of amusing, biting commentary and playful cynicism, all geared toward making people laugh. Jon has won twenty-one Emmys and two Peabody Awards, for coverage of the presidential elections called "Indecision 2000" and "Indecision 2004."

Jon connected with the audience in a way I had not seen, as his commentaries not only taught people but moved them. I will never forget the show he did after 9/11. Here is what he said, with tears in his eyes:

"The view . . . from my apartment . . . was the World Trade Center . . . and now it's gone, and they attacked it. This symbol of American ingenuity, and strength, and labor, and imagination and commerce, and it is gone. But you know what the view is now? The Statue of Liberty. The view from the south of Manhattan is now the Statue of Liberty. You can't beat that."

In July 2019, Jon was not just mad; he single-handedly took on Congress in his campaign to get compensation for life for the 9/11 first responders. "You should be ashamed of yourselves," he told members of Congress on Capitol Hill in a very emotional takedown of lawmakers who were not inclined to step up. His outrage, his angry words—"It is an embarrassment to our country," he said when criticizing members of Congress who skipped the hearing—brought his inflexible integrity back to the forefront. And he won. Congress voted, unanimously, to take care of the heroes for life.

Political humor has a long history in our country. Today we kind of take it for granted that, starting with *The Smothers Brothers Show,* and thanks to *The Daily Show* and *The Jon Stewart Show,* brave political commentary married to brilliant humor is available on late-night television. But Jon's work, his support of all those correspondents on his shows, is remarkable. It is sort of like he created a television dream version of Second City. Jon agrees.

"In many respects that's what it was, because that's the skill set of the individuals. In some respects, we're merely the professional outlet for those technical 'schools.' You see those performers move on to do all kinds of things. But that particular skill set, when you are a correspondent on this show, you have to have television chops, which is just sort of that mechanical sense of knowing where the camera is, when you want to interact with it, how you want to do it. And then you have to go out in the field and improvise scenes with people that do not know they are in a scene. You know, my general process is self-critical, so I don't go, 'People think what?' I would probably just read the comments section and feel, 'Nailed it. Yup. Wow, that was great.'"

This makes me think about social media and its effect on the commentary that was on Jon's shows. When Jon started out with *The Daily Show,* social media wasn't around as much as it is now, when it's become much more potent. "Communication was mostly through things you would write on the bathroom wall. That's how you found out you sucked. You'd go to a comedy club, and you'd go into the bathroom, and somebody would've written up there, 'It wasn't worth it,' and you're like, 'What?' As long as you didn't go to the bathroom, you thought your career was going great."

Continues Jon, as thoughtful as always, "Now you look at your phone and you remember. The Internet is, I think, a truly pure outrage machine. It's a beautiful example of something that self-perpetuates. The difficult part of that is, you never know where it's gonna come from, what dark spot of the Internet is gonna pop on. The good news is, I'm pretty sure they're gonna be mad at somebody else tomorrow."

I love that philosophy. Jon, of course, brings it back to funny. His usual brilliant humor combined with outrageous thought is always impressive. "Look, David, what's so interesting to me about issues is that people are talking about something that they believe, which is the most powerful force in the universe. But if you joke about it, it will crumble. For example, God. God created the world in six days, but if today, somebody, let's say, on day three, had made fun of His shoes, I think the whole thing would've been off. 'You have slandered God, so we must punish you.'"

I reply that there's never a presumption that God might have a sense of humor. You would hope so.

"I think the greatest example that God does have a sense of humor is the scrotum. I mean, if He doesn't have a sense of humor, why would He hang something so sensitive outside the body? Why wouldn't He tuck it away in some sort of cage? Was the scrotum God getting even in some way? Or just purely an engineering oversight? It's hard to say, in terms of design. Somebody has this blueprint, and all of a sudden you look around and go, 'Where are we gonna put that?' And He goes, 'Just hang it on the outside and hope nobody punches it.'"

More proof that every great comedian starts in stand-up: Jimmy Fallon, who is no exception, but his desire came from, you may have already guessed it, watching *Saturday Night Live*. He was just a little kid, maybe

Before going on *The Tonight Show Starring Jimmy Fallon,* 2015. It was great being back at the same old Johnny Carson *Tonight Show* set in New York City after so many years. It's still the same setup. I instinctively knew where to enter the stage. It was all so nostalgically familiar to me. I missed Johnny, but Jimmy Fallon belongs there now.

six or seven, he thinks, when "my sister would dress up in my mom's dresses. And we'd do 'King Tut,' from *Saturday Night Live,* you know, Steve Martin. And we'd say, 'We are two wild and crazy guys!' We would have no idea what the words meant. But I remember I did have a bunch of comedy records I just *loved.* I owned your records, David, and I would imitate Rodney Dangerfield. He was my favorite. My parents would pay me, like, twenty-five cents:

" 'Just do Rodney for everybody.'

"And I would go, 'Oh, I tell ya, my wife's cooking is so bad, I mean, since when does toast have bones? She told me to take out the trash. I said, 'You cooked it, you take it out, all right?'

"I did stand-up in high school. My mom heard about a contest on the radio: funniest impressionists. And you had two minutes to do your best impressions. My dad drove me to the club. I was seventeen. I got up and did what I had done at home—I used to do impressions in my room. I had a troll doll, you know, those dolls with the fuzzy hair? And I would do different celebrities auditioning for a commercial for the troll doll. So, I would do Bill Cosby or Seinfeld—and I won the contest. I think it was a seven-hundred-dollar prize, which was a lot of money for two minutes. So I thought, if I can make seven hundred dollars in two minutes, this is my future. I gotta be a comedian."

Jimmy loves the history of comedy, just like I do, obviously. "I loved knowing the history. I liked seeing where people came from. Like Rodney Dangerfield's history. He was Jack Roy, and not making it. Till he was forty, I think. I grew up in a perfect time for stand-up, because there was a big boom in the eighties. Everyone had a show, a stand-up show, so there were stand-up comedians on every channel, every night. And it was amazing to watch that. I built my whole stand-up act around this two-minute impression thing. And then I won another contest. When you won that contest, you won a manager. I'd never heard of such a prize. I go, 'I don't want a manager, can't I win money?' But this guy wanted to manage me. So, he started booking me places, like colleges and stuff. And I started working the Improv during the week, and then, if you had a Saturday night gig at the Improv, it was a big deal, because they paid you a dollar more than they do during the week, and you get food."

I just love hearing these stories—the passion, the hard work, the delight in small things like laughter and free food and any recognition we would get.

"I remember I took a photo of my name on the marquee outside. And I told my parents right away, 'cause I couldn't believe it. So, I'm at the Improv, my first Saturday night, and who walks in but Jerry Seinfeld? And I was like, 'Oh my god, Jerry Seinfeld just walked in,' and there's a big buzz around the club. This was at the peak of his show, *Seinfeld*. And he decides to do stand-up. Jerry Seinfeld! They announce him, and it's a standing ovation as he walks on the stage. Standing ovation as he walks off the stage. All his 'A' material. He hits it out of the park, destroys!

"And Jerry goes, 'All the comedians who gotta follow me are gonna go, I'm not gonna follow that. Later, take care, man.'

"And then Budd, the owner, says, 'Well, who's Jimmy Fallon?'

"I go, 'That's me.'

"He goes, 'You're up next.'

"I was like, 'I have to follow Jerry Seinfeld? My first night?'

"It was that famous Saturday night at the Improv. I ask, 'What do I do? Oh my gosh!' I was so nervous. And Budd was there watching. I got up, and I remembered that I actually did my impression of Jerry Seinfeld in my act. So, I just opened with that. I did! I opened doing Jerry Seinfeld! It worked, and that got me over, and I had a great set."

Years later, Jimmy asked Jerry if he had stayed for his whole set. He hadn't. Most comedians go home right after their set. But Jerry did tell Jimmy, "Good for you. You learned something. You're supposed to follow people that kill. That's what you do."

By the time Jimmy had his own late-night show, he was following two others. Jay Leno had his 10 p.m. show. Conan had the 11:30 *Tonight Show*. So Jimmy had to come up with something all his own—like musical parodies. "I felt they were all doing those monologues, and that they began to sound the same. I thought people would be saying, 'We heard it. It's an old joke.' One day, it just came to us, 'cause we just had to think of different bits to do. Bruce Springsteen was coming on and at rehearsal, I asked, 'Would you like to sing a song with me as Neil

Young? I will be Neil from the '70s, and we'll sing Willow Smith's song, "Whip My Hair.'"

"And Bruce Springsteen goes, 'I am not familiar with that song.'

"And I whip my hair back and forth, and I tell Bruce that he has to whip his hair. So he goes, 'I love it. I'll do it. I think it's good.'

"Then, a half hour later, I get a phone call that Bruce Springsteen's on the phone, and I'm afraid he doesn't want to do it.

"Bruce says, 'I got an idea. If you're doing Neil from the seventies, I'm gonna do me from the seventies, so let's get a beard for me, and I'll bring my sunglasses from the *Born to Run* tour.'

"And I ask, 'Will you get that floppy hat that you used to wear?'

"He goes, 'Yeah, the floppy hat! I gotta have the floppy hat!' He's laughing, and I'm like, 'Okay, see you later, Bruce.'

"So he comes in, and he's Bruce Springsteen, he's a rock star. He's there, he's got the sunglasses, the hat, and I say, 'Do you want to wear the wig?'

"He says, 'Nah, I don't wanna wear the wig.'

"I go, 'Okay, no problem, whatever you want, Bruce.'

"And so everyone leaves the room, and it's just me and Bruce, and I go, 'Bruce, do you want to try the wig?'

"And he says, 'Okay, let's try it.'

"So I'm putting the wig on him—on Bruce Springsteen!!!—and he's got the beard and the glasses, and bam. He looks just like Bruce from the seventies. Exactly the same. We head over to the greenroom, where his manager, Jon Landau, who's been his manager forever, was, and he walks up to Jon, and I swear to god, tears well up in Jon's eyes. I mean, when do you think you're gonna see your client thirty years younger?

"And that's when I got the idea to do the musical parodies as a regular opening of the show."

All this talk about various versions of late-night talk shows, and Jimmy then taking over from Jay Leno, makes me nostalgic for the king of late night, my beloved Johnny Carson. I wonder if Jimmy ever thinks of Carson.

Jimmy seems surprised at the question. "He was my guy. I remember asking my parents if I could stay up to watch Johnny Carson. I'd watch the monologue, and maybe the first guest or something, and then I'd fall asleep. It was a treat. So, the fact that there might be a kid out there asking their parents, 'Can I stay up and watch Jimmy Fallon?' It's an honor, that question. An honor."

It amazes me to this day (and you probably wonder why, since I have worked with and been friends with so many comedians over the last fifty years) that the same people who have influenced comedy are pointed to again and again, by virtually all successful comedians and comic actors. It is never a surprise, but it does validate the impact and contributions of these worshiped talents. Ask Kevin Nealon, who was on *SNL* for almost ten years but started out as a stand-up at, you guessed it, the Improv in LA. "The three that really influenced me the most were Steve Martin, Albert Brooks, and Andy Kaufman. 'Cause I liked that misdirection. I liked the absurdity of all of it."

That makes sense. Andy Kaufman, of course, played to the audience where half the audience didn't know what he was doing. "That's what I'm talking about," says Kevin. "Misdirection, I love that. I'll always remember the day I decided to come out to LA. I was raking leaves in Connecticut, and I had the radio on, and I heard that Freddie Prinze died. And he was such a big influence when he did *The Tonight Show,* the hunga-rican and all that. I thought, 'Comedy really is important. We need more of it.'

"And I liked doing it. I would memorize the jokes in the back of the *Parade* magazine section to tell at parties. When I came out to LA, I was a bartender at the Improv, which was the perfect platform to watch and get to know comedy. If a comic didn't come in, Budd Friedman would put me on. I wasn't a good bartender, I didn't have an act, so you know I wasn't well liked there. But if someone like Andy Kaufman came in, I would leave the bar and go into the office, because there was a little peephole where I could watch the show. Or you know, Robin would come in and blow me away. One comic had given me the best advice:

'Get onstage as much as you can, wherever you can.' All I wanted to be was a stand-up comic."

But first there were discos and flat stages and even cruise ships. "I was a little bit nervous about it, because it was still early in my career, and the comedy was in the adult lounge, and my act is not adult. They had a dance floor, and they were all dancing, having a great time, and then they stopped the fun to bring out the comic. Who was me. And my comedy was and is very subtle, very dry. So the first time I started doing it, they were not happy. The next time, just as I began my act, they brought up the anchor—clank, clank, clank! But I had this bit that I did that kind of saved me. I called it the easel bit. I get somebody out of the audience and I sketch their picture with charcoal. As I'm sketching, I tell them I'm not good at it, but I've always wanted to be an artist. So I'm shifting their face, and there's charcoal all over my fingers, but they don't know it. It gets all over me, and suddenly the drawing makes them look like Al Jolson. And I show it to the audience and they love it—it saved me."

And, again, like all comedians, Kevin just wanted to be on *The Tonight Show*. "You know better than anyone, David, since you have hosted for Johnny more than anyone. You do one *Tonight Show,* then you're thinking—when can I do it again? Six months from now, five months? Then Dana Carvey, who was a friend of mine from stand-up, was selected to be on *SNL* that summer. So he goes to New York to get ready to help Lorne Michaels figure out the rest of the cast, and he calls me and says, 'Kevin, I'm at Lorne Michaels's house in Amagansett. I told them about you. And I think they're gonna want to see your tapes, 'cause they're still looking for one cast member. And guess who's in the kitchen? Chevy Chase and Dan Aykroyd.'

"I said, 'Are you kidding me? Chevy Chase and Dan Aykroyd are in the kitchen?' Of course I never thought anything would come of it, because I'm a stand-up. I don't do characters. I have never been to Second City, Groundlings, any of that stuff. And so I send Lorne my tapes, never expecting to hear anything. And I get a phone call from Dana, again. 'Hey Kev, it's Dana. I'm back out at Lorne's house. I think they liked your tapes.'

"So they fly me to New York. I think I'm one of the few going out to audition, but the whole plane is full, 'cause everybody's going to *Saturday Night Live* to audition. So I get there and I know I'm never gonna get it. But I go to Studio 8H and I do some of my stand-up—a couple of things that Dana and I used to do, characters, but not good enough. I leave and I'm the least nervous out of everyone, because I know I'm not gonna get it. A week later, Lorne comes out to LA and I'm at Brad Grey's office—he's representing Lorne Michaels. I get called in, and Lorne talks to me for about an hour about how he'd love to have me on the show. And I saw him on that Monday in 1987, and I was on there for nine years. It was a good run. A great run. I loved being on *Saturday Night Live*. I wasn't really seeing it as a stepping-stone, 'cause, again, I'm a stand-up. We don't have high expectations. I'd see new cast members, and they'd get frustrated and leave. And I'm loving it. You understand! You get to work with a different host each week, different bands. I got to sit next to Paul McCartney while he's rehearsing, playing 'Lady Madonna' and 'Hey Jude' and 'Get Back' and all that stuff. I am working with some of my idols, like with Steve Martin. It was a great job, so I stayed there a long time."

Over the years, there were also many appearances on *The Tonight Show,* in films like *Happy Gilmore, The Wedding Singer, Anger Management,* and many of Adam Sandler's Happy Madison films. And that led to seven happy years on *Weeds* with Mary-Louise Parker, playing a city councilman who was also a stoner. I directed Kevin in *Weeds,* and he brought lightness to this dark comedy. He was the most delightful person to direct. Not only was he funny, but he helped everyone. Kevin is always a mensch, pure and simple. Everyone loved him, always and unanimously the nicest guy. And directing him was always a laid-back pleasure, because he was so receptive, even eager, to get direction he felt would make him better at whatever he was doing.

If you were guest starring on *Weeds,* trying to adjust to the rhythm of the show, Kevin was the person who was willing to give his time and help you. And Kevin loved working with Parker, whom he calls "a really great actress who was also superb in her theater experiences. I was embarrassed to do a scene with Mary-Louise Parker because she was

so good, and I felt like a fraud, kind of the George Plimpton of every show. I thought, 'When is she ever going to tell me to get out of here?' "
   Never.

Speaking of not fucking with comics, you never have to worry about that with Robert Klein, because he is a wonderful comedian with successful albums year after year. He was a graduate of the Yale School of Drama. Robert also began in Second City, became a beloved actor in television (recently in *Will & Grace*), his theater work resulted in award nominations for *They're Playing Our Song* and films too many to count, and he really doesn't care if you get upset at one of his routines. He has seen it all . . . as he started out making people laugh when he was a young child.

Robert Klein shares my history. We were in early Second City together. We were competitive and there were always rumors of feuding that never happened. We liked each other and were always supportive. We remain in touch and have stayed friends.

What did he think was funny as a kid? "I loved every comedian I ever saw on television. We got a television in '51, and it's been on ever since. I would say that *Sergeant Bilko* and *The Honeymooners* are two of the greatest sitcoms of all time (by the way, Neil Simon was one of the writers). Probably in the top four or five. Phil Silvers had a tremendous energy and timing. I never wanted to do sitcoms, because none of them were as funny as that. The show came on the air right after the Korean War—a comedy on the military, which hit the sweet spot of the time and caught the zeitgeist. It took a vaudevillian and put him in a comedy series. And the fast-talking, charming Sergeant Bilko, who was always trying to be successful at get-rich schemes, was a kind military figure, rather than hostile, and thus beloved by the audience."

I agree with Robert. You could hardly be as good as *The Honeymooners* back then. Same with *Bilko*. It was a different way of producing those comedies—and the way they shot those things. Always a group of people, never a close-up of anyone. You didn't cut to someone. Robert reminds me that during his first years in stand-up, "they had real troops watching in the audience, so the laugh track was real with military personnel. I still consider making people laugh a high calling in many respects, because for those few moments, people forget their troubles."

Not many people know, but Robert and I do, that, like Robert, Joe E. Lewis started out as a singer. Then he got into some trouble with the Mafia, and his throat was cut for a gambling debt. When he went onstage in Florida, with his accompanist at the piano, he couldn't sing. So, instead, he talked. And that's how he started his sort of stand-up. He was actually one of the first stand-up comedians. And all those Vegas comedians, like Shecky Greene and Buddy Hackett, then worked with a guy playing the piano. And Robert is a throwback to that.

"I do work with music all the time," explains Robert. "My parents say I could hum a tune before I could talk. I come from a very musical family, so I used music. Bob Stein and I have been working together twenty-eight years, and over forty-four, forty-five years doing stand-up. I've had four accompanists, and Bob is the longest. He's also a wonderful producer of my HBO special, and we've been nominated for two primetime Emmys, including this song 'Hymn to America,' about Obama. And also, the 'Colonoscopy.'"

Both Robert and I started out in the 1960s. Robert recounts, "I was hired in 1965 at Second City in Chicago with Fred Willard, when you were the reigning star there, David. And you were something to see. You were not delightful, David, but you were brilliant. When you and the company went to London, Fred and I had our chance to blossom. When you came back, I learned a lot from you. A sort of mastery of timing, because I had raw talent before I went there. I think I was getting paid $150 a week, so you probably got $175, easily. I think I learned more than at Yale, because I was immersed, night after night, in front of an audience, improvising all the time. It was just the greatest. Being in front of people all the time gave me a technique."

How did you then get to Broadway? "I was in my first Broadway show, the first one I ever auditioned for, when Mike Nichols gave me the job. The show was *The Apple Tree*. But I wanted to do stand-up, and there was a place down the street that you had told me about, owned by Budd Friedman [who ended up owning the Improv in LA for a hundred years], where they had professionals go up. If you were in a Broadway show, he'd put you on right away. So I went down there and did stand-up, and I killed. I was just terrific. And this guy comes over to me, dressed in a black suit and a red tie, and says, 'Lemme tell you, you were fuckin' brilliant, and I'm a tough cocksucker.'"

That, folks, was Rodney Dangerfield. And then he gave Robert some advice. "You gotta come here every night for three years."

"That's exactly what he said," remembers Robert. "And Rodney was right. That was my college for comedy. Rodney mentored a lot of guys, and I was his first. His eleven rollicking years were amazing. The techniques of holding the mic, writing jokes. At that time, he wrote his own jokes, like, 'I'll tell ya, I'll tell ya, our streets are unsafe, our cars are unsafe, our schools are unsafe, our parks are unsafe. But under our arms, we have complete protection.' He got me over my bombing dreams. I had two kinds of bombing 'dreams.' One is that the audience does not laugh. The other one is being onstage and not knowing my lines, not as a stand-up, but especially in an ensemble like onstage in the theater."

In case we only remember Robert's musical and comedic talent, it was his serious chops that were the talk of a moving episode of *Will &*

Grace, entitled "Grace's Secret." His wrenching performance as Grace's dad, Martin, with daughter Debra Messing—also heartbreaking—brought back Grace's trauma at the hands of her dad's old friend Harry, showcased by Martin's flirtation with a waitress at a restaurant that was Grace's last straw. Robert's pain at this discovery is unforgettable, and his final enraged words about Harry—"He's dead to me"—show the depth of talent that Robert has, as he combines that raging phrase with a little humor (since Harry is really already dead). Robert Klein—truly a fine actor, comedian, and an old important friend who shares our very special history.

John Candy was, to his followers, Canada's Jackie Gleason. He auditioned, along with a lot of other Second City Canadians, for my 1976 Canadian show, creatively called *The David Steinberg Show.* When he walked through the door for the audition, he was visibly shivering. When I asked if he was okay, he said yes and immediately stepped into

With John Candy, shooting *My Dinner with Duddy,* a satire of *My Dinner with Andre,* circa 1984. We improvised like crazy, as two Canadians from Second City would, and had the best time.

John Candy and his family lived in my guesthouse in Los Angeles for a year while we were writing and shooting the cult classic *Going Berserk,* circa 1982. John wrote most of the script on a napkin. That should tell you something. That was the whole script.

a Jackie Gleason imitation, saying, "I'm so excited and nervous to be here."

That was the beginning of a long friendship that continued when John and his family moved into our guesthouse in Los Angeles and parked there for a year. During that time, we improvised a movie called *Going Berserk.* John was supposed to be writing it, but if you knew John, you would know it was like kicking a boulder up a big hill for him. As a result, when the time came to shoot, we had no script. We had to come up with something, which ended up with John and me (the director) going on the Universal lot each morning to find a set not being used that day. We improvised and created scenes right then and there, on the lot. It was exhilarating and scary.

Originally our film was going to be called *Drums over Malta,* which, to us, was a perfect title, since no one would believe that would be a John Candy film. Pierre David, the Canadian producer, wanted to call the film *Numb Nuts* and, unbeknownst to us, gave that title to the press. Upon hearing that title, the next day every comedy actor in the film puked their guts out. We fought back and compromised and did the film our way. The title remained *Going Berserk*.

John Candy, as you know, was portly, but he never played off of his physicality or used it in his comedy as a comedic actor. You would expect a big person to be slapstick, but he was much more subtle, as he had trained with Second City. The audience immediately took to him, since he had an empathy in his performances. When I directed him in *Going Berserk,* he was completely outrageous, but he always had a warmth that enveloped the audience and extended to the crew as well. Everyone loved John. His laugh was contagious, inviting the audience into his humor. He was endearing. The audience always rooted for him.

John was also determined to lose the weight. And that could be what killed him. He claimed that when he would lose weight, people would mistake him for Clark Gable, then the handsomest man on earth—so he was motivated. John had a trainer he wanted to work with, a young guy in good shape, who guaranteed us that John would be in great shape for the film. I did begin to notice that John's nose was always running, and so was the trainer's. I assumed they had colds or allergies . . . I was naive enough to believe we were well on our way. So I just kept working on the film. It opened and, surprisingly, it was a hit, has a cult following to this day, and holds up if you have the patience. We also did a small film in Canada called *My Dinner with Duddy,* which was completely improvised by John and myself (it was a parody of the "artistic" movie of the time, *My Dinner with Andre*). That, too, became a cult comedy, especially in Canada. John loved playing the blowhard in that film. And he killed it.

I always loved being around John and his perfect, honestly sweet family. He was great with people. Always ready to laugh. So funny all the time. I treasure our time together. I miss him. He was forty-four when he died. To say I was shocked, devastated, doesn't come close. I remained numb forever, and to this day, I can't believe he is gone.

· · ·

When a comedian takes on the mantle of Johnny Carson, king of late night, joins the ranks of Jon Stewart in terms of enormous impact on political satire, and expands the reach of his late-night show to include news parody on a level that changes comedy yet again, he stands alone. That is Stephen Colbert. From *The Daily Show,* where he served as a correspondent character, not as himself, to *The Colbert Report* to *The Late Show with Stephen Colbert,* he continues to take what he learned in Second City, use his improv talents to parody politics, and make caricature the core of his comedy. Colbert has over twenty years of hosting and continues to change the landscape of television. For this work, he has been awarded nine Emmy Awards, two Grammy Awards, seven Producers Guild Awards, four Writers Guild awards, and two Peabody Awards.

Films came along, too, big hits, like *Bewitched, Monsters and Aliens,* various voices for animation, and a documentary about the creation and eventual cancellation of *The Dana Carvey Show* that I think is mesmerizing, titled *Too Funny to Fail.* But it is television that captured Stephen's heart and mind and keeps him at the top of all lists of successful comedians who have had, and continue to have, a huge impact on our world. And it is his honest, almost pure, sense of what is right and responsible in terms of personal and political behavior that continues to set him apart as he makes people laugh while calling them to action as people and as citizens.

Stephen and I often discuss our beginnings, similar as they are. Well, kind of. I was Orthodox Jewish. He was Catholic. I had three siblings. He had eleven. My father was a rabbi. His, the dean of the medical school at Yale. I lost my brother when he died in World War II. I was five. Stephen lost his father and two brothers in an airplane crash on a trip to enroll his brothers in boarding school. He was ten. I studied Torah. He studied acting and improvisation. I joined Second City. He did, too. I went before him, paving the way. He joined years later, as an understudy for Steve Carell, who, he remembers, could pick up any wind instrument and play it in a couple of days, while it took Stephen days of practice to be able to blow. Stephen, Amy Sedaris, and Paul Dinello became a trio of friends, and together, in 1995, they moved to New York to debut their sketch comedy show called *Exit 57*. It lasted twelve episodes but won awards and began Stephen's career as a writer—yes, *SNL*, and then *The Daily Show*.

What Stephen and I really talk about most, though, is improvisation: the impact that Second City had on all of us who started there, and where we learned what still is the core of our work.

"When I got to Second City," Stephen is quick to point out, "there were pictures of you on the wall, as a priest. Well, actually, I believe you were a rabbi wearing a priest collar." As a Reform Jew, I felt I could push that envelope.

Stephen continues, "I don't know about your day, but we had to go learn thirty years of what was considered the best sketches. Yours were in there."

I replied that I only had to learn a year and a half of sketches, as there was only one company before mine. But Stephen was lucky in that he got to learn the core of improvisation at Second City from Del Close, our hero, although he had already confronted improvisation at Northwestern.

"I was at Northwestern University in the theater program, and a friend of mine said they're doing this thing at a cabaret bar called Cross-Currents. A pure, improvised show. It's called *The Harold*, essentially one-act plays, purely improvised from a single word, a mundane suggestion like 'paper' or 'rock' or something like that. And I instantly thought this was something I would like. For some reason, I had an instinct, and I went and watched it, and I thought, 'This is for me. I have to find some way to improvise.' I had to get up onstage. And, honestly, in no small part because I didn't have to memorize lines. Now, I've got a very good memory. I can memorize lines quickly, so learning the lines has never been a problem for me. But I liked *not having to know my lines*. I liked the freedom of having to find another reaction in the moment, being a vehicle but not necessarily responsible for what's about to happen."

Stephen also found that he liked alienating people with his comedy, kind of surprising them. "I'm very conflicted," he explains. "I was raised by very nice people, very polite people. And I worked very hard to not make my character an asshole, to make him an idiot, which is a very different thing. I think an asshole is an idiot who thinks not car-ing whether you love him is adorable, whereas an idiot really doesn't know that what he's doing is alienating you. He really wants you to still love him."

I think this is a good time to tell Stephen that if he was at yeshiva, the Talmud that he just gave, between an asshole and an idiot, is exactly what goes on at a theological school. Stephen points out that the dif-ference is in the wording, which is at the core of how he reports on his shows.

> *On this show, your voice will be heard, in the form of my voice. 'Cause you're looking at a straight shooter, America. I tell it like it is. I calls 'em like I sees 'em. I will speak to you in plain, simple English. And that brings us to tonight's word: Truthiness. Now, I'm sure some of the word police, the "wordanista," over at* Webster's *are gonna say, "Hey, that's not a word." Well, anybody who knows me knows that I'm no fan of dictionaries or reference books. They're elitist, constantly telling us what is or isn't true, or what did or didn't happen. Who's* Britannica *to tell me the Panama Canal was finished in 1914? If I wanna say it happened in 1941, that's my right.*

The other discussions Stephen and I have are about cynicism and its place on *The Late Show.* I do not think I am a cynic. Stephen doesn't think he is, either.

"I am not cynical. I behave cynically. Here's the thing—you don't know if the audience is going to be shocked or surprised or disgusted, or throw up their hands, or have a double take at the same thing. And that's why I would say what's nice about the format of the show is that, certainly, the dive into the story that I learned from Jon Stewart is that you bring the audience along and educate them only to the extent to get them to the joke you wish to tell. People often say, 'Oh, you're a journalist?'

"I'm like, I know you mean that as a compliment, but stop it. Because what I'm trying to do is get us all on the same page so they understand what I've read. I'm curating the news for them, only to get to the final display in the showcase, which is my joke. And sometimes you can do it in one sentence, and sometimes it takes a two-minute explanation, which you have to pepper with jokes, in order to get them to your ultimate joke. But, really, it's just for the jokes. The education is just so, as you would say, David, 'We're all on the same,' implying, 'We're all on the same page, before I make my point.'"

Which brings us to the night Stephen hosted the White House Correspondents' Dinner. On April 29, 2006, now more than fourteen years ago, Stephen was what they call "the featured entertainer" at the dinner, when George W. Bush was president. In his role of the conservative character from *The Colbert Report,* Stephen was scathing in his words about the president and the media. Stephen explains, "I got a call in early 2006, when we had only been on thirty-two times, at that point. My agent said, 'Do you want to do this?'

"And I thought, 'My instinct is, yeah, I want to do this, but let me call you back.' So I called Jon Stewart, and I said, 'Hey, man, they asked me to come down for the Correspondents' Dinner.'

"And Jon said, 'Like as a guest?'

"And I said, "No, as *the* guy.'

"And he goes, 'Dude, have they seen your show?'

"And I said, 'I don't know, but I think I got to do it.'

"And he goes, 'I think you do.'

"So we called back right away and say, 'Yeah, he'll do it.' And then I didn't work on it for months and months, of course, 'cause I had my show to do.

"And then, just a couple weeks before we went, we worked on it for twenty-four hours, and we wrote and wrote. And, by the way, there were so many jokes we didn't do! We cut out what we thought were the harshest jokes. And we really thought that the president might laugh at it. I really thought he might enjoy himself more."

So don't pay attention to the approval ratings that say that sixty-eight percent of Americans disapprove of the job this man is doing. I ask you this—does that not also logically mean that sixty-eight percent approve of the job he's not doing? Think about it. I haven't.

I stand by this man. I stand by this man because he stands for things. Not only for things he stands on. Things like aircraft carriers, and rubble, and recently flooded city squares. And that sends a strong message. That no matter what happens to America she will always rebound with the most powerfully staged photo ops in the world.

"I really didn't think it was gonna be a big deal. I really didn't. There might be a whiff of brimstone, but that'd be it. As my executive producer, Tom Purcell, said, 'We were not throwing Molotov cocktails.' But people thought we were—we were just throwing a Nehi grape bottle that, admittedly, had a burning rag in the neck. But there was no gasoline in there, it was just Nehi. But we didn't know that the room was soaked with gasoline. And so the rag was all it took for people to perceive it as this vast attack."

Stephen continues thoughtfully, "I was there to do jokes. *My* jokes, which are essentially satire. It cuts. But I really was just doing what I do for a living. And they invited me, so I figured I would do it. I don't know if you've ever been in that room, David—it's a three-thousand-seat room at the Washington Hilton. And as a performer, I can't hear the difference between a thousand people reacting and three thousand. I think above a thousand sounds like bacon frying. That's all you hear. And so, at home, when you watch this dinner on C-SPAN, there are no mics pointed at the audience, the room is not wired by show business people. It's wired by C-SPAN. And so you can't hear that the audience was laughing for a lot of it. And if a third of the people laughed, that was a thousand people laughing, and so it felt pretty good. The only time I thought I was in trouble was when I made the mistake of looking at the president. I had already done like twelve minutes on him, so I did the next twelve minutes on the press, which nobody remembers. Everybody thinks it was just ragging on Mr. President. Then it was over, and I looked at the president, and he looks right at me, and he does this wink/tongue click and just gives me this little eye shot, and I'm gonna take that as extremely friendly, like, 'You and me are pals, and I really like what you've done tonight.'"

· · ·

Washington, DC, could not be farther from Martin Mull's mind, as he now spends his glorious days painting. Marty has lived in Santa Barbara for many years. He started out as an actor and comedian, became well known for his work on *Mary Hartman, Mary Hartman,* then on *Roseanne, Sabrina the Teenage Witch, Two and a Half Men,* and *Arrested Development.* He was a songwriter, acted in over thirty films, but his real passion has been painting ever since he graduated from the Rhode Island School of Design as an undergraduate and also with a master's degree in . . . painting.

"I went to school, got my master's, found out, 'My God! [I love to

Martin Mull is a very special person, gifted in so many ways. One of the most unique and original comedy talents and a remarkable artist. I actually have two of his paintings. He's a very special friend. We go back to the '60s, when we were both performing a lot at Max's Kansas City in Manhattan. Here we are on the set of *Inside Comedy* so many decades later, in 2012.

hear his "my Gods!" about everything—I miss hearing it.] There's no doctorate! I'm going to actually have to do something in the real world.' And I had been playing music all through school, just to pay my rent and keep me in beer and cigarettes and tuition. So when there was no more schooling, I decided to go on the road as a musician. I started writing my songs, and that kind of turned into a comedy act, because I'm an abysmal singer—before each song, I would make these kind of explanations about what you're going to hear, do the song, and then immediately launch into an even longer apology. So all of a sudden I realized I had an hour show on my hands that was basically music and comedy. It became an act, and I actually made some records."

Marty and I developed our friendship starting out at Max's Kansas City in New York City. We packed the house every night and held records for attendance. Our joke, between us, was who was going to open. I had the bigger audience, by two or three people, so we flipped a coin. Our friendship developed as he was a frequent guest on *The Tonight Show*. His first appearance was the result of a kind of cattle call—which the producers had when the show first started. They were on Friday afternoons, and anybody could audition—jugglers, lion tamers, anybody. The producer, Freddie De Cordova, would watch. Marty remembers that he sang "a French song that I had done in my act, that did well, only in order to make it more French, I put a red-and-white-checked tablecloth over my lap and a large loaf of bread, hung grapes off my guitar, had a beret, and a few other French things. I should mention that this song was roughly in French, but not really. And so I thought, 'That's the killer, I'll go in and do that.' And I did it, and then went back to New York and waited to see what would happen.

"Suddenly I hear Buddy Morra on the phone going, 'No kidding? Really? Well, that's certainly extreme, okay.'

"And I asked, 'What did he say?'

"He said that it was absolutely 'the worst freaking thing he's ever seen in his life; never send that man over here again.'

"And I thought, 'Well, there goes my *Tonight Show* career.'

"Then, two weeks later, my friend George Carlin was hosting. And as you know, when you're hosting, you can pick your guests. And

George said, 'I want to have Martin Mull on,' so I got on. And of course, you know what I had to do. I mean there was no question, I had to do the French song. Two weeks after that, I was guest hosting."

Martin Mull is yet another fan of Steve Martin. I figure it could be that they both spent a lot of time in Santa Barbara. Nope. It is based on the fact that neither one of them is Jewish. "Steve and I share that lack of a heritage. I think that's one of the reasons we're such good friends—we have absolutely nothing in the basement. You know, there's no history there. There's no nothing. It's that WASP lack of heritage. But what it does is it causes you to disconnect a bit, and I think that can translate into some form of comedic material."

We must get to Martin's painting career, because this is what he has been doing the last many years. And he has become a noted painter. He agrees, with some humility. "I actually live, support myself as a painter now," he says with some glee. Even though he is currently starring in a series (*The Cool Kids*), he makes the time to paint, and his works go for many thousands of dollars. The work is critically acclaimed and reminiscent of Norman Rockwell—realistic yet dreamy, bringing memories of history to the forefront.

"The whole show business thing was simply a means of supporting myself to be a painter," Martin says, somewhat seriously. "I never stopped being a painter, and every painter or visual artist I know has to do something vaguely tangentially connected to the arts. You know, David, for me it was never like, 'Get my agent on the phone, I gotta get this gig, I gotta get that.' It just kind of fell in my lap. And I'm extremely grateful. Finally, the work began to be collected by museums and some major collections. And they started saying, he's a painter, before they said he's an actor or a comedian."

To me, he is all.

Actor and comedian (but no painter) is the very definition of Eric Idle. But the label "comedian" doesn't really define him, because Eric Idle lives on a planet I am not sure I have ever visited. Every word is outrageous, every thought a surprise, every memory funnier than the one

You can't grow up in Canada, or anywhere, and talk about
comedy and not talk about Monty Python and Eric Idle.
Here we are on the set of *Inside Comedy* having a laugh about
"Always Look on the Bright Side of Life," 2013.

before. As Eric is very British, and his huge success, Monty Python,
was also created in Britain, with his partners, I ask him why he is now
living in Los Angeles.

"I like Los Angeles," he explains. "I do not have a place in London. I have a place in France. For forty-two years, actually, nicer than
London."

"But they worship you in England."

"No, David, the English don't worship anything, really, apart from
the queen. But they are nice to us. We're kind of the old farts, you
know, so they're kind of sweet to us. The policeman smiles and says,
'Hello, Eric.' We've got to 'Hello, Eric' status."

Does he have an apartment in New York? After all, *Spamalot,* his
award-winning, showstopping musical, created with and directed by
Mike Nichols, played in New York for 1,575 performances (five years,
not including all the national and international touring companies),
was seen by two million people, was nominated for fourteen Tonys
(and won three, including Best Musical), and included the huge hit,
originally from *Life of Brian,* "Always Look on the Bright Side of Life,"
which is one of my favorite pieces of comedy, ever.

Eric tells the story. "No apartment in New York. My partner, John Du Prez, and I had been trying to write a musical for a long time. We were always looking for a good subject, and one day in the nineties, I went, well, duh, Holy Grail is a perfect subject for a musical. *Monty Python and the Holy Grail*. We wrote the first song that we had improvised, called 'The Song That Goes Like This.' And then we got Mike Nichols, who apparently had some experience in the field. Actually, no joke, I knew Mike for a long time. He was one of my favorite comedians when I was at college, with Nichols and May. He's just brilliant, and, of course, he got a great cast and we won the Tony for Best Musical on Broadway in 2005."

From beginning to end, *Spamalot* was a smash. It had stars who became even bigger stars (Tim Curry, Sara Ramirez, Hank Azaria, David Hyde Pierce), songs that were classics and new ones that became classics, all those awards and critical accolades. And it brought Monty Python back to new generations, giving it additional life.

But back to Eric's beginnings, the Monty Python days. Eric doesn't really make light of the effect Monty Python has had on Britain, and on the world, and certainly not to me, as I cannot overstate the impact of watching Monty Python growing up in Canada. It was the most outrageous comedy, steps up from the more well-known slapstick of old, brilliant and funny almost beyond words. Their words. And it was then all about the writing, by the most well-known British comic writers of all time (who all later also developed huge careers in performance): Eric Idle, Graham Chapman, Terry Jones, Michael Palin, Terry Gilliam, John Cleese, Ronnie Corbett, and Ronnie Barker. Explains Eric, "We came out of universities, Oxford and Cambridge, where we wrote and then performed what we did at local festivals. Then we were dragged into the David Frost mesh world—he 'sharked' everybody up to write for him. He was very good that way, and he gave us jobs on *The Frost Report*. We were always professional writers, on little shows. And Python was just another of those that sort of came along until Terry Gilliam arrived. Mad fucker genius, he was. Before Gilliam came along, we had a TV show for kids called *Do Not Adjust Your Set,* at five in the afternoon—five twenty, actually, and adults were coming home to watch it. So we were getting enormous numbers from a TV show for kids, and we did really well.

"And then Gilliam came, sent by Cleese, and he was this scruffy guy wearing an Afghan coat. And I really, at first sight, I loved that Afghan coat, so, I said, 'He should join us,' for some obscure reason, and my other two, Michael and Terry, are going, 'We don't need this guy, he isn't, like, funny.'

"And I said, 'No, but there's something about him.'" And so he came in and started to do animations, drawing cartoons, and the rest is history, yes? Then it took us about a year to write *Monty Python,* and suddenly we were on the BBC. They changed our name from *Monty Python* (we did four shows with that title) to *Monty Python's Flying Circus.* And the BBC said to us, 'Look—you are on Sunday nights, nobody watches, everybody's at the pub. We just want to have an hour before the queen comes on and they say good night, so just do thirteen, go away, and come back when you've done it.'

"Which was fantastic. They didn't need to fear, they didn't read, they didn't see what we were doing. It took us about a year to write, and it was really at the edges of things. It was fantastic. Perfect. Executive-free comedy!"

By the time the BBC noticed, the troupe and the show were already successful. I believe, and Eric agrees, that because the troupe had grown up with radio, it affected their thinking. "It affected it fabulously," Eric says, nodding excitedly. "'Cause the imagination with words fills up in extraordinary ways. I mean, on radio, *The Goons* would have things like, 'They're setting fire to the Thames!' But you don't have film of that, it has to be in your head. So I think it makes for more surreal thinking, rather visually based thinking. You're thinking and creating pictures and concepts all the time. But we also learned from *Not Only . . . But Also,* which was Peter Cook (the funniest man in England, just a fabulous guy) and Dudley Moore. And *Beyond the Fringe.* All great influencers. There are so many memorable characters and lines that are truly bizarre unless you know the players. My favorite, and a huge hit, is the song 'Always Look on the Bright Side of Life.' Just hearing the words and I am prepared to sing it." Eric bursts into song, and then comes the story.

"We were writing the *Life of Brian,* and we were getting toward the end, and everybody was heading for crucifixion. And/or death. And we go, 'How are we going to end this movie?'

"So I said, 'Well, it's obvious. We have to end with a song.'

"And they said, 'Oh, that's a good idea.'

"So I said, 'But we should be crucified—it should be a ridiculously cheery song, it should be really cheery-uppy, like a Disney song, with an annoying little whistle, too, and me on a cross.'

"I went home and wrote it in about twenty minutes. I recorded it and I took it in the next day, and they said, 'That's the end, yeah.' So that was the end. And then I sang it on a demo. And we were in Tunisia filming it, and I realized that the vocal wasn't right, that it should be in the character of Mr. Cheeky. I'll play the character called Mr. Cheeky, who is being crucified. On a cross! 'Oh, look on the bright side.' We took the track into a hotel room, and we put mattresses around the walls, and the sound guy lay on the floor, and we had a little drink of this brandy, and then—what you hear is totally live from the floor of a Tunisian bedroom. 'Some things in life are bad, they can really make you mad.' And that characterized it as insanely cheerful. The irony is— *look on the bright side of what?* You're being crucified, idiot! So it is truly astonishing that it has become a kind of insanely cheery-uppy thing."

I almost sign off with Eric, using the line above as the last, kind of perfect ending with his iconic song, and then I remember the Olympics in England. Surely you do, too. Go to YouTube if you somehow missed seeing this in 2012, what I consider the absolute highlight of the opening and closing ceremonies of those games. Showstopping. Some 750 million people worldwide watched Eric sing "Always Look on the Bright Side of Life" at this performance, and over 100,000 were there live, including over 4,000 people who were onstage.

Eric tells the story. "What I admire so much about the English," says Eric, "is that they love their talent in a lot of ways, and when I started to sing it, the entire stadium knew that song. I can't think of any comic person that has a comic and satirical melody out that an entire America could sing like that one. It was incredible. And since then, it's become a sort of alternative national anthem for the Brits. They sing it all the time. At any place—I was watching cricket, and the guy was *out,* and I hear my voice singing, 'Always look on the bright side of life.' It is rather wonderful."

I ask Eric, given his amazing longevity, his talent at entertaining to an out-of-bound unexpected degree, if he is considering writing an autobiography.

"Yes," he says. "I wrote an autobiography. It is my autobiography. All the cars I ever owned. Starts with a Ford Popular, then there's the little Hillman, and there's a Triumph Herald."

You think Eric Idle is an ironic personality? He surely is, even with that brilliant and outrageous sense of humor and talent, but another level of irony might be the story of my friend Richard Belzer, the stand-up Jewish comedian who practiced his comedy mostly at Catch a Rising Star in New York City. Yes, I am aware, par for the course among

My dear friend Belz (Richard Belzer) sharing another intimate moment with our Izzy Steinberg, circa 2013. Belz always has his beloved dogs nearby, but not today. Izzy took time off from writing the best parts of this book to connect with Belz.

comedians. Catch a Rising Star is also where Richard and I shot *The Richard Belzer Show,* a sitcom for Cinemax with Billy Crystal, Tom Leopold, and other comedy friends. It is one of my favorite things I have done. He also warmed up audiences for *Saturday Night Live.* He was on the radio, did occasional acting gigs on comedies, and then here is the irony: Richard Belzer portrayed Detective Munch on *Homicide* for seven seasons and then had the same role on *Law & Order: SVU* for fifteen seasons. That is about as serious a dramatic role as you can have on television, let alone for over twenty years.

Some little-known facts about Richard: He is Henry Winkler's cousin. Both his dad and his brother committed suicide. And he is truly an expert on assassination theories about President John Kennedy's death, having written four books about what he calls the conspiracy theories, which, by the way, is a philosophy he brought to Detective Munch.

I first met Richard a hundred years ago when I saw him emcee a show at Catch a Rising Star. "Well, that was a gift. Because when you're emcee, the show starts at eight or nine, goes to two in the morning, bringing up twenty-five to thirty acts. And I have to do something between each act. I mean, I can just say, 'And now . . .' But as I got more used to it, I would do my act, my twenty minutes, twenty-five with a stretch, as they say. And I had no more material. So I started improvising, talking to the audience, you know. I did it for years, every night, five, six, seven nights a week, five to six hours. Staggering home at two, three, four in the morning. One time, I was introducing an act, and this was the record. Because people used to complain, 'He takes too long between the acts.' You know, fuck that. So, one night, I did fifty-eight minutes."

What kind of work? Stand-up?

"I toured with Warren Zevon, I'm proud to say, for almost a year. And we toured all over the country, small clubs, in the South, all over. This was when I realized—this was my epiphany about not being stereotyped—'cause I had been called the 'New York Jew comic,' or that euphemism for smart-ass Jew, 'New York comic.' I was going to South Carolina, Virginia, North Dakota, we were going everywhere. And I learned, hey, my shit works. It taught me a lesson that you don't patronize an audience. If anything, you educate them. And my favorite review, if I may, at the risk of being immodest: I worked at the Bijou Café in Philadelphia. And the critic the next day said, 'Richard Belzer is the only comedian I've ever seen where the audience leaves wondering if *he* likes *them*.' I'm so proud of that. It was so comfortable and easy for me to play myself. And we got Billy Crystal and Robin Williams, Pat Benatar, great guests. Here is the thing I liked about the conceit of the show. I love when celebrities get taken down, especially when they do it to themselves. And they're unaware of it. That's what I was playing with."

For those of you who know Richard only from his role as Detective Munch, you will be surprised at his talent for truly great comedy. "I think I'm handsomer than I am, I think I'm funnier than I am, but more importantly, I just like that conceit about it all. Because then I can be megalomaniacal. Like Jack Benny. The genius of Jack Benny was he wasn't afraid of having people around him being funny. Or Mary Tyler Moore. That's the way I feel. Just, you know, bring on the best."

So when Lorne Michaels came to New York City to cast *Saturday Night Live,* he came into Catch a Rising Star, where Richard worked. "So I befriended him, and he told me what he was doing. And at that time, I was in the *National Lampoon* show, with John Belushi, Gilda Radner, and Bill Murray. And I introduced Lorne to that world. So John and everybody got the show. But me. And I was even there when people were auditioning, sitting next to Lorne. We went out into the hall, and I said, 'Why not me?' And this is what he said, and I'll never forget this as long as I fucking live. He actually said to me, 'Well, you're too funny.' *You're too funny.*

"Now, then I was a neurotic, insecure Jew, and I thought I did something wrong. I didn't realize how absurd and bizarre that is to say to someone. But I later found out that some other people were worried and threatened. You know I don't have to say this, I don't give a shit—they were trepidatious about having me around. So Lorne threw me a bone, and I did the warm-ups. And I did this for two shows, and I've never told this story before, but after the first one or two, the guys in the crew were mumbling, 'Belzer's funnier than half the guys here.' And that kind of got out. And then, Don Pardo resented me doing the warm-up—he was threatened. But John, my 'brother' John Belushi, got me to do sketches. He tried to keep me there. John found out I wasn't making what the rest of the cast was making, and he threatened to quit. That was John."

For the last twenty years or so, Richard can't walk down the street anywhere without being stopped. I've been with him. People are turning their heads, running after him, just showing him love. And they love that character, too. "But after twenty-one years I should really fucking grow up and say, you did a good thing. In Europe, my wife and I took the Orient Express. And it was 'Hi, Inspector Munch!' In Turkey, 'Inspector Munch!' You know, wherever I went, it just built and built over the years. Literally, for me, it's been overwhelming, and I've been speechless."

I wondered how this stand-up got the part of a detective.

"They had been casting *Homicide: Life on the Street*. They couldn't find a Munch, and they brought in a lot of actors. And creator Barry Levinson said, 'Why don't we bring in Richard?' He didn't even know if I was an actor or not. And in my first audition, Barry says, 'I want you to take the script and come back, but you can't leave the lot.' I go in a big room in there, with a stack of VHS tapes, and the sign says 'Munch' on the door. This must be other people's auditions, I think. I open the door, and I do, like, a Spy vs. Spy thing. I did the thing from *Mad* magazine: I closed the door, I sat down, and I watched all the guys auditioning this scene that I was going to do. And the thing that I noticed is that they're all playing it very serious, like a cop. Like what they thought a cop would be. Some of them were good, and some were just okay, but it's like a one-note reading on these guys' part. So that just rang a bell in my head.

"So when I went back, I did this interrogation scene, and I took hold of my shoe, and I just went crazy. The way the character, I thought, would have. But I didn't change the script. I did all the lines in Paul Attanasio's script. The next day, my agent calls and says, 'You got the part.'

"And I say, 'That's great!'

"'You don't understand, this has been a big search.' And I'm so cynical, I didn't trust it for some reason. Twenty-one years later . . .'"

Richard was just a talented, clever, and witty comedian, and then all of a sudden he is an actor in the most popular television show. And it lasts forever. None of us who knew him then would have been the one to say, "Belz is gonna be hugely successful, with a house in northern France."

Drew Carey doesn't spend much time in the South of France. I doubt he ever leaves his working space—TV studio, writing desk, soccer meetings (part owner), and now as the new host of our TV series, *Inside Comedy*. I could not be more proud, as he is admired, beloved, and respected by all comedians—and he is the most fun to be with, whether working or sharing a meal at his favorite restaurant. Did I say "sharing a meal"? More like hosting a meal. Actually, more like hosting anything and everything—from *The Drew Carey Show* to *Whose Line Is It Anyway?* to *The Price Is Right* (twelve years and counting) to *Power of 10* to *Drew Carey's Improv-A-Ganza*.

Drew Carey, one of the best stand-ups, sitcom stars, and now host of *The Price Is Right* and soon to host the new incarnation of my show *Inside Comedy*. This photo says it all. Light-hearted, extremely generous, and always quick to laugh.

He started out like all of us, a common road taken, as you know by now. After he won *Star Search,* in 1988, he went on to perform stand-up in comedy cubs. And then, in November 1991, like all of us, he appeared on *The Tonight Show Starring Johnny Carson.* Johnny asked him to come to the famous couch on this, his first visit, and, as we always say, the rest is history. But it was not so easy—it took Drew three years from the promise of the first Carson date until he appeared. He tells the story:

"When I first auditioned for *The Tonight Show,*" explains Drew, "I'd done *Star Search.* And we sent a tape of *Star Search* to *The Tonight Show.* That got me an audition with Jim McCauley, who was the guy who picked all the comics. We went out to the Comedy & Magic Club in Hermosa Beach, California, and I auditioned for him there. Usually people audition three, four times, ten times, fifteen times to even get on the show. I went that one time, he meets me backstage, and he goes, 'Well, you got the show.' And word spread like wildfire throughout the little comedy community, 'Hey, Drew Carey got *The Tonight Show* on his first audition.' And I was like, 'Wow, I can't believe it. I got *The Tonight Show!*' Back in Cleveland, the *Plain Dealer* did an article about me, writing, 'Local comic to be on *The Tonight Show,*' and all that stuff. It was really exciting. What they did was, you would do a set, and they would put you on a list. And then whenever someone fell out, they would call you and you would step in.

"So I waited and waited, never heard from 'em. And I was out working at the Comedy & Magic Club that November, and the next day I went to see Bob Saget do a *Full House* taping. I was gone all day, and no cell phones back then, so nobody could get ahold of me. I went to see *Full House* and then drove to the Comedy & Magic Club. I get there and the emcee meets me at the door and goes, 'Hey, you all right?'

"I go, 'Yeah, I'm doing great.'

"He goes, 'Oh, I guess you didn't hear.'

"I go, 'What happened?'

"And he goes, 'I don't want to tell you.'

"I go, 'What, my mother died? Just tell me what happened.'

"And he goes, '*The Tonight Show* has been trying to call you all day to do *The Tonight Show* tonight, but they couldn't get hold of you. So they got somebody else instead.'

"I was like, 'Are you kidding me?'"

"I called Jim McCauley on Monday, and I said, 'I'm sorry I missed your call on Friday.' He goes, 'That's okay, but I'd like to see you again before we schedule another appearance.' So I went and I saw him again, and he saw me do another set. Now, I was still brand-new—I was only doing comedy for two years. And he said, 'You know what, there's something about you that's not quite ready yet. There's something about it that I just don't like anymore.'"

"So I had it, I missed the call, then I didn't have it. I said to myself, 'That's it, it's not gonna happen again, I'm not gonna miss one of these calls.' I ended up living out of my car for the next eighteen months. I didn't sleep in the car, but I traveled in it, doing stand-up. All I could think about was I gotta get back on *The Tonight Show*. I don't care what it takes. I want to get my act so good that they can't deny me. It took me three years. I didn't have an agent or anything. I did it all on my own. I then called Jim McCauley again, and I said, "Remember me, Drew Carey? I'd like to come see you again. I've been working on my act." He goes, "Yeah, come out and see me." I went to the Improv in LA, and I did a set for him. I do one of the best sets of my life. Like a killer twenty minutes, out of a good hour and a half then. After all that time on the road, I did my best twenty minutes.

"Jim McCauley comes out, 'You got the set.' Then I'm waiting and waiting, and this time I'm not telling anybody. I got back on the list, but I'm not as excited. I'm playing it a lot more close to the vest. And I finally get a call that November, almost three years to the day. 'You're gonna do the show next Friday.'"

"I get to LA, get a haircut, go do *The Tonight Show*, and I hear him introduce me, the curtain goes up, and it's just like I dreamed it. I was like floating the whole time. And we get done and the band's shaking my hand, the security guard's shaking my hand. And then Johnny calls me to the couch. MY FIRST TIME ON THE SHOW AND HE CALLS ME TO THE COUCH!!!!!!!"

"Here's what is in my mind. I used to go to a Pentecostal church when I was in junior high. And when I was twelve or thirteen, I got saved, and talked in tongues and everything. You shake and fall on the floor—things like that. It's a very emotional, but a very real, experience.

That *Tonight Show* thing was the only thing like it. It's like being saved in the blood of show business. I could just feel everything just wash through me. Like I was a new person when I got done with that *Tonight Show.* I wasn't the same person seven minutes later. And that is the torment and the magic of *The Tonight Show.*"

Drew and I have spent many hours reminiscing about our youth experiences. Turns out the kid from Winnipeg and the kid from Cleveland have a lot in common. First, we both were avid readers of *Mad* magazine.

"I never missed an issue," Drew says, quite emphatically. "Remember, David, when they had all their parody stickers? I loved the song parodies. All these years later, if I hear the song, I think of the parody because you could sing it and get laughs from your friends. I would sing them at school. I'd be like, 'Hey, wanna hear a song parody?' One was 'Ground Round,' to the tune of 'Downtown.' 'When you eat meat but hate the meat that you're eating, then you surely got, ground round. It's so unnerving.' That's a good *Mad* magazine word, 'unnerving.' 'It's so unnerving when they're constantly serving it in an eating spot, ground round.'"

I loved those parodies, and also Tom Lehrer's work. Drew agrees. "I love Tom Lehrer."

Drew: "I love 'The Old Dope Peddler.' Starts like a ballad. 'When the shades of night are falling, there's a fella everyone knows, he's the old dope peddler, spreading joy wherever he goes.' Tom Lehrer was the best; you know there's really nobody like him anymore."

Then Drew is offered *The Price Is Right*—seems like an odd segue, but it lasted for twelve years, and is still going strong. I wonder if that was an easy decision for him to make at the time.

Drew shakes his head. "I said no first thing. I was kind of retired then. I was really into photography and chilling out and watching soccer games. And I had been taking acting lessons, 'cause I thought I might want to do movies. And my agent goes, 'I got the most interesting call from CBS casting.' And first thing I thought was, like, *CSI?* A detective of some kind? But no. My agent explained. 'What would you think about taking over *The Price Is Right* from Bob Barker?'

"And I went, 'Are you fucking kidding? No.' That was a whole different thing from what I was thinking. So the first reaction is, 'Are you kidding me? No.' It was the quickest no I'd ever given. And a couple of weeks later I get another call from him, and he says, 'I got another call from CBS casting, and they said, 'What if we really went after Drew?''

"And I said, 'What does that mean?'"

"And he goes, 'I dunno, probably money or something.'"

" 'Well, how much money we talking about?'"

"He goes, 'I don't know.'"

" 'What's the work schedule?'"

" 'I don't know.'"

"So I thought I should at least have a meeting with them at CBS, 'cause I felt like I kind of owed them that. I met with them, and then the ball started rolling from there. The money was right; the price was right. And I was excited about the stuff we could do on the show, and I *really* thought it would be a good fit for me, since I had done improvisation, had had my own series. And I talked to my friends and I ask, 'Do you think I'm gonna be ruined as a stand-up comic because I'm doing daytime game show stuff?'

"And they go, 'Are you kidding?' And they started giving me reasons why it wouldn't ruin my career."

And here's the kicker, to me. Drew smiles.

"I pitched my show as the anti-*Seinfeld*. Now, I love *Seinfeld*, but it bugged me that in all these shows people seemingly had copious amounts of money, lived in really nice places, never had anything to worry about. And I was like, 'You should have a guy who's working. Where's the working-class guy? There's nobody like that on TV.' So we were the anti-*Seinfeld*. We were not as popular, didn't make as much money. But, David, it turned out *perfect*."

When a comedian/actor is known as much for his enormous talent as for his charitable heart, for over $50 million that he helped raise with Robin Williams and Whoopi Goldberg through Comic Relief since 1986 for the homeless nationwide, you might forget that he, Billy Crystal, is a comedian and actor, improviser, stand-up (everywhere), sitcom star (remember *Soap*?) with six Emmys, theatrical actor (like in his one-man show, *700 Sundays,* which won him a Tony, toured around the world for two years, and then became a ratings blockbuster on HBO), actor in films that are classics (*The Princess Bride, Throw Momma from The Train, When Harry Met Sally, City Slickers, Mr. Saturday Night, Analyze This*—and that's all the room I have), television host (*SNL* was nothing compared to hosting the Oscars nine times).

Billy would never forgive me if I didn't mention that he is a New York Yankees maniac, that he signed a one-day minor league contract with the Yankees and once went to spring training. Why do I think he values this more than his seven American Comedy Awards? Because I have known him for almost fifty years.

More facts? Married to Janice for fifty years. Graduated from NYU, a film and television directing major. One of his teachers? Martin Scorsese. And in his class? Oliver Stone and Christopher Guest.

And how did Billy go from a degree from NYU to stand-up?

"I didn't really start doing stand-up alone until '74. I started off as a single at Catch a Rising Star in New York. Jack Rollins came to see me for the first time. I was really nervous, but I did my twenty minutes and just destroyed. We went out afterward, and he said, 'I didn't care for it . . . because the audience loved it. But you never said the word "I" once. I don't know how you feel about anything. You didn't leave them a tip. Leave something on the table, Billy—something that's you. Tomorrow, come in again. Don't do any of this stuff. We know this works. I want to hear what you think. Be prepared to bomb.'

"Truly, David, that was the best advice I've ever gotten. It changed my whole approach to what I was doing and, ultimately, it's the culmination of everything I've prepared that became *700 Sundays.* They're getting a piece of me that becomes a piece of them and becomes about their family, their experience."

It was so much fun for me to see Billy turn into these characters. For example, it was incredible when he did Sammy Davis Jr. Explains Billy, "Sammy was the funniest, best, coolest, and strangest cat ever. We did thirty nights straight. So now it's opening night. I do my thirty-five minutes. I walk into the wings, and Sammy would just follow me

Billy Crystal and I share a great love of the history of comedy and the same references (most comedians do). This is right after I interviewed him on *Inside Comedy,* 2012. His impressions of Muhammad Ali and stories of sitting on Billie Holiday's lap as a child while watching the movie *Lassie* are flawless.

out. He says to the audience, 'Is that the white Richard Pryor or am I nuts?'"

So it is always a particularly joyful occasion when Billy and I sit down to chat. Nonstop. Catching up—always takes us back and also to today. We start with *700 Sundays,* a wonderful theatrical experience. It is Billy's brilliance that turned his life experiences into this one-man show. What is *700 Sundays?* Billy's dad, Jack, died when he was fifty-four and Billy was only fifteen. They shared seven hundred Sundays, a number most precious to Billy.

Actually, says Billy, "you, David, were a big help to get me back onstage. I had not been onstage on a steady basis for around sixteen years. I'd gone into movies, and the lifestyle was better. But I'd been through some losses in my family, and I needed to get back up. You and

I started doing these benefits, right after 9/11, for kids who'd lost their fathers at the towers. We were supposed to do an hour. We did two. And then we took a break, and I came out and said I want to do more by myself. It freed me up, and we did four or five of them, so I started to get confidence again. We started to talk about the things that ended up becoming the root of *700 Sundays*."

Billy toured with his show for about two years, all over the world. "We perform wherever we can, sometimes six cities, one after the other. For me, even after all these years, *700 Sundays* is still the greatest thing to do, because it's mine. My characters, taken from my family and friends. Some funny. Some tragic. And it is really funny and very touching."

Billy wrote the music for the show as well. How did that happen? "My dad produced jazz concerts, and my uncle was a great record producer. The family business was this little record store that everybody hung out in, so I grew up with jazz guys. I started imitating them almost as well as I could imitate the immigrant Jewish relatives. By the way, and you, David, the son of a rabbi, will identify with this: our house always smelled of brisket and bourbon, because I was around all these Jewish relatives and the cool jazz guys at the same time. It was a really interesting group—the Yiddish of it all and the ethnicity of it all, and the cigar smoke and the schnapps smell. My two brothers and I were always doing something together. My brothers were all funny. But I *needed* it more."

But why comedy? How? "It was always about being funny," remembers Billy. "From the first time I saw Sid Caesar on television. *The King and I* was the hit movie of the year, and on the *Show of Shows* they did a *King and I* sketch. Sid came out with a bald wig and calypso pants, barefoot, and screamed, 'Who is smoking in the palace? There's no smoking in the palace!' I thought it was hilarious. That was my first memory of laughing uncontrollably. Before I went to bed that night, I rolled up my pajamas and started screaming, hitting my little bare chest, 'Who is smoking in the palace? There's no smoking in the palace!' So Sid was my first influence."

The others? "Jonathan Winters was gigantic for me. He was funny because he was crazy, but it was structured. For a little kid, that was the greatest. And that time on television was the best time for comedians because there were very few situation comedies. It was all variety shows." Variety shows were life changing, because they gave us access to all kinds of personalities, all kinds of music that never interfered with the comedy.

"For me," emphasizes Billy, "I was so influenced by Carl Reiner, Cosby, Lily Tomlin, Alan King, Laurel and Hardy, Chuck McCann, Jack Paar, and Johnny Carson. There was an aristocracy about Carson. He was a little terrifying until you broke through and realized he was just really shy. He was so smart and quick-witted and generous and really enjoyed funny people. If you made him laugh, you had a career the next day. My first *Tonight Show* was really terrifying. I was doing it on a Tuesday night. The Sunday before I was in Las Vegas doing one of those roasts—this one was of Muhammad Ali. Orson Welles was on. I finished my set, and it went very well, and Orson Welles is sitting backstage going over his jokes. I walked up to him and said, 'Mr. Welles, I just want to say—' and he finished my sentence for me: 'That I'm a great influence on you. Thank you very much, and now basically go fuck yourself.'

"So now I go to do the *Tonight Show*. My first time. Welles is the guest. I get called over to the couch to sit with Johnny (which was a *huge* honor) and Orson Welles. And Johnny says, 'You're on this upcoming Dean Martin roast . . .' Before I could say anything, Welles jumps in. 'Wait till you see him on the show,' he says to Johnny. 'He's hilarious. He steals the show. This guy's got a big future.' And that was basically how Orson Welles apologized for dissing me."

And so I have to bring up hosting the Oscars, since the man has hosted them nine times. I love when Billy hosts the Oscars. Everyone does. What is that like, Billy?

"I liked doing it most of the time. But after nine times, it became too much a part of my year. You've got a billion and a half people watching you. I tried to do something different with it every time. There was one moment in that show where Hal Roach was supposed to wave from the audience. He was a hundred years old, the man that gave birth to Laurel and Hardy, really one of the fathers of silent comedy. I introduced him, and he got up and started speaking without a mic and kept talking. I see crew running to get a mic out, and everyone looking at him, and then they look for me to say something. I see the red lights on me, and I said, 'This is only fitting because he got his start in silent films.'"

But I can't leave without bringing up Billy's most wonderful, classic character on *SNL,* because it was not just iconic but original then, and it's still original now, years later. And I bet you may not know that what Billy was doing when he coined that unforgettable phrase on *SNL*—he was parodying the actor Fernando Lamas. I just can't leave without hearing him say, "David—*You look . . . mahvelous!*"

You, too, Billy. You, too.

It is always dangerous to say someone is the best at anything, because you will get an argument from a lot of people who have their own lists of greats. Including me. And yet, you will get a hard time from every comedian I know if you don't insist that Marty Short is at least great, perhaps one of the greatest. Ever.

First of all, he is always funny, no matter what he is doing. No matter where. One time, a friend asked if we could reach out to Marty to just do an hour of stand-up at a casino. The company flew Robyn, my wife, and me, along with Marty and his wife, Nancy, on a private plane to a casino in Las Vegas. First class all the way—so far, so good. Marty is then led to the stage, which is in front of a pool, strewn with a bunch of tables and chairs, and a huge crowd of people sitting there, waiting for him. Marty starts to speak—and within fifteen minutes, the management leads in a crowd of young, barely dressed women, who begin to party, ordering drinks and hanging out with the crowd. Noisily. At this point, Marty calls out on the microphone, "IS DAVID STEINBERG HERE? DAVID! IS IT A STROKE WHEN IT IS GOING UP YOUR LEFT ARM? DAVID?"

To his credit, Marty finished the show, through all the noise. And we never stopped laughing about it—for years! That's Marty. He doesn't get flustered when the venue falls apart—he goes with the humor and always finds the funny at a moment's notice. The consummate pro.

Find him poolside at a hotel—all the other guests around him are laughing. Really laughing. Find him at a restaurant having dinner with his three kids—waiters are dropping dishes, nearby diners are holding their sides. It's just who he is. Joyful, kind, generous, smart, inclusive, fearless, aware, successful, celebrated—did I emphasize "joyful" enough? Because he really is joyful. Oh, yes, and talented beyond words. His comedy, always resulting in audiences' roaring-out-loud laughter, is cheerful, free-form, unexpected, jubilantly funny, and the best of what was called slapstick in the days of the Marx Brothers—a little insane, totally outrageous, sometimes risky, always seeming to be out of control—and it is that taking of chances, that feeling in the audience that no one knew what Marty would do next, that made, and makes, his comedy exciting, a little scary, and just absolutely memorable.

The man is everywhere. Comedian, actor, singer, writer, stand-up, television, Broadway musicals, film actor. Canadian through and through (he also has the Order of Canada), he was one of five Catholic kids and began his show business career at age fourteen in his living room.

He says he was very good, and even then, uninhibited, brilliantly original, fearless, and always generous to his audience, giving them more than they ever expected. Where did that come from? His steel-selling dad? His concert violinist mother? ("My beloved mother was the concertmaster of the symphony, so absurdity and eccentricity were not criticized.") His siblings? Well, the sarcasm and jibes around the dinner table were memorable.

Marty has an easy answer. "When you go home, and you're loved, you can go into the real world, and if people don't like you, you say, 'I don't care—I am loved!' Being the youngest of five, I was adored, fueled with confidence. And that got me through everything."

When did it begin? "I was twelve, and we were on in prime time," remembers Marty. "It was 'The Martin Short Variety Hour.' My brother Michael and I practiced it in my bedroom. We were on at eight-thirty p.m. every other Tuesday. And I would do a medley of songs that weren't nominated anywhere, interview Eldridge Cleaver, or someone like that, from the *Playboy* interview ['What's going on with your people?'], or watch Jonathan Winters and mimic his act. And we had an applause record," he recounts, his grin wide with delight. "I had a rocking chair in my room and the arm was broken. And I had a tube of glue and I kept gluing it. And my brother Michael went to my parents and said, 'This is not normal. I really think that we have to be open to the idea that he's sniffing glue.'" (Michael and Marty have been writing together their entire working lives. Michael has also gone on to win awards for writing, most recently on Eugene Levy and his son Dan Levy's hit show *Schitt's Creek*. More talent from Canada, I might add.)

Foreshadowing the future? Who knew? Marty did. Although he got

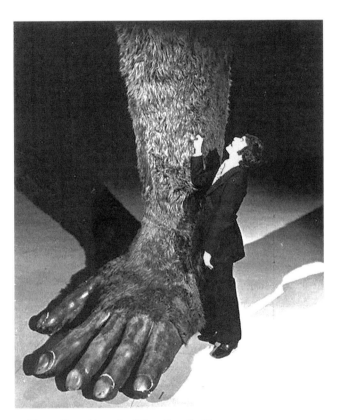

This is Kong (short for "King Kong"). Kong was my monologue go-to. Sometimes I would talk about current events, and I also would do a Dietrich-like rendition of "Falling in Love Again." One of the many places Kong and I went was on *The David Steinberg Show*, the CBS summer replacement for *The Carol Burnett Show*, 1972.

The ever-adorable Dick Van Dyke on the set of *Inside Comedy*, 2014. One of musical comedy's treasures.

a degree in social work in 1972, from McMaster University, where his fellow students were Eugene Levy and Dave Thomas, as it often happens, at the same time he auditioned for and was cast as an actor in the Toronto production of *Godspell*, with Paul Shaffer ("I always wanted to know what made them have such a good time") as the musical director. As they say, luck would have it in that others in the cast included Victor Garber, Eugene Levy, Andrea Martin, John Candy, Dan Aykroyd, and Gilda Radner. (Yes, they dated: "Every other guy wanted to go out with her. She was just a magical person, adored by all, including me.") They also did *The David Steinberg Show* in Canada, where I played a—this is a redundancy—but a narcissistic version of myself. I was egotistical, and they were the company.

The David Steinberg Show was one of my greatest pleasures, because all these people on it were being discovered, and they were phenomenal. I cast John Candy, Dave Thomas, Andrea Martin, Richard Pryor, Jon Voight, Elliott Gould, Tommy Smothers, Milton Berle, and, of course, Gilda. (Actually, Gilda was cast on *The David Steinberg Show*. After she signed her contracts, she got a call from New York from a show called *Saturday Night Live*. Gilda had gotten a role there and needed a release, so she asked me if that would be okay—and of course, I said, "For you to have this break in the US, I won't hold you back. But I won't be able to replace you.") Marty reminds me, "Canadian comedians work all the time. Their definition of 'variety' is to try everything. And that's how I continued my life—trying everything, doing everything, films, television, Broadway, stand-up—that was and is me."

When I first saw Marty in his audition for my show, he came in doing the wildest and weirdest character I had ever seen—high-pitched voice, screeching and jumping around. Everyone was laughing hysterically—they realized that he was doing an impression of me. I loved what he was doing and said, "I don't know what you were doing, but you and I are going to be working together on this show." And that's how Marty Short became my sidekick on *The David Steinberg Show,* his first big break (which Marty talks about in his book, *I Must Say*). *The David Steinberg Show* was a comedy series that took place behind the scenes at a talk show (which was actually the forerunner of *The Larry Sanders Show*—Garry once apologized to me for "borrowing" my idea and making it better—eventually he hired me to direct *his* show). *The David Steinberg Show* is now available on Amazon, Roku, and Tubi.

During my show, every time he spoke to me, Marty started and ended the sentence with "Cousin David! . . ." That was my name on the series. I would cringe. But most importantly, Marty courted his wife, Nancy, on that show. They were married for thirty years, shared three children. We were all heartbroken when she died in 2010. Marty, who had already dealt with three devastating deaths in his family when he was just twenty—his mother, dad, and brother—had to face it again with his beloved wife. "It gave me a kind of a cockiness in the world—tragedies that kept happening. I had my siblings, then I had my kids. But these things make you stronger—I developed a newfound fearlessness—not hesitant or afraid of things. I mean, what could happen? Would it kill me? The truth is, I have chosen to treat my life more like a party than something to stress about."

Then Eugene Levy encouraged Marty to try out for Second City in Toronto (owned by Andrew Alexander, populated by John Candy, Dan Aykroyd, Paul Shaffer). "All I wanted to do was find out what was it that made them have such a great time in their lives," which he did, and of course got in, and then he and a group of improvisa-

I learned from seeing Lenny Bruce perform at the Gate of Horn that a comedian could be dapper and still be funny (rare for the time). Lenny was a genius. He was soft-spoken and never pandered to the audience. He was never afraid of being controversial. He was my comedic hero. He was everyone's comedic hero.

tion actors produced a show for television called *Second City Television,* better known then and forever as *SCTV.* You know these characters, because they remain as stars in the history of comedy. Talk show host Brock Linehan, old songwriter Irving Cohen (people think he was based on Irving Berlin, but in his own book, Marty says the character was inspired by Sophie Tucker), and, of course, the very, very weird man-child Ed Grimley, who later became a staple on *SNL* and then became an animated series (*The Completely Mental Misadventures of Ed Grimley*). *SCTV* had a rough audience—we worked hard, mean audiences of drunk businessmen—a rough crowd. By 1977, Marty joined *SCTV.* "I loved the audience, and I loved the work ethic."

It was on *SCTV* that Marty had the chance to develop the characters who remain iconic today. "It was so ideal! I was with all my friends, in my hometown of Toronto, and could do anything I wanted to try out. I impersonated Jerry Lewis," he remembers with glee. "I hadn't met him yet. I remember the first piece I did: 'Live at the Champs-Élysées.' And it was a satire of Richard Pryor's documentary that Martin Scorsese had done. The premise is that it was a concert. It was good in a way because I could celebrate what was great about Jerry. Then, around ten years later or so, in 1991, I interviewed Jerry, and I was nervous to meet him, 'cause I didn't know whether he was gonna hit me. But he was so polite, and very nice, and then in the middle of the interview he says, 'Didn't you do me on *SCTV*?' and he kind of went [chuckling], 'That was good.' So, I passed the test." At this same time, there was a new show in the US—you may have heard of it, it is still called *SNL*—by another Canadian, Lorne Michaels.

Marty gave *SNL* new life, but "it was punishing. I was full of anxiety. It was a tight schedule, limiting creatively because there was so little time. It was one hard year of live TV." And then he had three versions of *The Martin Short Show* on TV. One of my favorites was his creation Jiminy Glick, where he interviewed celebrities in that character. "Hilarious and unpredictable, the most uninhibited comic creation," said *The New York Times* at the time. And then Marty expanded his world, as a guest and co-star on dramas such as *Damages, Weeds, Law & Order,* opening the world's eyes to his ever-expanding talents. And that was only television. Movies and theater followed, and not small stuff. His films include *Three Amigos, Innerspace, Three Fugitives, Father of the Bride (I* and *II), Mars Attacks!,* and more. He created unforgettable and now iconic television characters. He was a star in both comedy and musical theater work, which became his passion, brought him many accolades and Tony Awards, and remains his love to this day. *The Goodbye Girl, Little Me,* and *The Producers* were only a few of his hits.

Throughout his work, frenzied and as courageous as it is, Marty is still so thoughtful. "The thing in comedy is that if you start worrying about something, some people will say, 'Oh. That's too silly.' Then five years later, silly has become hip. It's then considered art. So I never comment on anything I do, because if I say anything negative about a film or a TV show, people who saw it and loved it will say, 'Well, am I an idiot?' Comedy is a weird thing. It's the weirdest thing you can do.

There's no consensus. It's not like people say, 'I saw *Saving Private Ryan,* and that scene on the beach is just so moving.' I can't imagine anyone who would say, 'I don't find that moving!' But in comedy, whether it's *Laurel and Hardy* or *The Three Stooges* or *Jiminy Glick in Lalawood,* some people are going to look at it and say, 'That's the funniest thing I've ever seen.' And some people will say, 'I don't get it.' Who's right, who's wrong?"

Marty and I see each other all the time. I love the time we spend together. Just the other month, we needed a host for a benefit for the NRDC. I called Marty, and he jumped in immediately, and he was probably the most successful host we have ever had—and we raised lots of money. In the last two years, Marty has been touring nationwide with Steve Martin, which became a Netflix special.

He gave—and still gives—his all. Some of my favorite Marty lines, to this day (as Rosie and Conan and David and Johnny always said, "the funniest man on the planet" and "the king of all guests") include:

"I skewer the narcissists. Not the good guys—the morons with power. But not our Mel Brooks, although I really don't understand, what's his beef with the Nazis?"

"People think I am Jewish! Even all my friends think I'm Jewish! Everyone I grew up with thinks I am Jewish! Why? Maybe I have their rhythms, their style. Or maybe I am thrifty. But I will give you an idea of how Jewish Mel Brooks is—that's a nose job."

"I love musicals. But the truth is, the musical is only as good as its director. The same can also be said of the CIA."

"A few years ago, I won a Tony for *Little Me,* and I learned two important lessons from that experience. One is that fair-weathered friends are so much more interesting to be around . . . and two, it is amazing what this Tony fetches on eBay."

I tell you these stories, before I forget, because they explain why I love comedy and why I love comedians. They have been by my side in my work, and in my life, for more than sixty years, and I am honored to still be working with them.

I remember, as a child, sitting in my neighborhood Winnipeg movie theater, all day, every weekend, watching the same Marx Brothers movies over and over again, and laughing and laughing and laughing, worshipping this great, odd, funny man with the funnier name, Groucho.

Cut to eighteen years later, meeting my childhood hero, my new friend, Groucho. He could still make me laugh, but this time I could reciprocate the gift of laughter.

To share a stage and laughter with the likes of Richie Pryor, Robin Williams, Larry David, Jerry Seinfeld, Tim Conway, Don Rickles, Dick Van Dyke, Jonathan Winters, Bob Newhart, Jon Stewart, Billy Crystal, and Marty Short—the laughter legend list is endless—that's more than a good life, that's a dream built on laughter.

ACKNOWLEDGMENTS

I want to personally thank the following people for your wonderful contributions and enthusiasm in making this book happen. And of course all the remarkable people in comedy who have touched my life. I cherish them all.

Robyn Todd, Rich Russo, Jeffrey C. Briggs, Esq., Dori Stegman, George Shapiro, Amanda Sidney, Nicky Ferguson, Josh Etting, Stan Rosenfield, Pearl Lieberman, Sam Kashner, Jeff Sotzing, Roz Wolfe, John Slotkin, Marc Jaffee, Ziggy Steinberg, Graydon Carter, David Kuhn, Laura Sedrish, Lisa Halliday, Jill Adams, Leslie Sank, Annie Gilbar for her unending dedication and love, & the remarkable Victoria Wilson for her pitch-perfect guidance.

INDEX

Page numbers in *italics* refer to illustrations.

ILLUSTRATION CREDITS

A NOTE ON THE TYPE

This book was set in Adobe Garamond. Designed for the Adobe Corporation by Robert Slimbach, the fonts are based on types first cut by Claude Garamond (ca. 1480–1561). Garamond was a pupil of Geoffroy Tory and is believed to have followed the Venetian models, although he introduced a number of important differences, and it is to him that we owe the letter we now know as "old style." He gave to his letters a certain elegance and feeling of movement that won their creator an immediate reputation and the patronage of Francis I of France.

Composed by North Market Street Graphics,
Lancaster, Pennsylvania

Designed by Soonyoung Kwon